Lee Harwood

Collected Poems

Books by Lee Harwood

POETRY
title illegible. Writers Forum. London, 1965; reprinted 1996.
The Man with Blue Eyes. Angel Hair Books, New York, 1966.
The White Room. Fulcrum Press, London, 1968.
Landscapes. Fulcrum Press, London, 1969.
The Sinking Colony. Fulcrum Press, London, 1970
Penguin Modern Poets 19 (with John Ashbery & Tom Raworth)
                               Penguin Books, Harmondsworth, 1971
Freighters. Pig Press, Newcastle-upon-Tyne, 1975.
H.M.S. Little Fox. Oasis Books, London, 1975.
Boston-Brighton. Oasis Books, London, 1977.
Old Bosham Bird Watch. Pig Press, Newcastle-upon-Tyne, 1977.
Wish you were here (with Antony Lopez), Transgravity Press, Deal, 1979.
All the Wrong Notes. Pig Press, Durham, 1981.
Faded Ribbons. Other Branch Readings, Leaminngton Spa, 1982.
Monster Masks. Pig Press, Durham, 1985.
Crossing the Frozen River: selected poems. Paladin, London, 1988.
Rope Boy to the Rescue. North & South, Twickenham, 1988.
In the Mists: mountain poems. Slow Dancer Press, Nottingham, 1993.
Morning Light. Slow Dancer Press, London, 1998.
Evening Star. Leafe Press, Nottingham, 2004.
Collected Poems. Shearsman Books, Exeter, 2004.

PROSE
Captain Harwood's Log of Stern Statements and Stout Sayings.
         Writers Forum, London, 1973; reprinted 1995.
Wine Tales: Un Roman Devin (with Richard Caddel)
         Galloping Dog Press, Newcastle-upon-Tyne, 1984.
Dream Quilt: 30 assorted stories. Slow Dancer Press, Nottingham, 1985.
Assorted Stories : prose works. Coffee House Press, Minneapolis, 1987.

TRANSLATIONS
Tristan Tzara – *Cosmic Realities Vanilla Tobacco Dawnings*.
                   Arc, Gillingham, 1969. 2nd ed, Todmorden, 1975.
Tristan Tzara – *Destroyed Days, a selection of poems 1943-1955*.
                         Voiceprint Editions, Colchester, 1971.
Tristan Tzara – *Selected Poems*. Trigram Press, London, 1975.
Tristan Tzara – *Chanson Dada: selected poems*. Coach House Press /
                       Underwhich Editions, Toronto, 1987.
Tristan Tzara – *The Glowing Forgotten : A Selection of Poems*.
                   Leafe Press, Nottingham, 2003.

LEE HARWOOD

Collected Poems
1964-2004

Shearsman Books
2004

First published in the United Kingdom in 2004 by
Shearsman Books,
58 Velwell Road
Exeter EX4 4LD

http://www.shearsman.com/

ISNBN 0-907562-40-X

Acknowledgements:

The texts in the section 'Wine Tales' are copyright © 1984 by
Richard Caddel and Lee Harwood, and are reproduced here
by kind permission of The Estate of Richard Caddel.

Poem 9 from 'Ten Poems for Downbeat' by Jack Spicer, which
is used as the opening lines of 'Afterwords to a poem by Jack
Spicer', is copyright © 1975 by The Estate of Jack Spicer, and is reproduced
here with the Estate's permission.

CONTENTS

title illegible / early work. 1964-65

The man with blue eyes. 1965-66

The white room. 1966-67

Landscapes. 1967

The picture book open. 1968

The coast. 1968

In the mists : mountain poems. 1988-93

Morning Light. 1989-96

Foreword

These *Collected Poems*, or collected poems and prose, include most of my work written between 1964 and 2004. A few poems have been cut as not all poems last the course. I've also added some that haven't appeared in book form before – mostly from the 1970s – as well as some recent unpublished work. The section titles in this volume generally correspond to the original books where the poems first appeared, though not always.

Over these years I think, and hope, I've changed in the way I see the world. It would seem natural that there should be a parallel development in my writing. Re-reading these poems, however, I realise there are often repetitions and echoes, insistences that remain throughout on or under the surface. A reader will soon recognise them, despite shifts in the scenery.

The poems, I imagine, harbour curious stories, questions and explorations, instructions for assembling pictures, declarations of love and other obsessions, elegies, and often enough a collage of all these things. They set off, one hopes, into the unknown or barely guessed at. It's in the reader's hands.

Language is never perfectly reliable but – obvious enough – it's all we have to talk to one another. It's to be used as well as possible, as precisely and clearly as possible, but not to be wholly trusted. The complexity of language and people and "life" is to be worked with, accepted, and all their contradictions to be relished. I learnt this, and ways of mapping it all, early on when still in my teens from reading Ezra Pound, and then a year or two later from Tristan Tzara, Jorge Luis Borges, and John Ashbery. After that, the list of writers I'm indebted to spreads far and wide, whether it be the thought and imagination of Jack Spicer or the sharpness and heart of Anne Stevenson or the amused tenderness of Constantine Cavafy. My thanks to them all.

I would also like to thank the editors and publishers who over the years have brought out my books. Bob Cobbing (Writers Forum), Lewis Warsh and Anne Waldman (Angel Hair Books), Stuart and Deirdre Montgomery (Fulcrum Press), Nikos Stangos (Penguin Books), Ian Robinson (Oasis Books), Ric and Ann Caddel (Pig Press), Peter Hodgkiss (Galloping Dog Press), John Muckle (Paladin), John Harvey (Slow Dancer Press), Peterjon Skelt (North and South), Alan Baker (Leafe Press) and, finally, Tony Frazer (Shearsman Books). My thanks too to all the editors of the magazines where these poems first appeared. Their work and care is a generous encouragement for any writer.

Lee Harwood

In memory of
my grandmother Pansy Lee Harwood (1896-1989)
and Paul Evans (1945-1991)
who showed me so much

title illegible / early work

1964-1965

Cable Street

    blood
    dripping slowly
    from your throat.

    how can I watch you anymore.

Certain individuals frequently suggest that I should write about
Brick Lane and Cable Street, two areas that I know intimately, having
lived in the same these last six years. The two streets are situated on
the western extreme of the Borough of Stepney, now renamed Tower
Hamlets under the Greater London Scheme. (MEMO: Are we really
expected to live up to this pastoral name retrieved from the archives?
Captain Jack is dead.)

    mid-afternoon
    in some top floor room
    sunny day outside.

Perhaps, or rather, the reason why these individuals make such a
request is that they are romantics. *nostalgie de la boue*. Wilde's opium
dens still doing good trade in their heads. X street (ref. Dorian Gray)
now renamed Y street, the haunt of 'low lascars and chinamen'. The
romance of the slums, all very romantic.

    The County of London (Grace's Alley, Stepney)
    Compulsory Purchase Order. 1963
    No. 37 Wellclose Square.

        I am writing with reference to your letter dated 12 January
    last and would confirm that 37 Wellclose Square is included within
    the above-named Compulsory Purchase Order, which will shortly
    be submitted for confirmation to the Minister of Housing and Local
    Government.

        Subject to the Minister's confirmation of the Compulsory
    Purchase Order, general rehousing by the Council would be undertaken
    at the appropriate time of those eligible residential occupiers who
    would qualify for rehousing at that time. I would mention, however,

that it might be some twelve to eighteen months or more before the Council would be in a position to begin general rehousing.

Yours faithfully,

The square at night – all wind scudding and black cobbles. sound of fights in Cable Street, and another drunk or cursing woman staggers round the square. one more lap. and sometimes this scene is so clichéd, it could be out of some Brecht opera or Zola. It's too absurd. people dying, and crowded, and hungry.

Walk down nearby alley Sunday afternoon. hardcase men in blue suits and white shirts. Ford Zephyrs and Zodiacs round the corner. all standing round in the sun, outside jukebox cafés. smell of stuff hits you one end and by the time you're half way down you're high too.

And anyway Cable Street – half pulled down, only its shadow left. All the melodramas that might and have happened. the whole scene like some stage set for social protest 'movies'. the crumbling buildings and boarded shop fronts.

'Well, well,' said pussy twinkletoes, 'isn't that a surprise!' And it was a surprise too. Everyone in Woodland was talking about it for weeks after. 'Fancy Wendel coming back after such a time. He must have had some rare adventures.' And wherever you went the only talk was that of Wendel.

a hundred night cafés. jukeboxes. the whole street vibrating. Algerians twisting in the arab café. cafés filled with everybody. what's the difference at night. Mod kids keep calling me Dennis. Why? Do I have some other side that I don't know about? Am I king pusher of Cable Street? Dennis the walking pleasure dome. Have I commandeered a colour machine. roses growing green.

And summer mornings children singing and hand in hand as they ring-a-roses in the asphalt playground. fat women teachers somehow on their wave length.

the moon so clear in the sky
above these city trees
your lips and eyes
so tender filled with love.

Hunger marchers. mid '30s. columns of grim pale men silent.
just a drum beat as the column moves by.
A coffin from Jarrow.
Or, May 1926. General Strike. armed food convoy moving up East
India Dock Road and Commercial Road. Pickets silent beneath navy
machine-gun positions. armoured cars and Coldstream Guards in
each truck.

Small meeting of strikers outside Seaman's Institute, East India Dock
Road, when covered lorry drives up. stops just past them. then tail
board goes down. and out pour the police. and from other direction the
mounted police. both charge into the crowd. Father Grosser running
out arms extended to stop them. his fingers smashed by police batons.
Thank you. Everyone running in all directions. for safety.

what humiliations and pain. the fat men laughing in their clubs.
Churchill wanting to slaughter every striker. Odessa steps. Thank
you.   Thank you.

the hum of factories. lorries unloading at the warehouses. people
going in all directions. carrying and moving crates and boxes and
barrels. hooters wailing. horns blowing. The cranes grinding. ships
moving into the quays.

According to Lenin part of the reason previous revolutions failed was
due to poor organisation, as he explains in the case of street fighting
and barricades. The former revolutionaries' mobility often being
hampered by their own barricades. This was also the case with the
1871 Paris Commune. In fact Lenin published in *Vperyod* the memoirs
of General Cluseret of the Paris Commune on the tactics of street
fighting – 'considering it extremely important to spread knowledge
and understanding of military tactics and war technique among the
working class', if a revolution was to be successful.

(MEMO: How was it Verlaine survived the Commune, passing daily to
and from his office? In fact – why did he? N.B. this is an even more
relevant question.)

The raising of barricades and street fighting were also a frequent
occurrence in London during the anti-fascist riots of 1936. especially
in East London in the Stepney and Bethnal Green areas.

A witness I know, then aged sixteen, can remember seeing whole
gangs of men prising cobbles from the street to throw at the mounted
police detachments at Gardeners Corner. The police were trying to

clear a way for the fascist march. This was just one incident in the Battle of Cable Street, 5th October 1936.*

I turn on and then re-read your poems. a fly buzzing round the wall and room centre. the mystery of stains at the bottom of a glass. eye slowly swivelling round. yet so soon I'm lost in your world as I read. the room is gone and all your words and pictures fill my head. and look out the window – children playing games in the school yard. the factory girls sunning themselves. their hair and breasts obscured by white overalls. man eternally repairing his car – just the sound of his hammer striking the metal. so loud and important. pigeons swaying in the tree tops.

floating through space. velvet black. my rocket ship slides to distant white stars.

---

*The Battle of Cable Street was caused by the British Union of Fascists, led by Sir Oswald Mosley, aided by the police, attempting a propaganda march through the 'East End'. This was opposed, naturally enough, by the Jews, Socialists and Communists. There were three main battle points – Old Mint Street, Cable Street and Gardeners Corner, though numerous skirmishes took place in the many side streets in the vicinity. On the one hand the police were trying all ways to get the march through, first along Mile End Road via Gardeners Corner, and alternatively along Cable Street. This, on the other hand, was opposed by the anti-fascist forces. The dockers turned over lorries to form barricades across Gardeners Corner and elsewhere, and crowds erected barricades across Cable Street, 'ripping doors and furniture from houses and pulling up paving stones'. An ingenious device were planks with nails knocked through which successfully stopped all charges by police horses and motorcyclists. (MEMO: Marbles rolled under the horses' hooves proved equally effective. Also the waving of sheets of paper in front of a horse's eyes would invariably cause the horse to rear and so throw the rider. (NOTE: One such unfortunate police officer when dismounted was chased by the crowd which pelted him with his horse's own dung. The reason for their anger was that the said officer, issued with rum by his superiors previous to the riot, was striking with his baton any person within reach – old women and children included. In fact, he went berserk.)) And if police tried to penetrate a side street a group would rush to defend it, and form a human if not a physical barricade.
The fascists, who assembled 3,000 strong in full uniform at Old Mint Street, were unable to move – the police having totally failed to make any passage whatsoever, despite numerous baton charges. By early afternoon the police retreated and Mosley was ordered to disperse. End of battle. (NOTE: It is interesting that the Communists rallied their supporters using the Spanish Republican motto – 'They shall not pass'.)

the light over my navigation table warms the charts and instruments I've left there.
now smoking in the break and watching planets slowly turn. the beauty of this clear plastic slab in the port-hole.

> sea noises outside
> and you in my arms
> among the cool milk sheets
> distant car lights sliding across the room
> high tide and the moon boats
> swaying in the night
> wind
> sea wind
> such peace
> the strength of your loins
> pressed to mine
> our seed mingled

CHECK: Is the chemistry right? Are all the factors taken into consideration before we take further action?

> the silence of the ship at night
> the coast fading
> and black smoke from the funnels
> sweeping into the dark night sky
> our topless towers burnt
> in orange flames
> in the distance

The atom is split in order to find its exact nature, and in turn the fundamental nature of all matter. The main research technique is the observation of the interaction of matter and energy, for instance the effects of radiation on the atom. Bohr, Planck and Schrödinger (Quantum Theory, etc.) explained the behaviour of electrons, and this, in the 1930s, answered many of the questions related to the atom (nucleus and electrons). But it has only been in recent years that the nucleus itself has been seen to break up.

EXAMPLE. A piece of radium placed on a photo-sensitive plate gives off particles – the tracks of which can be traced on the plate. These particles are not all electrons. What is being witnessed is the decay of the radium nucleus.

Up to 1962 thirty-two different and distinct tracks (distinct in length, curvature, etc.) had been recorded. So the nucleus, far from being unique, is, in fact, an elaborate mechanism made up of at least thirty-two particles. And every day more particles are discovered. Early in 1964 at the Brookhaven Laboratories, USA, the omega-minus particle was discovered. But this, more than any earlier discoveries, marked a major breakthrough. Whereas previous particles discovered were unplanned and unexpected, this was a predicted particle. A theoretical chart had been made which could tabulate the whole scheme of the particles of the nucleus. Obviously there would be gaps in this classification, but these could be found, as was proved by omega-minus, the discovery of which verifies the possibility of a chart, and so is a step nearer to an understanding of the nucleus.

sometimes lying on my bed at night ships hooting on the river.

On the Sunday of 9 May 1926, Cardinal Bourne, Roman Catholic archbishop of Westminster, said at the high mass in Westminster Cathedral – 'There is no moral justification for a General Strike of this character. It is therefore a sin against the obedience which we owe to God ... All are bound to uphold and assist the Government, which is the lawfully-constituted authority of the country and represents therefore in its own appointed sphere the authority of God Himself.'

At the East India Docks a mass of strikers outside the gates were intimidated by the sight of bluejackets manning a machine gun that was directly pointed at   them.

wondrous dream hashish visions of the quiet and beauty of just every minute article and detail that surrounds me

and what can you do. every noise going through the whole house. and cat crap and dustbins on every landing. and the stink of people and decay. one toilet for the whole house. fifteen people in six rooms. all the kids reeking of piss and black with dirt.

This is an all-white house.

'Sorry. No coloureds.'

wailing indian music coming from the cafés below. Brick Lane. and standing grey faced at the window – no flowers, no blue skies. peeling off my overalls after the night-shift of cleaning out office blocks. The sky is grey. the rooftops are grey. the roads are black. Red neon signs blink.

the river slides smoothly
under many bridges

THE CATS   are here again

in molecular biology . . . . . . let us be basic
    a big fat rocket is taking off
    from the launching pad.

    Do the presidents know what they're doing?

    space conquests?

smoke and the sound of my own chest lungs breathing. the decision to
turn my eyes to look at another corner of the room. the ginger of my
ginger cat assassin ten times brighter.

    O I am of noble birth
    noble family
    we are poor.

this chaos, total and illogical. put all the plans and patterns back in the
box for they're quite irrelevant.
                                cat saxophones.

sitting in the dark on this summer night. turned on. window open and
cars passing. people walking by below. the slow rise and fall of my
chest. you reading me Blake in the half-light. man in house opposite
kicks a ball round his yard

an ark is moored somewhere in South London.

        O   Prince your days are done
        The Revolution's come.

                                        1964

22

This morning

for Harry

this morning
leaving you
in a crowded street.
heading off to start the late shift
I just couldn't think.
the pain of your leaving
and my love for you
      as hopeless as ever
my stupidity as ever
thinking I could forget
and re-arrange my memories
while you walking round happy
in the afternoon sun
and tonight warm in some bar or cinema
or driving back home feeling good
or maybe – like me – sad tired
and scribbling it all down
to make it feel like
something had happened today.

Angel rustling in the dry ditch

ah   the bamboos sing

not for you
              not for you

and sadly

                  not for me

in this café
where angels drift
from table to table
whispering their lovepoems

waiting for my angel
who's late as usual
who never comes

frogs and green fishes
whistle their lovewords

when they do
I only catch the last word
but hope some day
              to hear it all

a quiet rustling
behind my shoulder

h-64

tiger and me danced ecstatically
it was love at first sight.
the orange and reds of our joy
chandeliers glitter in the diamonds
in my love's eyes.
and they collapsed so easily.
my own eyes gone.
and a sweet dew pond in stead
                    in my head.

Poem for Roger Jones

children playing in the trees' branches
large fruits sucking them in
with liquid sighs.
the plain is deserted
except for my own dust-trail
that chokes the remaining life.
I stop my metal horse
gear in neutral
and pace my domain.
a saddle-bag full of plans
for the future.

The man with blue eyes

1965-1966

As your eyes are blue...

As your eyes are blue
you move me – and the thought of you –
I imitate you.
and cities apart. yet a roof grey with slates
or lead. the difference is little
and even you could say as much
through a foxtail of pain   even you

when the river beneath your window
was as much as I dream of. loose change and
your shirt on the top of a chest-of-drawers
a mirror facing the ceiling and the light in a cupboard
left to burn all day   a dull yellow
probing the shadowy room   "what was it?"

"cancel the tickets" – a sleep talk
whose horrors razor a truth that can
walk with equal calm through palace rooms
chandeliers tinkling in the silence as winds batter the gardens
outside   formal lakes shuddering at the sight
of two lone walkers
                              of course this exaggerates
small groups of tourists appear and disappear
in an irregular rhythm of flowerbeds

you know even in the stillness of my kiss
that doors are opening in another apartment
on the other side of town   a shepherd grazing
his sheep through a village we know
high in the mountains the ski slopes thick with summer flowers
and the water-meadows below with narcissi
the back of your hand and –

a newly designed red bus drives quietly down Gower Street
a brilliant red   "how could I tell you..."
with such confusion
                              meetings disintegrating
and a general lack of purpose only too obvious
in the affairs of state

28

              "yes, it was on a hot july day
with taxis gunning their motors on the throughway
a listless silence in the backrooms of paris bookshops
why bother   one thing equal to another

dinner parties whose grandeur stops all conversation

but
     the afternoon sunlight which shone in
your eyes as you lay beside me watching for. . . –
we can neither remember – still shines as you
wait nervously by the window for the ordered taxi
to arrive   if only I could touch your naked shoulder
now   "but then ..."

and the radio still playing the same
records I heard earlier today
                       – and still you move me
and the distance is nothing
"even you –

The white cloud

the white cloud blinds me
passing through your blue chair
and eyes

why does the bird fly?

why is this wall so white?

      why do you cry in my arms?

why these interminable questions?

my love   my what?

        another passing bird

rattle of typewriters
spending the afternoon
      when one ray of sun
      light waves
a clattering shoe
in the street below

no –
one does exist outside this town

          dove   love

swaying in the television masts overhead

and my love eyes studding the walls
of your room
centuries watching our ritual

Before Schulz the Kiteman

Paris clambering through the chimney pots of your dreams
harpsichord slicing eggs
     into flowers
flowers into tumbrils
tumbrils into towers
towers bursting from lakes
        in remote mountain districts
a peasant walked dazed into the village
        a dog couldn't avoid his boots
    a hay stack collapsed
    crying
        when you passed

"oh it really twists within me" he said
a tear enveloped the village
I couldn't discipline my troops enough
so the campaign lagged through a winter schedule
rain obliterated a trail
    in a water sun
    a man emerged with rabbits in his shirt
and passed through the city walls
"let me tell you how this curse came upon us"
a dam was breached
and ever since people couldn't stop
you know the winter also collapsed in tears

walking along the avenues

my stomach arches you
and a love army marched across
occupying us hopelessly

this was only the beginning

31

For John in the mountains

In a mountain sun
pursued by my own phantoms
monsters lurking in the forest
                            in my head
an innocent forest out there
mountain flowers and meadows
the swirl of grass and pines hissing

at each open bush a terror
behind me   a dark snow
darker than your eyes'
dark snow
in which some flowers
can grow into me
a night when your river
could have left its bed
a desert awakening
a maniac pyramid
settle into a newness

your kiss holds such towns

Rain journal: London: June 65

sitting naked together
on the edge of the bed
drinking vodka

this my first real love scene

your body so good
your eyes sad love stars

but John
now when we're miles apart
the come-down from mountain visions
and the streets all raining
and me in the back of a shop
making free phone calls to you

what can we do?

crackling telephone wires shadow me
and this distance haunts me

and yes – I am miserable
and lost without you

whole days spent
remaking your face
the sound of your voice
the feel of your shoulder

The sun burning its own fur

when the museum crumbled
    parrots rocketing fluttering

your eyes shining
    sad love stars in the night

stuffing falling out everywhere
floorboards lolling in the dusty sky

a piranha perhaps

      if a cage should

and to return to windows collapsed
answers lost
and to return to
and to return to

the interrogation lasted the night
    and long into the next day

red and white and green feathers
still fell among the rain drops

let me build you in a house
    and then come in

Green light

for Michel Couturier

the night tingling
sleigh bells arching you

    is it?

this star within your mouth

a love eye burst from a mist
hanging
tinkling glass tree
           downward
erratic rhythms

    is it?

whining geysers
and the softness of a clean blue shirt

watch – is it? – a movement
in the streets a train and shop-fronts

an instant blasted in pinkness
    of London squares roses flashing
    from the slots of pinball machines
    arcades dressed in greenery

let a bison ramp its hill
into one small star speck
carpet patterns shuddering
claws caught in metal fissures
and torn off near their roots

a night tingling
the ghosts within me
a black wall circling

No – all the temple bells...

No – all the temple bells
can only kneel
groans and chantings

a purity neither lost nor found
only a further dumbness with words

I can kneel here
        with no special ritual
but my own
a carpet design
        or a twisted heap of metal
my obsession god this minute

cymbals dulled drums
        my clothing so ornate that
        I have to move with ceremony
    gold and silver
        silks at my throat
a minute explosion puffing
from a small top window

whoever you are
let me shelter you

        and with this
        drumming rhythms grew
    until the entire planet was woven
            into

an elaborate stringball
rolling across a green desert
whose orange and humid night
I now eat and offer you

"let us reconsider ... I mean these
mountain problems"
a car starting in a quiet side street

Journal 20 May 65

the new angels ...
oh fuck these angels
an eye closed half vision
of black smoke clouds
        in my red sea
white shredded feathers falling
        through the night
of your gasp

angel body twisted like rope
old homestead photos of fishermen
        plaiting rope with creaking
        papuan wood machinery
gun slingers riding in
and messing up the whole show
"don't take our father away"

let his cock droop warm and clean
        in his denims

I don't know . mental fingers
        goosing him in wood-shed
        ecstasies
why should the bandits want him
        – when I'm here
the first to come in all situations.

Lausanne 26 July 65

a cat twining itself round a mountain-top
the mountain crying
tears set in the long black fur
a lake so cold
that palms keep their respectful distance
on hotel balconies overlooking this scene

this couldn't be
yet the cat's eyes – I know – have shone
in so many towns
shadowing me and so many others

if lions tigers forests could spring
from such an earth

and the train's restaurant-car with
knowing smiles exchanged over the wine
and signals so often repeated
that they've lost their meaning
and the response becomes a mere formality

dark woods with orange creatures
flitting through like forest rangers'
lanterns in the unending storm

but only repeating themselves
and other nights
and so lost again in the fur of nights
half-suffocated
but the plan always working out
and a head bursting from the lake
gasping
and catching breath
the submarine escape-hatch stuck
but a way round this difficulty was found
always given that last chance
when the pressure gets too much

so the idiot's grin and the calm return
of the sailors to their ship
and the mountain curling round the same
or another cat
in its well-meant and sadly clumsy fashion

The white and blue liner left harbour and began to cross the ocean again

the lone hunger of wolves on ice blue days
a sleigh with tugging yapping dogs passed through the
forest
and I was still nowhere near you
autumn was the same in seaside towns
as it was in the dark mill-town valleys of the north
the rain beating down on the sodden hill-side
to tell you of the warmth indoors seems
too irrelevant –
                    a kiss gone forever
is too easy to understand that I have to stay
silent
the leap back into cafes and juke-boxes
again is too simple a reaction that I
follow it and am surprised that it works

"the deserted houses and empty windows
what can I say"

just fold it up and pack away
a tangle of circumstances

Summer

these hot afternoons "it's quite absurd" she whispered
sunlight stirring her cotton dress inside the darkness when
an afternoon room crashed not breaking a bone or flower.
a list of cities crumbled under riots and distant gun-fire
yet the stone buildings sparkle. It is not only
the artificial lakes in the parks ... perhaps ...
but various illusions of belonging fall with equal noise and regularity
how could they know, the office girls as well
"fancy falling for him ..." and inherit a sickness
such legs fat and voluptuous ... smiling to himself
the length of train journeys

the whole landscape of suburban railway tracks,
passive canals and coloured oil-refineries.
it could be worse –

at intervals messages got through
the senate was deserted all that summer
black unmarked airplanes would suddenly appear
and then leave the sky surprised at its quiet
"couldn't you bear my tongue in your mouth?"

skin so smooth in the golden half-light
I work through nervousness to a poor but
convincing appearance of bravery and independence

mexico crossed by railways. aztec ruins
finally demolished and used for spanning one more ravine
in a chain of mountain tunnels and viaducts
and not one tear to span her grief
to lick him in the final mad-house hysteria
of armour falling off, rivets flying in all directions like fire-crackers,
and the limp joy of the great break-down
which answers so many questions.
a series of lovers – but could you? –
all leading through the same door after the first hours
of confused ecstasies.
the dream woman who eats her lover.
would suffocation be an exaggeration of what really happens?

the man who forgets, leaving the shop
without his parcels, but meaning no harm.
"it's all a question of possession,
jealousy and ..." the ability to torment,
the subtle bullying of night long talkings.
what artificial fruits can compare with this
and the wrecked potting-sheds that lie open
throughout the land? gorging their misery
and that of others ... geranium flowers hacked off the plants
by gentlemen's canes and now limp on the gravel
    paths wandering through empty lawns and shrubberies
afternoon bickerings on a quiet park bench while
families take tea at a convenient cafe, so nicely situated.

engines and greased axles clattering through the shunting-yards.
fluttering parasols running for cover
under the nearby elms as the first heavy sweet raindrops
lick the girls forehead. the slightly hysterical
conversations crowded beneath the leaking branches
waiting for the july thunder to pass. The damp heat
and discomfort of clothes, a tongue passing the length
of her clitoris ... and back again ...
erections in the musty pavilion which should lead to a lake
but doesn't. the resin scent and dry throat in the pine wood
across the meadows.
                "surely you remember?"
but so long ago.

strawberries lining her lake in the dark woods
an old picture slowly fading on the wall
as if a flower too could change her face
as a dusk cloaks our loneliness

Poem for Peter Ruppell

naked girl breasts silhouetted against
racing screen of trees swinging bridges
and leaves falling softly on crashed motors

all this confusion and now when a warm
numbness mind blanks
leaving a body operating automatically

a girl breast against my cheek
an obsession with cars starting in quiet side streets
in the centres of cities

a helpless wing flapping
inside your eyes and my eyes
the last petrol coughing through the night wind

letterpoem

nothing happening. I don't do much.
fix every so often
and a couple more days drift by in cloudy footsteps.
I go to work each day and come home in the evenings.
sit around and listen to the radio.
It's colder these nights.
the piles of old newspapers become less
interesting each day. I've done all the crosswords
and read how the Wild West really began.

lunch-times I sit in the park
watching the sun and damp grass.
there's no big fiery blast to end this poem,
no sudden revelation – "more's the pity"
– and even this sounds too neat.

That evening Pierre insisted that I had two roast pigeons at dinner

The loon house woke up
it was as if in the late afternoon and the exercise was repeated
some days when the streets were overgrown
the odd mail coach got through and a
bear was sighted on the outskirts of the marsh town
your sentimentality is better now than
    the earlier cynicism complaining at the
quality of omelettes

that solitary flag on the skyline and the
grey public buildings that surround the park
how you hated me but now we could embrace
it was and you saw it sunday papers
spread over your bed and my shy clumsy introduction
fleeing to another's arms usage can mean safety
I can tell this from photos
hasn't this battle field been too often re-visited

"hasn't this fool game gone on too long?"
we locked the hut up for the last time
and walked back down through the pine forest
the melting snow-line a thing of the past

"New York will welcome me"

the blue cadillac
sweeps round the sky
into its tower sun setting
people file out of the offices
and crocodiles move into the subways
a grey man standing on a column
of sponge cakes
shook himself awake
and continued counting the pigeons
while a red cat
twirled his tail
on a bar stool
sucking the scotch
still left in his whiskers
"life gets tedious ..." he said
as the last indian arrow
passed through the breast pocket
of his last check-shirt
one dollar is seven shillings and tuppence
and at present there is a water-shortage
in new york meaning water cannot be
served at table unless requested

so the love song and finger strokings
and eyes meeting on the stairs
of eastside tenements
all at a meeting planned a year
                                    a head

Interrogation

1

a crackling in the next room
the officer quickly rose
I could hear him talking quietly

we folded the house
        and moved to another site

2

the plain was deserted
a few stunted fir trees
the first snow falling
mottling the landscape

that day it was my duty
to polish the sledge runners

I sang quietly as I worked
my breath in small clouds
the barn empty
it was then that

3

a list slowly mounting
crossed out
remounting

a cherokee fusillade
in his eyes
a warm hand
suddenly found in the bed

4

"you will either say A or B"

    I could see he was getting angry

"you will either say YES or NO,
you do or you don't –
you understand me don't you?"

    his distress was painful to watch

    I left the room
    and danced on my own
    to rock'n'roll records
    slowly in a larger room

    a temporary block was achieved

"you see we have to know …
"it is useless your continuing like this …
"we can help you … you need our help …"

    he was practising in the next room
    he worked so hard

    did he ever rest?

5

or was it that fencing job
         over by Snake Creek
must get me some new gloves
that wire can rip a glove apart in a week or less

6

the snow began to settle
and I returned to the main room
the table was set
we began again

but first a quiet
the wind outside
the transmitter humming
the officer finishing his cigarette
I sat in the usual place
the light was set
the papers sorted
we began again

it was still very quiet outside.

Landscape with 3 people

1

When the three horsemen rode in
you left me
there was no great pain at your leaving
if I am quite honest
you disappeared back into the house
and I mounted up and rode out with the men

It is strange that now many years later
aboard this whaler I should remember
your pink dress and the crash of the screen door

2

The roses tumbled down through the blue sky
and it was time for us to go out
Our horses were saddled and the peon waited patiently
The morning was still cool and quiet – a low
mist was still staring at our horses' hooves.
So we rode round the estate till 10 o'clock
– all was well.

Later at my desk – the accounts settled – I would
take a thin book of poems and read
till he brought me my dry martini
heavy ice cubes clattering in the tumbler
and vodka like sky-trailers gradually
accepting the vermouth and sky.
but this was a different ranch

and my dreams were too strong to forget
a previous summer. And what did it matter
that the excitement and boredom were both states
to be escaped except a grey   lost   and on
these mornings a ship would sink below the horizon
and winter covered the islands   a deserted beach

3

Once it was simpler, but in those
days people rarely left the city
It was quite enough to stand on the
        shingle bank when the tide was out
and the sun was setting and workmen
would lean forward to switch on television sets.

4

on winter evenings I would come across her by accident
standing in bookshops –
she would be staring into space dreaming
of – that I never knew

And most of this is far from true –
you know – we know so little
even on this trite level – but he – he was
more beautiful than any river

and I am cruel to myself because
of this and the indulgence it involves.

I loved him and I loved her
and no understanding was offered
to the first citizen
when the ricks were burnt.

The white room

1966-1967

The book

1

It is so much a question of isolation and machines
and the systems never quite work out
and we're glad of it   or half-glad
through fear   the confusions when faced with "logic"

"the nervous touch of sickly women"

and the motorcyclist started his machine and
putting the bike into gear left
and rode fast along the big highway
that led in a hard inflexible line to the
dock gates   drunken captains finally
sobering and breaking down with real tears
in the mahogany ward-room
while the chintz curtains were drawn by a fresh breeze
through an open port-hole and the heavy brass
catch glistened in the sunlight

"you're not fooling me or anyone else"

2

The 5.25 Pullman train, painted chocolate and cream, or
rather, burnt umber and cream, left Brighton station
on time as usual. It was October and dusk was just falling.
Autumn had taken the countryside and produced the
classic scene of woodlands whose leaves
slowly turned yellow.

The spire of the village church could
be seen behind the hill but we
had to hurry and so couldn't stop
this time. She drove the car
as fast as she could in silence
purposefully ignoring me. I
would have liked to have seen that
particular church – early Norman

has an innocence of its own.
It was the brown of the ploughed
fields, with rooks in the elms
and seagulls following the tractor,
it was...   No, you can't see
and the...   my contempt was equal
being a city-dweller by nature

3

The churchman was still leafing through his sermon
        notes when the tea was brought, and even this
did not wholly distract him.

I sat opposite him trying to read your book
and, really, your poems have never had a better setting
than this. The staff of the restaurant car were
discreet in the extreme. Their activities as
        expected went unnoticed. Things went
        accordingly and no real upset was allowed.

Our separation seemed only temporary

The main door was locked on that afternoon
but we were still able to walk round the churchyard
examining the inscriptions on the tombs. Later it rained.

I put down the book and carefully poured another cup of tea
avoiding spilling any
as on this section the track was very uneven
and the carriage rocked a great deal
The churchman was not so successful
but his minor irritation was only passing
I couldn't help but love him for this
and it seemed a reflection of my love for you
with your words still so close to me

The woodland outside at last disappeared
and then there was only the blackness broken
by the occasional orange light from a farm window

4

It was not the same and when the end was realised
with all its implications   I had grown calm

We had both avoided the logical sequence and were
glad of a breakdown in negotiations   The rest
would be taken care of –
imagined loves and the riverside farewells
are only left for our weaker moments
the tears and longing were real enough until
a corner was rounded to meet a new distraction

We parted at 1st Avenue and 51st Street – it was July.
Wearing a cream-coloured suit and dark glasses
he crossed the street and then turned to wave – twice –
the lunch-time traffic was very heavy and I soon
lost sight of him.

The maturity

"When I come home
tell me all about it."
                    Stevie Winwood

When the tractor had started up the hill
farm machinery was left lying all round the yard
the orchard was old and diseased
and many of the trees had to be uprooted and sliced with
                              the yellow buzz-saw

the dull maturity weighed so heavy

the dead lover *really* failed

and now the hard slanting rain made it impossible
to even see the tall hedges that surrounded the meadow

But this was leading us nowhere....
though the occasional sight of distant cities
produced the idea of "hope" and intimate dinners
in the best restaurant which was only
filled with the natives of that city, and with no
foreigners except myself and our friend – a fact that
was both strange yet genuinely understandable.
So many good things are carefully withheld
from "common knowledge" and kept for "the few"
who sought more than mere sensation
but this exclusiveness was in its own way a disease
that fed more on the memories of past summers
than any present reality, and even the reality
of these "summers" was doubtful –
Pictures of loving couples had been enlarged beyond
all recognition

The city too was a picture and an image –
yet this was so attractive when compared
with the endless complications of a "maturity" and
independence that became a bad-tasting medicine
that was sure to be good for the subject

of the struggle in the private nursing-home
where sickness was politely ignored and
life took on an unsurpassed gentility

Yet it was so obvious that eventually
the melodrama and its adolescent hero's role
must come to an end, and in the same way
that the relationship between the young
man and his older patron would cease
just as the young man would cease
when he became a "grown-up"

The grown-ups were waiting in the theatre lobby
for the last of the children
in the audience who were reluctantly leaving the auditorium
– their hearts still beating from the thrills of
the pantomime and drunk with the
theatre's orgy of plush and gold

Many years later he grew a moustache
but it was a very frail barricade
and the questions only multiplied
as soon as they were asked.
Not being a vine, it was hard
to know where and what to grow into.

His July return

"rushing to embrace we were
at last in each others arms
I kissed his ear
and the sun reflected in my
gold ring making it glow even more
as I gripped his wrist
I saw how much darker my hand
was than his
but with our arms round each others shoulders
there was no question of inequality

The public buildings sparkled white
and the green of the park could be touched"

When I had finished writing this, I looked at
my watch. It was 2.30 in the morning.
I decided to go to bed. The rain had
stopped and I could see, when I parted
the curtain, that the streets were completely
deserted.
Tomorrow tourists would ride in small pleasure boats
down the river. I would be at work.
But it is still worth considering what this
means to both of us, if anything,
though both our meeting and this poem
are not free from a note of triviality

I wish I had a cat

The late poem

Today I got very excited when I read some
poems by Mallarmé and Edwin Denby, and later
in the evening, by F. T. Prince.
I don't get "very excited" very often,
but today was an exception;
and the fact I got "excited" was only
increased when I realised two of them – Denby
and Prince – are still alive and are probably
now asleep in their beds in nice apartments.

Ted Berrigan has met Edwin Denby.
I don't know anyone who's met F. T. Prince.
I wish I could meet F. T. Prince;
maybe I will one day, but it will have to be soon
as he must be getting old.

This poem is rather silly
but there is a place for silliness
even today when it rained
and was too cold for July.
It is a rather silly day,
in fact, it's damn stupid.

Do you really think it's worth getting angry
though

The seaside

You wrote such a love poem that I was
dumbfounded and left to scratch the sand
Alone in the surf   I couldn't join the bait diggers
I'd left my fork and bucket at home
and I am not rough by nature

You were sitting on top of a boulder deep in the forest
it was taller than a man and surrounded by pine trees
I think there are pine trees in Fire Island
but I've never been to Fire Island, though
I can imagine and we all know what could happen

there, but......
and the world that started in a parked car
was really a fearful one – It would only lead
from one confusion to another
and I couldn't do this to you on the giant highway

She was a reason in herself, and women need
the menace of ambiguity in their actions
so one action might well signify the opposite
– an act of sacrifice really the act of killing and revenge –
and this much was true

The exercise book was green and the distance
saved much embarrassment though you were
in many ways ignorant of this
I still can't find my bucket and bait-fork
but this is only an excuse

Pastoral

"Today autumn was especially beautiful
the sun shone and bright leaves lay
happy on the pavement.

"I don't question this, and my reward
of pleasure is duly given – just as
the triple rainbow came so a
small girl called Celeste could see it.

"She too deserved what she got –
sooner or later we deserve what we get
and all our patience is rewarded.

"Celeste and her father left the bookshop
without any books. They needed none
in *this* world that I'm making now.

"I have to work in the bookshop
but long ago I stopped reading books.

"Instead I wait for the autumn sunshine
and the pale city square drunk with
its own lushness and the scent of dying leaves.

"And in this world I can put many other
people I love, besides Celeste and her father;
so the bookshop and square are really quite full.

"This all lasts until spring
when everything has to be changed,
but I can wait and spring has its own surprises.

"Summer of course follows. There is no
winter in my world.

"Perhaps as you read this poem
you will be pleased, and the smile of
memories and hopes will come into your face.

"I do hope this happens as it's the first
time I've written nature poetry."

The separation

The time came when the desire to return
grew so strong that certain songs would automatically produce
the physical pain of real longing
just because they were markers of former street-days

the restraint was hard to bear
when the cold closed in for the year

when the thaw might come was a speculation
too distant to have much reality

The orchestra would come and go
and there seemed no regulation by which
one could plot or know their movements
yet at each appearance they never failed to chill
me with their blank faces and uncompromising playing
It was as though "I" wasn't there,
as though it was all a self-supporting film
The leader of the orchestra would advance
towards me yet his eyes were set beyond me
It was so unbearable that I was forced to stay –
though the pleasure of mute acceptance was denied me
– their movements settled this
Many days were passed waiting in suspense for the next
appearance

When the sun shone you could see the cliffs
and seashore across
The little boats bobbed in the harbour

That the pain was doubly hard to bear since
it involved such self-restraint as to
not gulp down the remedy which was
a bottle with "answer" crudely printed on the label –
the symbolism of this almost went too far

If a ticket was bought it could only mean one thing
and there waiting on the other shore
was a table loaded down with childish treats

and lots of cuddly bears romped all round the table
I had almost packed my knapsack
before I realised the spell might break

I had tooted the car-horn for almost half an hour
outside their new house before I realised
    they might not want to come out

The old photo had faded and was now very worn
It was more than a matter of mere recognition

Yet underneath the forest even when the glacier
threatened imminent extinction
the desire to return to a warmer land
was as fierce as ever and no dangers
even in the form of pawnshop windows that displayed
neat rows of pistols and automatics – each with its neat blue
price tag hanging down so prettily – could deter me

It was a necessity to be continually reckoned with
even at the height of ecstasies;
The ice-cold chewed deeper
It hurt when the "answer" was realised
and the whole camp stood silent for a minute

The ferry leaves

The ferry leaves, winds buffeting,
but in the end –
a skyline sparkles and her body is more beautiful than ever,
her curves among the park's flowers and
my joy at the sight of the bleached wood piers
is really only a reflection of my joy in her
when the statue turned green
– even though the word may not be spoken.

The mystery began
yet never lessens – in fact,
it increases from an earlier acceptance
to a later wonder.

The unicorn and fading kings are only symbols
of her body, my lips
kissing the inside of her thigh.

Who would imagine that a memory
could have covered a mountainside
with wild honeysuckle – yet it did,
and I love her for it.

The voyage was planned, but

An apple tree, young and uprooted, stood on the boards of
                                                a small rowboat

"Soon I'll be across the lake
you will be waiting in the forest cabin"
The scene had been well rehearsed
but the set is very expensive
like my cabin and the drinks I never pay for

and with all this –
it is so strange to see all one's life spread out behind
like some vapour trail and the plane's destination
or whereabouts are still far from clear
left pouring over maps as the night drones on
the kings were not on time
nor did they find what they expected
They passed through a series of parks and buildings
and ended drinking beer in the street
and eating cheap cakes whose freshness was doubtful

but where does that lead?

they were glad to get home
though no one could fail to be impressed by the
forests and deserts of the continent – and, in
a way, their lives had gained a wholeness,
and a purpose in loving was clear to everyone

That the man loved the woman, and that
she loved him, became the only theme of importance
in both their lives

"How I love you ..."

for Jenny

1

the fountain played long into the night
"how I love you..."
the house backed onto a large courtyard
which was filled with trees, plants, and
flowers in profusion. Wistaria climbed all the walls
and covered all the balconies, producing an atmosphere of
unreality that

In a park a long way downtown the chess-players finally
put the pieces into the yellow box –
the box had a sliding lid on it –
This only left the drummers
but it is hard to know if they count
or if anything counts in these terms
when the basic qualities are still unknown
perhaps a comparison with a mountain landscape
with wild honeysuckle – perhaps – and boulders scattered

2

Riding back across the continent
just to lay beside the fountain again
my boots well worn by now and listening alone to
rock'n'roll on the radio usually saddens me
horses will have to be changed soon
but there are other things that won't

3

The night had passed and morning found us lying
naked in a large white room. Lifting a corner
of the blinds, it was noticed
that geraniums flowered and the fountain

still played surrounded by greenery.
On the opposite side of the courtyard a famous painter is known to live.
But her body, most of all, contained the infinite
in tenderness and wonder

4

The town became so tempting that I could easily
have stayed and forgotten forever that I had
come there as a stranger.
Yet more beautiful towns had known stagnation,
a series of pointless acts, a complete wrong-headedness
that was only to later be realised with regret.
There were plans of sorts – or rather –
the time had come when I knew
what a love meant and must be.

The courtyard may or may not exist,
yet fountains and greenery will always be there
when our bodies meet. Beneath her eyelids
the bright red of geraniums, and the wistaria's
blue flower in her breasts' delicate veins.

The journey

a prose poem

1

I left Taos early in the morning – the sun was
rising and the first indians were entering the town.
I could leave now – I knew that Kit lay at rest
with all the peace a man can expect.

It was strange – getting used to the rhythm of my
saddle again after the long period of inactivity.
The hard stained leather when carelessly touched
burnt the fingers. Of course, I remembered other
towns, and was half afraid of the planned journey.
An expedition …

Tucson *was* hot *and* dusty. The arid mountains looked
on impassively. I found out the truth of the 1871
Apache atrocities when I read the farmer's accounts.
No holds were barred and the feats of cunning astonishing.

Riding across country – Fort Worth at last appeared
a low silhouette on the plain.

My death was near, but I had to find …
My love was left behind in the quiet sea town, and
I knew I would never return – and if at all, not for
many years to come, and this is a long time in which
memories can be completely lost. "Tucson was inevitable"
and now Fort Worth had its own answers.

As I passed through the outskirts of the town I let
the reins lie slack, leaving the horse to walk at
the pace it chose, and enter the town as she willed.
When we turned into Main Street the body of a
recently lynched bandit was still sat in a chair on
the boardwalk. Flies crowded and crawled through his
beard and around his eyes. I could see the town had
still kept its sense of humour, despite the continual
threats. He was still wearing his hat and pistol.

I dismounted and according to the local law, checked
my rifle and pistols in at the sheriff's office. He
was a pleasant man, and we talked for a while. In
our conversation, we discovered that we both came
from the same town, and I took note of this as such
a bond could well be of use in the near future. I
decided to cultivate this friendship if I could,
despite his aloof nature.

All this travelling wearied me, and it seemed far
from its end. How was I to know?
But it was when entering the livery stables that I
realised who had passed me in the street only minutes
before. The realisation and the shock at being so close
– at last – to a finality. But was it that final?

Many resolutions had been made in the past and within
months had been allowed to quietly melt away
in the back of my skull.

Would I be able this time to see it through?

2

Adjusting the long tight cuff on his blue shirt –
"Parting and travelling both include equal measures
of fear and joy."

(That statement is so firm that it is almost final,
but really it doesn't mean much. What does matter
is that I am frightened. "He is frightened" – these
words? their very inadequacy yet finality only leads
this problem further.

And – to be quite "Honest", is it worth any effort?

I could leave now – the desert is still there. Sage
bush scratches the road's hot back when a wind is willing.
There *is* a real feeling of sureness when pulling
tight and buckling the wide strap beneath a horse's
belly, and the final act of parting is the last tug

on the saddle-horn to make sure all is secure.
But whether this mood goes beyond the town's outskirts
is another matter.

The line between escape and pursuit is so covered in
ground mist.)

Once in the mountains, I dismounted, secured the reins
to a stunted tree, and sat down on a boulder, and cried
– for no special reason. And this made my tears all
the more violent. I don't often cry, and when I do it's
always when alone.

One's own indulgences are not for strangers.

3

The stranger had passed me. Though, was it him? –
certainly I heard stones clattering under a horse's
hooves nearby in the night. But the small fire I had
built in the rocky hollow only produced enough light
for the most basic domestic activities.

Imagination can lead anywhere, and this can be another
cause of grief.

How long will we be dodging each other. Long ago the
distinction between pursuer and pursued was lost. We
were both chasing and fleeing from one another. The
whole affair became a matter of style. At times I
wonder if he really exists. Unreasonable accidents
can so easily be taken as proof, when desperation is
there, or lack of desperation.

The journey involved no symbols or allegory. It was
real enough. The story went on …

The mountains were by now blue smudges on the horizon,
and any discomfort felt just had to be borne. "You're
not back east now."

It would be many weeks before we reached Cheyenne.

4

To hide was necessary
and many grottoes existed in that region
when they came the citizens greeted them warily
and with a reservation that at first could not be understood
except by a few – later in the day
a building was seen in the middle of the plain
Many old men were driven out

I rode by

I couldn't tell them

Come now, let us walk in the garden
It was a mild evening
based on very little experience

Really there were few emotions involved in the telling
just as the final meeting was one in which
the departing could only smile and continue to watch the
river while the one who had to stay in that city
grew more agitated talking in a way he had
never done before and this was a pity

Yet when the time came and I was at last slowly riding
down Main Street I turned in my saddle and looked back
he was walking back across the street
into his office
"We both waved"

Still in the mountains I could see the road
stretch out before me for many miles
It would be three days crossing the desert
and then again the mountains which were now
just a blue smudge on the horizon

5

Many boats on that shore were already too rotten
to ever float again. The village had lain in neglect
for too many years. There was nothing for it. He
would have to wait there till the ferry was service-
able again, and that would not be for two days.

He spent the time mostly lying in his room. The
sun slanted across the white walls. At meal-times
he would rise from his bed and walk slowly into the
cantina, return to his room when he had finished
eating, or walk down to the stone jetty to see how
the work was progressing. One of the villagers would
stop hammering, look up at him, and wave.

It was a time when boredom could almost make him
give up the chase, and return – to where, he was
not even sure, but self-disgust and despair always
are homeless. It would merely be a change in his
direction.

What remained was the weight of his pistol as it
rubbed his thigh. He never took it off by day, and
at night he slept with the whole gun-belt at his
shoulder.

So many precious things had been lost; and what now?

In the evening he stood on the outskirts of the town.
The blood red sun was now resting on the horizon, and
the sky reared up in strata of white, yellow, blue
and purple. At such a time it would be very easy to
give way to tears.

The perfect gunman had to be met, set down and passed
through

6

Several months later I saw him, and for the first
time he saw me. It was almost too sudden for us
both. By this time we had grown clumsy. The years
of preparation and pursuit had wasted the earlier
tensions and energy. We just stood looking dumbly
at one another. All our resolutions were frozen.
If we had been able to move our hands, our fingers
would have been too clumsy to even get a pistol
from its holster. At last I reached for my gun,
but it was useless, like I said.
Trying to speak – that too was hard – but after …
The shock was so great, and the answer almost too easy.

Yet, finally, we agreed that evening to settle it,
to shoot it out standing six paces apart.

The evening came, and we both were now ready. The
delay had been necessary. We paced out the distance
and took up our set positions.

The only sound was that of the night birds preparing
for their evening's hunting.

A borrowing

The cranes stayed set as they were
a bridge went up and 3 barges came into the dock
It was only too obvious how the kingdom was
steadily shrinking. Without taking
too easy an escape, it was hard to know where to go.
I was often near to tears. Many believed …
and then I returned to the locked door
A cymbal clashed and golden rays sped out
with many sinister and conflicting meanings
It was never the same as the previous day
but nothing appeared

Weakness was admittedly the soft key
I could rush into court and hang on the Chancellor's neck
but he was so much a comforter, softly patting
my shoulder – "There, my lord" – there was not
the drama of "Fare you well, my lord".
My sword was never built for such things
another beautiful decoration

Rip your garlands or your garments – the shriek
of tearing fabric would at least startle those who
were completely asleep.

When an ambassador comes I am always tense
and put on my best clothes, but they have never
yet lived up to the expectation. A quick
dismissal is the one saving grace and faint
proof of strength

The court was poured in and out of the palace,
like so much milk being poured from jug
to cup, and cup to jug, and so back and forth
as is the custom of Sikh women preparing refreshment
for guests

and so everyone would stream forth into the
surrounding countryside, only to have the film reversed
I could not laugh at the shock, it was only a

larger mirror
crumpled paintings were carefully strewn about the floor
It was only the painters who laughed
and started again
"On this matter it is difficult for me to advise you,
my lord, but I am sure your wisdom will come to your aid."

At this, he respectfully retreated,
but it wasn't the answer
and I was getting desperate
and far from able to stand outside the situation

Yes, I cried; but when, at last, I raised my eyes
from the wet palms of my hands
It was still all the same
Everyone stood exactly where they had
before my fit
They stood quietly and respectfully
waiting

The tractors are waiting

in the pain of silence
the meadows ...
and from the barn's top loft
but nothing rustled among the bales of straw
the tractor is waiting in the meadow
but flowers arranged in a vase are no real comfort
      despite their scent

if an obsession were carried to its limit
then there would be a clean sky across
which grey clouds lovingly – and a lone
farmhouse stands out on the flat horizon
its plank walls bleached and the wheat
coarse and hard

For Robert Motherwell

the white and then the black oval
and then the white and then the black
and then the white around the black
oval or rather the white overhung
by the black the white and then the
white and then the black oval form
within the white oval and then the
black and then the white and the flurry
of snow as the body fell and then
the white.

The Encyclopaedias

1

As the sun was setting like a red ball behind
a net of black pine trees that I'd seen
in a picture in the Children's Encyclopaedia
It was impossible to avoid the realisation

So many opportunities were missed and this meant
that certain people were disappointed
It also inevitably meant that on other occasions
it was the totally wrong thing that was done
This could only be realised afterwards when
the ruins and havoc were there for all to see

The dead "Sea-Hawk" was laid on top of
the royal pyre, and by this time
no one really believed anymore that
the weapons and gold served their latest purpose
All that hurt was the tears
which could not be denied the leader

There were other pictures and …
All our talk … yet I saw so little
of what was really happening in the crowded room
and the first crumbling of a famous monument
began with a few hurried words in the narrow kitchen
when he … and surely it was obvious
the next move waited patiently for me
But I failed and was at a loss
and didn't see the full significance of the immediate –
She …
there are obviously limits to the extent
of action and passivity we are willing to undertake

2

The real regret was later, when stories increased,
and there was one picture entitled "What could have been"
It was a clumsy utopia and crudely aped
Moreau's "The Chimeras" subtitled "Satanic Decameron"

76

but was this a truth? or another myth
only too ready to hide and decorate the object
that alone was already too complex for the casual observer
to even *see* let alone experience

In a later volume were a set of miniatures
that told a story of a series of intimate scenes
– the first showed the interior of an apartment
It was mid june and an unusually hot night in that city
The scent of creepers vines and flowers filled the room
There was a balcony beyond this room and a garden below it
lush with summer and the night – a fountain spluttered
in the darkness.

In the last 4 miniatures we are shown a man dressing
with care – obviously he is afraid of waking someone
He then leaves the apartment …
(It is very tempting to suggest more than can actually be
shown by the paintings)
The man is then shown outside in the street walking
towards a subway station with "96th Street I.R.T."
written over it.
The third miniature merely shows the interior
of a subway car which is completely deserted.
But the last miniature has much more of interest in it –
the man is once more seen in the street.
He is apparently nearing his destination.
The dawn must be approaching
since the sky is now much paler than the previous
street scene mentioned. – also he is in a very different
area to the one he has just left, as is evident in the nature
of the street and buildings painted here
This is finally confirmed when the observer notices another
subway station entrance shown in the top left hand corner of
the small canvas – but this time the name of the station is
much more difficult to read, yet using a magnifying glass
he will read "Astor Plaza I.R.T." and in even smaller
lettering below this – "Lexington"
The air is warm and soft – but it is impossible to know the
feelings of this man walking along the deserted street

3

Her face was no longer clear, though the history was agreed on
... and all that remained
was for the seal of our two bodies to be gently added
to the document – but what happened in reality? –
Maybe ...
He stood awkwardly wanting the excuse
only I could give him   the events and their sequel
        as he imagined them
His attempts at selling me were so transparent
and there were so many tasks to perform
before I could even approach her surrounded
as she was by others
No clear sky or street was open – and it meant
an involvement in a kind of power struggle
– this ritual could only strike me as grotesque

"Choice" and "perception" somehow looked ridiculous
words in these circumstances. The bowl of punch was
now quite empty, and as the party started to break-up
I wasn't sure who I should help on with their coat –

as I too had to go somewhere ... though the decision of where
was getting beyond me
and no one had looked through those volumes for so long

I think I went on with him to dinner somewhere
... where did you go then?

The Argentine

1

Of course I was discontent with the ranch
the pampas was only there for one purpose
that the whole land knew of

The green continent groaned and stretched
while its brown rivers charged round in all directions
only to settle down as before
when the land fell asleep again

A single tree dominated the mountain top
but went no further than that

So many wrong and arrogant statements were
made in the geography books – and I
was not alone in resenting these

Brown chaos charged the towns and finally
smashed through into the very heart
of the people – they were terrified and some of
the people died too

"Can't you understand my difficulties?" was
whispered as I put my ear to the ground
"I wasn't prepared, and she could not wait
for ever"   the voice went on and on
with an endless story

I kicked every door down in the house
but found no one
It was opportune that at this moment
the group of horsemen galloped into
the court-yard. I had seen them at this
same time last year – but this time
I was prepared to ride away with them.

2

This was not the first migration
nor would this country be in anyway final –
the movement had been an agony dragged across
many lands   it was a well known process

The dead and numbed tundra or the sleepy estuary
with its brown banks and heavy jungle
"The grass was always greener on the other side"

She understood, I thought, that the ritual was grotesque
as it was necessary – and all this belonged elsewhere
just as the real love was elsewhere, but
this through accident and not desire

3

"He never visited the ranch" – and so in isolation
I continued as best I could. No profits were made
but neither were there any losses to talk of
What made it bearable was the memory – and hope –
an airport lounge with its automatic clock
and the milling crowds at the bus terminal...
He had a way of looking across a dinner table
– it at once commanded and yet asked for kindness.
Love and tenderness were the dominants – and the ceremony
of social acts was all that separated a fulfilment.
In fact pleasure was gained by the very anticipation,
by the polite dinner conversations and the easy talk
in the bars afterwards
The brief touch of his hand
or the caress of legs under a table
gave more than any previous experience

When these memories grew unbearable ...
The mountains   the long ride and brief visits to other ranches
where nervousness made an evening pass quickly enough
in a series of laborious politenesses

On the way home, rain beating on the car roof
the essential notation of details like

the car's head-lamps and the night – their effect on one another
All this seized in weak desperation to distract
a realisation, and sometimes even a regret

Such an image had been set so deep in my heart
that its destruction would inevitably cause
much more than local damage
and the fire chief didn't exaggerate when he said
"keep all those people well clear. That building's
going to collapse any minute.
It's little more than a burnt-out shell"

4

How could the two see reality as far as it meant
the truth of their situation or rather how true
were their words and sensations – both come and go
quite rapidly after all.

On the sidewalk in Fifth Avenue just below 12th Street
3 men were parting outside a German restaurant.
The older one had to go uptown – it was late –
and the 2 young men were
separately going to drift round the Village for a few hours
Then, as the taxi arrived, Joe reached up
and kissed John on the forehead.
The 3 split up. It was a hot june night – of course.

The second young man left outside this action
evidently felt something
It would seem that he was really the more concerned
with the older man and that he now regretted
his passiveness in that street, but he had had a reason
– though now it seemed a mistaken one.
He had feared to embarrass, where in fact a spontaneous act …

The frustration at a missed chance is universal
and a slight jealousy of the successful equally common
There were other days, and usually the older and the younger man
succeeded in gaining some degree of harmony

But …

the pressure of a train and a plane schedule
put a simple end to that development

Finding a torn letter left in a hotel room
he read – "she must have felt something for me,
but I was torn in two,
and in the end I just waited for her to come to me
– and this got me nowhere, as she too had her fears
and I was not the only answer in that town."

5

Mist rose from the marshes
and the rider was forced to skirt the estuary
and keep to the higher ground. Dew was heavy on
the coarse grass. The grazing lands stretched as far
as the eye could see in all directions.
And above this vast open countryside rose a hot sun
that soon thrust the mist back into the ground.

The cocks crowed and the horses grew restless
for the coming day's work. The dogs barked
and strained at their leashes as the first men
fed and watered the horses. This was the beginning...
Then midday.   Evening time   the faint sound of voices
from the other side of the yard

6

The rare view from the mountain pass
suddenly made everything seem clear
and the whole geography somehow too simple
The answers were obvious and the route through
all the country ahead

The journey had to be made and the horsemen were right
But the weight of possessions held on to,
if not for love of them, then for some sense of duty
and fear

These accounts of past and future journeys
became boring ... and any violence that might have been
has now grown limp like the vase of dead flowers
that the efficient house-keeper will surely clear away

White

for Tom Clark

It all began so softly and white was the
colour that showed the most dominance
In fact – it was a glorious white
This meant that the toy soldiers had to all be rearranged;
confusion on all levels and "no one was really prepared"
My arms were no longer tired – the rest had been good

It was a happy occasion
but you were so surprised to see the same flags still hanging
limply from the long balcony of the state apartments
In the end the ritual remains unaltered
and that too is comforting and like the "last words"
of an important general's speech
talking of history, religion and tradition

The only sabotage was the irritating acts of open vanity
performed by women consciously or unconsciously

The paintings would have to be winter landscapes
and this means lots of white paint –
I've bought it for you already. He said "look in that cupboard"

The New Start is near
and white is so tender anyway
like the little sail-boat in the large round pond

The doomed fleet

1

The entire palace was deserted, just as was
the city, and all the villages along the 50 mile
route from the seaport to the capital.
It was not caused by famine or war –
"It was all my fault."

The troops of desperate cavalry were ridiculous.
The naval guns could pick off
whatsoever their whim dictated,
but there was only one commander-in-chief.

2

The grey battleships lay in silence
anchored in the middle of the harbour.
They were ready all the time –
the only necessity in all this was decisions.
That may appear laughable – it's all
so simple.

The wounded was a subject never touched on
in the officers' mess. And the question of
occasional small but brutal outbreaks of
disease was similarly treated.

Nothing that could disturb the carefully planned
vanity was tolerated. That was the new order.

3

Grey waves slapped against the sides of
the iron grey battleships. Seabirds screeched
above the wind; they don't sing.
Even the ships appeared deserted, except
for the occasional dark figures that would
hurry along a deck and then disappear
through a hatch-way as abruptly as when they first
appeared. It was their continual menace,
however, that undeniably asserted their presence.

The menace. The power that vibrated
from the ships. The grey harbour.
Power. Menace. All terminals irrelevant.

In such a setting, it is not surprising
that tears or tenderness, shown by a small
but delicate gesture or caress, were of no consequence.

The men's minds were set –
they didn't understand "pity". The very word
had been deliberately deleted from all the books
scattered among the fleet. They needn't have feared.

4

With so few exits left ...
"That was really ridiculous, wasn't it?"
Murder was just one of the expected events.
It would be carried out with the precision
of any naval operation and with the coldness.
Everyone knew their place and to disrupt the
series would be not so much reprehensible
as an admission of bad breeding in the extreme.

It was only actual closeness to the event
that allowed any levity. The midshipmen were
only boys, after all. And the officers and the men ...?
– who is ever free from the fears and shadows
so firmly established in every childhood?
The point of "safe return" had long since been passed.
There were no maps in existence
for this ocean, nor were there any charts
of seas, harbours or sheltered estuaries
where the least clue or news-item
might be found concerning "The Successful Voyage".

Maybe they never did get there and, instead,
the whole expedition lay at the bottom.
This already begins to sound like a very bad boy's story.

5

Age began to show … and the divisions widen
and become even more resolute and rigid.
"What could have been" became altogether another story
like the family photos in the captain's wallet
– there was no room for sentimentality now.

The heavy service revolver seemed somehow too
melodramatic to be real enough for its purpose.
I suppose there was no doubt about efficiency
– only about motives. Wasn't this word
"melodramatic" something of a key?
How *real* was the death to be?
Was it an act of necessity or escape, or
one last weak self-justification, self-gratification …?
The scene was, apart from superficial changes,
only too familiar, and tired.
The unwilling audience would at least be glad
of the concrete finality of this latest show.
It couldn't have much of a sequel, thank God.

The chart table was cluttered with empty coffee cups
and a haze of cigarette smoke filled the navigator's cabin.
It was very late at night, and the navigator
had fallen asleep, fully clothed and exhausted.
But even now, with so much unanswered and so much confusion,
there was in the atmosphere a feeling of finality
whose very grimness brought a strange joy
and relief. The death would not be that dark –
The dead body somehow would know a sweetness
that can be compared to the parable of the
bees' honey inside the dead lion's carcass.

The fleet steamed out beyond the point.
Nothing was free from the ridiculous and "pain."
The laughter was not disrespectful,
nor was it really that inappropriate.
The night sky was a dark blue and most stars visible.
Salt waves broke over the rusted iron decks.

"Goodbye Tom"

The dull mist that ... the castle stands still
within its moat   "Wild One"
and the sadness leads the same way when facilities
are there   the work of their provisions

The radio plays more music, though it is the
soldiers in the castle who select the dance records
and the nature of the provisions is still a secret
The whole network was clearly set out on the wall chart
by the use of brightly coloured pins and narrow red ribbons
that linked certain points – but the next morning
all that remained was a faded wall

and the "dull mist" – what became of that?
It could always be put down as an omen or, even
more disturbing, as a symbol
of the approaching dream that marked the couple
for life.

No pity need have been wasted on the castle
its walls were beyond all hope of restoration
The people really were glad and the tourists sighed ...
with relief the Wild One and the provisions
were destroyed and so was the confusion and the sadness
The number of loose ends to be tied and tidied
also were destroyed – everything was destroyed –
until the orgy of destruction itself became ludicrous and upsetting

When the site was at last at peace
there was only "the dull mist" left
What else happened was forgotten

"You will soon lose sight of me
sleeping or awake. It is too much to expect.
Goodbye –"

It is all as though the whole
land decided upon this, that "the tribe

should once more be scattered"
The words when printed in a text book grew
as cold and distant from events as the
illustrations of traditional tribal tattoos
whose magic and power ...

"Are they scattered?"
"That was a stupid question, sir."
The dull mist parted by the approaching dream
like a new plough-share slicing the air
and black earth   Soldiers playing cymbals
The Words were left there singing "Keep on Babylon"

The Blue Mosque

a poem to Gus

1

The blue mosque had one tower higher than all the others
and it was from this that the muezzin called the faithful
to prayer and thoughts of God:
"There is no god but the God."

The city which contained the mosque
is unnamed, as it is unmarked on the map.
The school atlas was equally useless, and history was more
of an amusement than most would admit.

If you will accept this story for what it is,
then you may well be amused or even pleased;
the actual reality is of no importance.

The facts and words – even whole lines –
could so easily be seen as matters of pure style.
Even the cheapest trinkets can mean more,
in the end, than any heavy act of conscious gratitude.

The towers, I believe, are called "minarets" – but this
accuracy is completely lost as it progresses.
All there really is is a deep concern for "charm"
and the "pleasant surprise".

2

Despite appearances and the first reflex reaction to this –
there could be more love in this acceptance
of the ludicrous and obvious
than in the many books with titles like
"Morals" or "Morality" or "Truth" or "Logic" or …
and so on down the book shelves.

3

And now that the expedition was safe –
surely it was time for all the merchants
to thank their saviour and God?
– quarrels broke out almost immediately
over this order and precedence.
With the wilderness safe behind the city walls
it was not really unusual to see how quickly
memories and resolutions burst like soap bubbles,
and already few of them could even remember
the blackness of the storm clouds and,
least of all, their own helplessness and terror.

It was only a matter of days ago –
there was no question of it all being part of
some ancient riddle or alchemist's anagram.
It was all *too* simple, and that was why …
books of authority and accepted formulas
were so violently seized.
The obvious and simple were like two men who
stood open-handed at the doors of the mosque.
It became essential for the merchants
to ignore them, if they were ever to continue as they were.

No one wanted the blood stains
on their own saddle cloth – yet …
The expedient had to be insisted on in private.
And the tanned hands' very openness –
that revealed pale tender palms
capable of so much love and gentleness
– was an unbearable threat.

4

The dull red neon in the bar windows and the "other things"
were left behind as they walked up Avenue B
to the brighter lights – there was no real malice
in this, nor in most actions in that city,
or any other town nearer or farther from home –
though "home" unfortunately is meaningless.

Is so much repetition always necessary?

When put bluntly again the question was
finally answered by "the man".
He said: "When faced with basic but *deep* emotions,
 like (obvious, and so "extreme") love or fear, the common reaction
among this social and age group is to –
ONE: regard the experienc*ers* with hostility;
and TWO: urgently seek explanations (i.e. refuge)
for (i.e. from) the experience in the "copious realms"
of established reactions and common prejudice or
ignorance."
This was all pretty obvious …

5

The muezzin, I'm sure, knew this,
and did not he proclaim the greatness of God
over the rooftops and the whole city every day
from his minaret in the blue mosque?
And, surely, when in the quiet of his study,
he knew that "the greatness of God" embraced
far more than the power of one individual?
Rather couldn't it be the power of this very openness,
whether in hands or love? The doors of the mosque.

There were so many books and already his head
began to ache. "Such is the life of a muezzin,"
he said, and laughed.

The sound of a fountain splashing in the courtyard
soothed him. This whole scene though
is only taken from another book – but
do the circumstances and scenery matter?
The mosque, the muezzin, even the expedition
that was claimed to be safe –
there can be no difference to their final reality
whether they exist only in the imagination
or in the physical world. It's only a matter
of the story holding people with its style
and lists of events, either curious or tender.

6

This preoccupation with words can only be boring
for the onlooker – painters arguing over the different
brands of paint – useless parallels.
What have any of these words to do with
praising a good man or a love?
No matter how exotic the decorations
and materials – the words always fail.
It's all been said before – and this
very questioning now heard only too often.
Even the clichés seem to contain less conceit
than the poem, and now the poem about the poem,
and the poem about the poem about the ...
and so on and on deeper into the cheap gaming house.

What has this to do or say with any weight
of the two men with open hands at the mosque
who will be murdered by the merchants' assassins?
or the good man that still knows how to love?
or the loved one whose kiss alone is beyond words?

The whole poem book must be left behind
(while I go to help the two men
and thank the good man), and then let it
be forgotten now we've become men and women.
And surely it's obvious to the simplest of men,
as it is for the muezzin to cry "There is no god but the God",
that I should now leave writing this poem
when it is so late at night,
and go lie with my love.
It is late, but such blindness
could not go on forever, thank God.

Plato was right though

for Ed Dorn

1

The empty house – the empty country – the empty sky.
Reverse it to A–B–C.

A: The large house
filled with many people – servants and guests –
it is now a country mansion.
It is white and has extensive grounds and woods.
There are many people.
They hunt and shoot. They laugh and talk.
In the evenings they play games.
It is all like a picture-book
that teaches vocabulary to foreigners –
each different object in the picture is numbered,
and below is the list of words that correspond
to the many numbers. So – 12 is table;
5: vase; 16: father … and so on.

B: The full country.
The map blocked out with the red of cities
– that's the agreed colour in the atlas key.
This continues into the 3rd dimension with
"concrete and neon" parodying themselves.
Countries, armies, "The People" struggling with
"The People". The borders on the map look
so pretty, with dotted lines in bright coloured inks
– all yellows and reds – dot dot dot – and in practice
nothing more glorious than a stretch of
ill-kept road with a line of battered poplars
one side and strands of barbed wire on the other.
The bad spy story continues … The plot is very obvious
and stupid, even if it *is* all true.
No one could look at this and take it seriously.
And it wasn't just that the generals and borders
were ridiculous, but that the whole situation,
– including the very existence of the cities –
was wholly laughable.

The atlas became the one truly funny book,
and it did not escape our notice that what was portrayed
should be regarded in the same light.
To be totally "negative" in believing the
countries as they were (and the cities) were
painfully absurd and grotesque seemed
perhaps the saner and more realistic.
It was a very pompous speech ...

C: The sky was crowded with airplanes of all colours –
a totally unreal picture with dozens of
happy red, blue, orange and green
airplanes filling the sky in a mechanical
rainbow. Each plane, painted entirely in its
colour with no other markings, flies through a series
of aerobatic stunts, diving, climbing,
rolling over and over, and "looping the loop".
This is happening in a clear blue summer sky –
there has been no trace of a cloud all day.

2

All the previous locations are now impossible.
There is only this confusion in which no one
knows exactly what is going on.
The planes or the hesitating crowd on the lawns,
the house party going its usual way –
but this only in a vacuum.
Outside is total darkness
dominated by the sure knowledge of Death
that takes on an almost human persona
and vibrates like the engines of an ocean liner at night
that can be felt many miles away and yet never seen.
(Black, as you know, is the negation of colour
and strictly it is not even a colour,
while White is all colours.)
And white is the love and only light that can be seen
to really exist besides the blackness.
The White is the only sure and real force
in an otherwise brutal chaos, and the only
home when all else has been lost.
(This new "simplicity" was, in fact, a blessing

and advantage never before possessed, and that now
made the struggle easier and brought a sure relief
in the victory that before was confined to day-dreams.)
A lone parachutist drifting down through the blue ...
And even if he *is* shot dead in his harness
by the border guards, who really cares?
He has the same chances as anyone else.
"When you're facing death or junk, you're always on your own,
and that's exactly how it is," he said. It became daily
more obvious that such clichéd truisms were only too true.

It is not a question of doubts or a lack of faith
in the forces of Good ... but from this black and white
landscape, what is it that will finally be launched?
There is an obvious and reasonable impatience
at the slowness of the expedition to set out and,
at least, attempt an exploration ... an examination
of what had happened in the past and what
could come out of the Interior afterwards.

3

The fact that there should be this co-existence
of opposites ... A desert, a barren plain, or,
to reduce this to its basic elements, a complete emptiness and darkness,
– faced by a crowded world of absurd objects
and events, and a tangled "confusion"; and this portrayed
quite clearly in a desperate heaping-up of words
and pictures. The brightly coloured airplanes flying low
and at great speed over the countryside and approaching the towns
brought a wave of "cold fear" upon all who saw them,
that the jollity of the planes' appearance at first denied.

It was this fact, above all, that was finally realised –
and no matter how painful the realisation, it had to be accepted
that what had gone on too long was due entirely
to a mental laziness that could live with this "co-existence".
There was no expedition to be expected or any news
of it to be eagerly awaited. If anything
was to be found or gained it would only come through
a "personal action".

"All the necessary equipment was there.
I had only to dress and begin.
And it was not a matter of fierce lions from the story-book,
or navigating my sampan through a wild and thundering gorge
only to have to fight 300 Chinese rebels the other side
single-handed with only a revolver and my walking stick.
The fun of these jaunts was a thing of the past.
What it meant now was to live like anyone else
– getting up in the morning, washing, eating meals …"

The convalescence, though once necessary,
was now over. All the wounds had healed and
the neat white scars could only be mementos.
This left no real excuses or causes for further delay.
"And the one simple and basic fact that love
had become a supreme power that radiated from me
was now the key to everything. And no matter how much
time would be needed, the struggle to deal with this
and other pressures was there and only waited to be
used. Like the quiet in the ship's engine-room,
this inactivity seemed wrong."

For some reason the word "LOVE" does not suggest
a strength, or grace, only a mild ineffectuality.
Yet beyond the romantic charades and the gaudy neon letters
outside the theatre – when the Real, and
the True essence is gained (or found), it's only this
love that creates a joy and happiness able to finally
dismiss a cruel haunting by Death, and meet the "world".
And what the words and poems attempt degenerates into this –
a clumsy manifesto in which the words used
appear emptier than ever before and the atmosphere
more that of an intense but bad Sunday School.
———————————————— PLATO was right to banish
poets from the Republic. Once they try to go beyond the
colours and shapes, they only ever fail, miserably –
some more gracefully than others.

Landscapes

1967

The paint box

What did you do? We all know how tired
you were, but you did, didn't you?
I mean the formula can be turned most ways
and it's only a matter then of local colour
to give *that* touch of distinction.
The surface then appeared different –
but under the paint?
Canvas was universal – everywhere.
The tubes of paint were so fat
and funny, as they didn't matter so much.
It was "the rose mist floating down
on the white mountain crags"
that was in everyone's mind.
The poem was printed out like a neat label
and stuck below the picture.
We've been here before, haven't we?
Yes! And it's now one more poem.
That's funny, isn't it? or maybe
it's not so funny, but scary instead.
I mean the whole routine of bare
canvas and the paints all squeezed out
on the palette and then it's just for someone
to step out and say "GO" in a loud voice.
And the day goes by in slapping noises
as more and more paint is used up.

When the geography was fixed

for Marian

The distant hills are seen from the windows.
It is a quiet room, and the house is in a town
far from the capital.
The south-west province even now in spring
is warmer than the summer of the north.
The hills are set in their distance
from the town and that is where they'll stay.
At this time the colours are hard to name
since a whiteness infiltrates everything.
It could be dusk.
The memory and sound of chantings
is not so far away – it is only a matter
of the degree of veneer at that moment.
This is not always obvious and for many
undiscovered while their rhythm remains static.
It's all quite simple,
once past the door – and that's only a figure
of speech that's as clumsy as most symbols.
This formality is just a cover.

The hills and the room are both in
the white. The colours are here
inside us, I suppose. There's still a tower
on the skyline and it's getting more obscure.
When I say "I love you" – that means
something. And what's in the past
I don't know anymore – it was all ice-skating.
In the water a thick red cloud
unfurls upwards; at times it's almost orange.
A thin thread links something and there are
fingers and objects of superstition
seriously involved in this.

The canvas is so bare
that it hardly exists – though the painting
is quite ready for the gallery opening.
The clear droplets of water sparkle
and the orange-red cloud hangs quite seductively.

There is only one woman in the gallery now
who knows what's really happening on the canvas –
but she knew that already, and she
also instinctively avoided all explanations.
She liked the picture and somehow the delicate
hues of her complexion were reflected in it.
She was very beautiful and it soon became
obvious to everyone that the whole show
was only put on to praise her beauty.
Each painting would catch one of the colours
to be found in her skin and then play with it.
Though some critics found this delicacy
too precious a conceit, the landscape
was undeniable in its firmness
and the power that vibrated from the
colours chosen and used so carefully.

During the whole gallery-opening a record of primitive red
indian chants was played – and this music
seemed to come from the very distant hills
seen in every painting – their distance was
no longer fixed and they came nearer.
But recognitions only came when all
the veneer was stripped off
and the inexplicable accepted in the whiteness.

The house

The rain over the hills – the shades of blue and grey
in the clouds on the horizon with evening coming –
The house is on the outskirts of the town;
and the view is something unknown in the capital
and these colours in the clouds are meaningless there.
It is different – a horizon which is formed by
a line of green hills and a solitary tower.
It's all like the early landscape in the city gallery.
And this question of painting and vision
and which seems the more real is fascinating –
I can't explain this. But beyond the hills
are the moors.
The brown and green in the hills shows
there is a forest up there.
This is getting mysterious, and the tower
is certainly not free from a magic awe.
The rain is so good and soon it will be night.
The clouds have almost gone and the sky
is taking on a pink colour.
It's as though time really has ceased, and
all I have to do is watch the bird
I disturbed by the river fly off through
the trees. The river has many eddies
and I can stand by the weir fascinated
for a long time – but I must return
to the house with its view of the hills.
Time really has ceased and
the simple mechanism of the revolver is stuck.

Sea coves

Sea coves and cliffs, the deserted beach –
they all mean so little
You are there and that is what it is
The clumsiness of my actions
We care for each other and love.
The sea is quiet and the streets
in the small port so narrow,
but somehow we get through.
It's only belief – what else
can words do? "Love."
This isn't a parable – the objects
are real enough, they have powers.
Allegories are in the past – there isn't
the luxury or time now.
This sounds brusque – what is the sound,
of our love? The words collapse again.
That was weak, wasn't it?

I can't get my paints out now.
It's not the time. You know –
we both collapse, but somehow
it's as superficial as the waves
and the whole seascape.
We're here and stay put.
It's our move; we paint what we like
and do what we like,
and all the words like "somehow" and the
objects and the "powers" are so little.
To talk of the plane now
would be unlucky – it's just there,
and the tarmac is so pretty with its oil slicks
and the orange wind-sock beside the white hangar.
"Yes, that sounds right, doesn't it?"
I do like oil slicks, but I love you.

Landscapes

The ridges either side of the valley
were covered in dark pine forest.
The ploughed hill sides were red,
and the pastures were very green.
Constable's landscape entitled "Weymouth"
is always in my mind at such times;
my memory of this small part of the
National Gallery surprises even me,
and maybe only I know how inevitable it all is.
The horsemen are riding through the forest
and at dusk they will halt on its edge
and then, after checking their instructions, ride carefully
down into the valley – delicately picking their way
through the small wood and fording the shallow river.
From then on it is not very far
to their destination. We both know this.

Somehow the action has at last gone beyond
the painting and this is for real.
But there can be no self-flattery on this account
– it has all been decided for us.
The illusions of freedom are at last
shown to be so obviously ridiculous that
most people cry at this point.

What it left is a canvas and paints
and a little time for distraction before the event.
It is not so much a justification – but saying
"Goodbye" now appears irrelevant.

All the lists and secret worlds have now been
exposed – there is little left to say.
"I did care, and the love I claimed
was and still is the miracle that continues
to astonish me. I love you.
It is only that death has forced
me into obeying its commands.
I am powerless and in its power."
And that's a personal statement and as true
and honest as I can force the words to be.

The saddles creak and it's almost dusk.
It doesn't really matter whether this is
the real or a symbol – the end's the same.

The "utopia"

The table was filled with many objects

The wild tribesmen in the hills,
whose very robes were decorated with designs
of a strangeness and upsetting beauty
that went much further than the richly coloured silks
embroidered there could ever suggest; ...

There were piles of books, yet each one
was of a different size and binding.
The leathers were so finely dyed. The blues
and purples, contrasting with the deceptive simplicity
of the "natural" tans.
And this prism and arrangement of colours
cannot be set down – the fresh arrangements
and angles possible can only point through a door
to the word "infinite" made of white puffy clouds
floating high in a blue summer sky;
this has been written there by a small airplane
that is now returning to its green landing field.

The table is very old and made of fine mahogany
polished by generations of servants.
And through the windows the summer blue skies
and white clouds spelling a puffy word.
And on the table the books and examples
of embroidery of the wild hill tribesmen
and many large and small objects – all of which
could not help but rouse a curiosity.

There are at times people in this room
– some go to the table – things are moved –
but the atmosphere here is always that of quiet and calm
– no one could disturb this.
And though the people are the only real threat,
they are all too well trained and aware
to ever introduce the least clumsiness
or disturbing element into the room.

At times it is hard to believe
what is before one's eyes –
there is no answer to this except the room itself,
and maybe the white clouds seen through the window.

No one in the house was sure of the frontiers
and the beautiful atlas gilded and bound with blue silk
was only of antiquarian interest and quite useless
for the new questions. The whole situation
was like a painting within a painting and
that within another and so on and so on –
until everyone had lost sight of their original landmarks.
The heath melted into the sky on the horizon.
And the questions of definition and contrast
only brought on a series of fruitless searches
and examinations that made everyone irritable and exhausted.

Once the surveyors had abandoned their project
the objects once more took over.
It would be false to deny the sigh of relief
there was when this happened and calm returned.

The bus bumped down the avenue
and ahead were the mountains and the woods
that burst into flower as spring settled.
The plan and the heavy revolver were all quite in keeping
with this, despite the apparent superficial
difference and clash of worlds –
there was really only one world.
It wasn't easy – admittedly – and someone
had to stay behind and…
The word in the sky had slowly dissolved
and was now nowhere to be seen.
But instead the sun was flooding the whole room
and everything took on a golden aura
– this meant we were even aware of the
band of horsemen now riding through the forest
that surrounded the valley.

The many details may appear evasive
but the purpose of the total was obvious
and uncompromising

The final painting

The white cloud passed over the land
there is sea always round the land
the sky is blue always above the cloud
the cloud in the blue continues to move
– nothing is limited by the canvas or frame –
the white cloud can be pictured like any
other clouds or like a fist of wool
or a white fur rose
The white cloud passes a shadow across
the landscape and so there is a passing greyness
The grey and the white both envelop
the watcher until he too is drawn into the picture
It is all a journey from a room through a door
down stairs and out into the street
The cloud could possess the house
The watchers have a mutual confidence
with the approaching string of white clouds
It is beyond spoken words what they are
silently mouthing to the sky
There was no mystery in this – only the firm
outline of people in overcoats on a hillside
and the line of clouds above them
The sky is blue The cloud white with touches
of grey – the rest – the landscape below –
can be left to the imagination
The whole painting quietly dissolved itself
into its surrounding clouds

Question of geography

Facing the house   the line of hills
across the valley   a river somewhere
hidden from view   the thickets there
I can't remember   the colours
green   a rich brown   as the sun shone
turned to slate grey   at times a soft blue smudge
with dusk or rain clouds   the details obscured
but like a long ridge setting the skyline
Months gone by   the seasons now almost full circle

It was spring and our garden was thick with
primroses
Each morning I would go out and...

Ridge in the distance   everything the same
as before   it must be
The moors edged with pine woods
in the south–west province   a repetition
but the cathedral town unchanged
It makes no difference who was there
all inevitably reduced to the question of
geography or memory

And now awaiting the next spring
set in yet another place   this too with
its own colours and forms
the others seeming somehow irrelevant in the present excitement
but still real like a very sure background
– you paint over the picture and start on
the new one   but all the same it's still there
beneath the fresh plains of colour

The picture book open

1968

Central Park Zoo

for Marian

Looking at the zoo   the great white park
of a misty winter's afternoon   "You're great!
and I love you for it"
All the animals have their thick winter coats on
– the childish humour of this is so enjoyable –
A brass clock strikes the hour of three and
sets in motion mechanical chimes that are
beaten out by rampant bears and prancing monkeys
with heavy metal limbs jerking to the rhythm
– this obviously moves the crowd of children who're
watching– some laugh with "joy ", others gasp with "wonder"

Let's call this charming story "A day at the zoo" –
all essays to be handed in by the end of the week

But back to the winter and coats
It's very crisp today and the air is clear
The *buffaloes* are magnificent and beautiful – they are a rich
        brown, and the hair is not matted as it was in summer
        "alas"
A pair of *bobcats* lie with their front paws round each
        other's necks – like lovers – they lick each other's
        fur (in turn) – it is a golden yellow
A pair of *badgers*
A pair of *lynx*
Two pairs of *racoons*
and the *grizzlies* and *polar bears* lie sleeping in the sun

Let's call this "The Peaceable Kingdom: A Painterly Reference"
or "Winter in the Zoo" or "A Day at the Zoo"
In fact let's forget what we'll call this
Instead let's ...   returning to
the zoo in the corner of the park
the white mist hanging over the trees
The fact we can become children again
shows how right we were in
believing in our love despite the canyon
which we entered stumbling along the dark bed

of the Bad Water river
But we climbed out the other side
though taken by surprise on topping the rim
never having realised the end was so very near
But there it was – the herd of buffalo
grazing on the lush plains
Geography in our sense *is* exciting
Plotting the whole course now
Sunlight and the shadows of fast
moving clouds sliding across the grassland
I imagine North Texas   or even Dakota   Montana

"The end" only of this canyon   but a continuation
of something greater   compare it to a plateau
of great size and richness laced with gentle
deaths at its edges   the spirits of the tribe
waiting with a deep love for us
It's not so much of a descent either – but these
details can wait   you see

"You're great! and very wise" we laugh as
we reach the top of the rock outcrop
"and I love you for it"

We flower   we continue from where we left off before
though the statement of this can only be
something secondary for us and therefore decorative
There's no worry
                        "People of the World, relax!"
We walk among the animals
        the cages upset you
When I really think I know you're always right
there's no worry   we're on the same planet
and so very lucky
that the poem should end like this
is very good

Halos

I wait   the madonna slowly glides across a gold surface
the icon's doors half open   a trumpet   an angel's wing
"and Mohammed is His prophet"   beyond the blue sky's floating
even the pure patterns that stay free from any sin of imitation
You can understand   the magic of flowers
painted in a formal enough setting yet
the very radiance of these gathered flowers   the woodlands

Your strength   and "independence"   the accompanying childishness
is admitted part of this   but
This mixture can only excite   you stand beside me
no one weighs or sucks the spirits in

The novelty can bring many dangers   a nakedness
among sword points   yet the alternative can only be
a disturbed sleep   the crossroad choice
"Sooner murder an infant in its cradle than nurse unacted desires"

At the third tree you begin again
a small pastel sketch by Redon
and after the vase of flowers some sort of silver –
or is it golden? – maybe – aura round your head

Telescope

The army advanced by night
at dawn the pearl grey of the sea
a large bird flying too slowly   I may be tired now
but lying in bed watching thin white clouds
passing through the window in a clear sky
Your smile is inside me   I wait
In this morning stillness everything seems at peace
the white sheets   the delicate ring of my watch
ticking in a bare white room overlooking the sea
One direction the harbour and the green band of waves
below the horizon – the other the heavy roundness
of the hills, the darker green of the Downs
The army subsides and melts like the night at dawn
– it's in the past now. Thoughts of you glow inside me.
A pale late winter sunshine floods the whole landscape
in a harsh white light and so makes it
look totally bare – the word "naked" can even be used now –
and this same air of nakedness in the sunlight
is like an announcement of the coming spring
The comparison expands and I see this all as a
reflection of your coming return that I now wait for
and how I lie here this morning thinking of you
Far from the shore a small cargo boat presses on
– from here its progress looks painfully slow
but this doesn't matter   neither I nor the boat's crew
can be ruffled with such good things so obviously in store for us

"Camels"

the camels fly   the tents had been folded–up long ago   all this sand
                                                        of the night
even the harbour lights glow orange at this time of the night
your face is always there beyond the clouds
through the large white window the sky's stretched out like a canvas
some days you smile   others you're sad and I miss you terribly
I look at the pictures on the empty cigarette packet
and can see all of this story portrayed there so clearly
and with such colour   how I'm always watching out for you
the creamy surf rushes up the beach dragging the shingle
and filling the sand with a heaviness as soft as the grey
waves swelling behind the foam
at night that is   it's all peaceful somehow
seeing your smile in the clouds   the orange lights

The backwoods

The steamboat approached the quay   "a room full of trees"?
about the lesson   there was a letter aboard for me
Telegramme to stop the process, m'lud
but nothing was learnt from all the mistakes
The steamboat – toot toot – approached the quay
white smoke puffing from its bright funnel
What a bright picture this all is!
And so on into the backwoods

The convicts were led ashore – toot toot –
and the steamboat pulled away
The mail box was as empty as the convicts'
striped uniforms – they started off into the backwoods
until like zebras they were indistinguishable from the trees
I tried to learn my lesson and remember it carefully
so that there would be no mistakes at all this time

M'lud, stop the process   "May it please your grace"
The steamboat returns on the timetable
As the turnpike is quicker, though perhaps the more dangerous
With a letter for me? To write a reply
I go off into the backwoods and send telegrammes
about the lesson   "Come, come, …

New Zealand outback

for Marian

"The three horsemen" is written down in the book
You gave me the book   I love you
My great-grandfather, his brother and a friend
rode out and someone took their photo.
Snap.

It is Sunday and the scent of lilies
really floods the room. It is also a sultry afternoon
in summer.   I love you.
The picture-book is lying open on the table
and shows an engraving of a lily,
your poem about a lily and our love.

The three horsemen disappear over the horizon
I feel as confident as my great-grandfather
that I love you.
Snap.

Sheriff's star

You out there   the dust getting everywhere and the old badge
lying on the table in this particular horse opera
Wyoming

Inside it's warm   it's cold   it's warm
shut the door   you sneeze
The dust or another cold?

Up there   pushing aside the moon and mountain crags
not a coyote, most certainly not.
"git along"

Some place the streets are empty
I crawl into bed when it's this late
it's like day   the moon's so bright
the whole desert floor a pale yellow

Formal portrait

The Emperor Shah Jahan is shown in his garden
in a small portrait painted with tempera and gold
Soft green hollyhocks with pink flowers, a marigold,
daisies and small plants, and flowers so delicate
and whose names I don't yet know

Ladies sit delicately on the swings
hung among the trees under chosen branches heavy with cool shades
– quiet attendants pushing them to and fro;
the only noise in the garden
being the creak of the ropes and the birds' cries.
On such hot afternoons

One thing for certain, the princess must not be harmed
under any circumstances   Negotiations for this
are at this moment in progress   The guards have young faces

A mirror made of highly polished metal
I see your reflection in this and in myself
The moon shines too above the many seatowns strung along the coast
It is coloured a clear white cream
and dominates the entire night sky

In Kashmir and other Himalayan foothills
Bichitr the artist in "1633" came to see
you swim naked to the waist in "a lotus pond" –
the hills behind the colour of a sliced blood-orange
I watch you undisturbed – your neat firm breasts.

The same lady is on a swing now
in a courtyard – steel grey storm-clouds gather
above the Kangra Valley
The same lady is caught in a storm as she hurries
through the woods – the snakes hurry for cover as well
"At the tryst" she stands below the orange flower tree
It is hard to know if these are exercises in grammar
or attempts at communication of sorts
either by the painter or the lady maybe
Sometimes you are the lady, but most often

you are even more beautiful than she is
or ever could be.
The long black hair and clear forehead
your dark brown eyes set between narrow lids

The number of possible scenes and descriptions
seems nearly as unlimited as the ever changing light

As you sleep the fine garden is deserted
except for the moon and a few tigers
The Emperor wears rich scarlet slippers
as he stands beside the hollyhocks unnoticed
Perhaps tonight he thinks of the war on the plains
or remembers when his palace was eaten by fire
You are quite safe and there is no worry

Tibet

Your temple music is fine
and there is such weight and ceremony in the actions
the swaying voices of faceless religious
Coming down the trail the yaks and behind them
the dazzling gold of the monastery roofs
high up the valley   When you fall silent
there's only the dark brown of your eyes – at dawn
I find flecks of green   Whatever it is …
the white rocks were very slippery
Chalk   Dark woods beside all this
In the distance vague lines of colour
caught by the sun   So many small bells
tinkling in the sunlight   the brass flashing
You are beyond this
Not in the desert though I am at fault
the morning only reveals further cruelties
after such richness   you are faced with
the coming night and a long trek across the plateau
where the darkness is cut by loud reports
from boulders cracking with the ice
Though I act as guide it is your light
that radiates from the sanctuary
I let you enter then wait outside
knowing what your return could mean
It is a matter of stripping these animal hides
from the walls of our hut and feeling their strength
once more

Return of the native

The clouds descend so warm and heavy   again
A rigid number gives time to the day but with no
certainty except the recognition of being here before
Once more facing   being engulfed even
"I never thought it would be this good"   and consequently
sway held up by a soft "greyness"   is that it?
eyes narrowing and the lids growing heavy too

There is piping music in the tents   the horses?
Can the stories ever be told once too often?
a new freshness radiates from the change perhaps

Slowly the clouds thin and…

The horses to be seen grazing far across the grasslands
dead zebras lying in the deep grass
and in the distance the roar of surf pounding some coast-line

the giraffe is a bright gold

A wind flicking over the pages of this picture book
in which time seems to go backwards
"early lithography"   "pursued by furies"?
a volume bound in coarse blue cloth whose spine is so faded
the dust settling outlined against the shafts of sunlight
dividing the room
and all this despite various private emotions
whose relevance cuts only too deeply for those who…
looping–the–loop

"The tents have been cleared and there had been
no one there to leave even the simplest message with
So, starting from the very beginning again –
the menfolk sat round the fires examining their bodies for lice
and other parasites. Each success met with roars of approval."
Closing the book

And on the return, after taking in the view from the window
once again, even praising its beauty,
yet all this more a formality than any fresh response –
an old lady's pilgrimage rather than JERUSALEM flashing

Reports continued to flood the warden's office –
throughout the entire district, on and off the Reservation,
carcasses of large and small game were being sighted
and in increasing numbers. The heavy clouds
no longer decorated the distant horizon – "love you"
what does that mean? in God's name in the distance –
they filled the air like snow–drifts
a soft "greyness"   where WHITE had dazzled

The picture–book's colours had so easily drugged us
with their richness that only the vague glow of the present
backed with irrelevant and totally unreal dates suggesting history
appeared to exist until an unexpected gap in the clouds
revealed the proof of rumours once so quickly dismissed
It was not a matter of the odd death by accident
but of a whole bloody trail stretching back into the distance –
beasts trampling in their panic   "Irrecoverable Damage"
totally inadequate if ever a "judgement" – and the time
unrepeatable and lost beyond the plodding repetition of cruelties

With dawn approaching, the birds singing in the darkness
– a young woman talks in her sleep, then laughs –
a happiness even in her dreams

The coast

1968

This year

The children playing on the front step
the sea is green
today   the power games
can't be gentler

The walk along the beach at night
shingle   back home the animals
all playing games underlined with violence
maybe cruelty

Everyone gets very religious
this year   it even opens out
but the desire to give out messages
has to be suppressed in favour of

A neat square is moist and green
its trees each have their
thin black branches that glisten with water
found by accident   it's very warming

To be here   the sea is green
at times grey   there are two empty houses
in the neat square   the windows   a black enamel
Surprised

As she undresses   the children playing in the street
the sea is green   her young body womanly
loose clothes hid her great beauty
at times grey   "olive" she said

Everyone gets very religious
I can understand why   even the power games
gentler   when play stops
what then?   gentler   surprised

Undressed   it's very warming
her young breasts fuller than   no messages
in favour of   nor against
her nipples are small and a defeating pink

Today   green power games can be
gentler than the sea   on the beach
shoo the animals   your lap
her beauty undresses   the sea

Soft white

When the sea is as grey as her eyes
On these days for sure   the soft white
mist blown in from the ocean   the town dissolving
It all adds up   her bare shoulders

Nakedness   rolling in from the sea
on winter afternoons   a fine rain
looking down on the sand   and shingle
the waves breaking on the shore   and white

It is impossible to deny what
taken by surprise   then wonder
the many details of her body
to be held first now   then later

In body and mind   the fine rain outside
on winter afternoons   the nakedness
of her bare shoulders   as grey as her eyes
the sea rushing up the beach as white as

The whole outline called "geography"
meeting at a set of erotic points
lips   shoulders   breasts   stomach
the town dissolves   sex   thighs   legs

Outside   then across her nakedness
it rains in the afternoon   then the wonder
her body so young and firm   dissolves the town
in winter   grey as her eyes

You become a star

Your face so near   your body
at the sea's edge   many continents
away in the distance   the whole shoreline
vibrating   the blue grey sky at night

A single star   through the large window   bareness
nakedness   in the sky   in you and I
the star   the nakedness   "is the work of God"
leaving the very essence   so pure

No matter what the trigger on this occasion
that fires the lightning bolt   the flash
in our bodies   it illuminates the same
landscape

The night is as quiet   your sureness
our bodies shining stars   and beyond
and within   the physical positions no more
than where or what we want

Your return   through the winter
the orange lights of the harbour seen in the distance
I await you patiently   the tide drags the shingle
down the beach   then returns it

So close even now   the shingle
dragged by the waves
fixed in the night sky   as clean and fresh
small pebbles washed by the sea

the night so quiet

Blue glow

As rich as ever   the dull red cloud
billowing up through the clear crystal
A year ago we … the time blurs
There are a series of white lines that vibrate
here   and time becomes patience
almost waiting calmly   it melts   going both ways
east and west   As a back-drop
all the cruelties we perform and later regret
In the blue glow of the mosque one way
and the other to the clear light of the seatown
beyond the high mountains   the bus
making a cloud of dust across the desert
You're gone   the water
warm and flexible   whichever way there's only
what arrives

The cliff walk

In the distance   the cliff walk
decorated piers now antique   you lie away
the ocean is so vast   someday
I am waiting   is your patience enough?

Ghosts haunt the sites of our past
I   someday soon
across the ocean   coming
such love goes far beyond

Green seas look soft and turn grey
the white chalk   a cap of dark woods
it is a matter of wonder
and what comes with time?

Such hands   silhouetted in the window
with a sea coast stretching off into the distance
then maybe it falters   the window   in a white glow
such a blue sky   in all this

the cliff walk turning from side to side
and soft winds brushing   ghosts
distance of the sea-town
you filter the pine woods   there you ...

green paint wet on the railings
your clothes will be marked

H.M.S. Little Fox

1967-1968

The situation

for Stuart Montgomery

"Dear Doctor…"   So many…   Galileo…
and all the worlds in The World and his telescope was now useless
At the beginning of a story there are so many raised hopes
This letter began "You've been too kind"

The empty country house burst into song with
"O sinner-man, where you gonna run to?"
But by now so many of the fine gauze screens
had been broken through and it became only too evident
that the "good" people were not so good
and that "Goodness" was still an ideal which no one had realised
The gardens all gone to seed, and nobody's fault, though …

And in 'Timothy's Space Book' there's no mention
of the monk Copernicus. Everything seems wrong.
The gardens all gone to seed and in the last
crudely coloured picture the returned astronaut waves
a *handkerchief* from the capsule's door.
The grounds so vast and in the middle of all this
the house. It had all been allowed to deteriorate
without stop, until it had gone beyond the point
of any easy or simple remedies. Now the whole operation
would have to be both drastic and costly, if at all.

"The prison of images pursuing, with beautiful
women, the hero of the ritual." That was another story.
History had to be forgotten with so much work at hand.

So far, you see, there can be nothing but confusion
and misappellation, which in turn causes a neglect
now only too evident. To ask for forgiveness is absurd.

If he named a dark dream "the sea of honey",
then why not go on?   though with the reservation
that perhaps there are too many words.

An ancient freighter painted black and red
blew her sirens as she left the dock and steamed
slowly down river to the sea.
You can now add this to the list of symbols
already provided – the large house and the boy's 'Space Book'.
Yes, it brings us all back to "the beginning"
and "the confusion" again. Yet, in fact, each is a separate
world, despite repetition blurring the edges.
"You've been too kind" is your world, and
it is not vanity, only time, that makes me
say yours is the simpler one at present,
while mine is the reverse, through my own fault,
with all escape routes blocked and trapped;
the group of viciously conflicting emotions and fears causing
a general inability to cope, to say the least.
Is it surprising – this retreat into the house
and a mass of trivial details?
But as this is too neatly explained, the question of
the "wrongness" and "good" stand out even more
as remaining unanswered.
Even a retreat has to end somewhere.

You will not be surprised if I leave now.
To stay longer would only …
More words would be useless. Our talk …
"Forgive me, you're too kind" – with such clumsiness
and a self-disgust that embarrassed everyone.
So let's let the ship sail through the house.
Forget the 'Space Book'.
It doesn't matter.
"Dear Doctor, the pain …"   If even the exit could be graceful
and nothing else, then …
All escape routes blocked   The undergrowth so thick
"A matter of time"

Dawn of the monsters

The sky grows pale with dawn
the birds sing there – maybe only three or four distinct songs –
but with more clarity in this than anywhere else
At this hour the sky is a soft blur
with black silhouettes on the horizon and pale stars
scattered – no one caring if they do move

In a different town far from here …
I'm not sure why I should be aware of you
– a common "wretchedness"?
more imagined than real?   You forgive me
there's nothing else to do   "I give in."

Paleness soaks deeper and deeper into the atmosphere
like an admission of collapse where nothing is touched

Chemical days

"The fix" can only mean
the man with two blue flags who stands all day
on the cliff top. Now he's waving them at
the aircraft-carrier, H.M.S. Blue Flag, that is
as hard and clumsy as most machines.
This process is called an "euphemism".
The wars, fathers, spacemen, soldiers –
just so many toys to be broken or dismembered.
Even the flag man and his strange obsession …
What there is …   I mean, couldn't it really be
a matter of compasses like fixing the sun or
the stars, or the hour for the "fix"?
This process is called a "smoke screen".
When it's raining and the isolation of the day
can only mean "the fix" or a studied chaos
of words and pictures in the hope of distraction
or, even weaker yet more honest, justification
for existence. Tears are so much of the past.
"Shall I have them all shot?
or just the leaders? That's quite a question."
Click! went the heels. A door banged in the yard.
Blue flags fluttering – "What's happening?"
It was all there waiting – a complete change of lives
– why the delay? Courage wasn't even
relevant, only "common sense" for a change.
She was still waiting in the yard patiently.
Everyone acknowledged her beauty and love.
"this stupidity"

The revisitation

Despite the dazzle of the New
– its own great and unique beauty –
(her long black hair reflecting a summer morning)
when the past's too roughly torn away
you can't deny the deep pain that
runs the length of my body
like the crack from an earthquake
that splits the new tarmac road
right down the middle for half a mile
Plate 56 in your geography text book
Its ragged lips have already tasted death
many times
An equatorial republic asking for aid
a large ship at anchor in the sound
a new pipe-line and harbour installations
the black capstan

(As a footnote – the escape was made
through a slim steel pipe which even you must know)
and that's enough said for now

Yet with this there is certainly no reason
for bitterness or resentment – they have no part
in this.
In fact there is nothing but the endurance,
there's not even a neat conclusion or clichéd saying
to draw on for cheap comfort –
only time and the inevitable process of a darkening
memory.
No one can be truly put at ease by this
as such inconclusiveness is always discomforting

The poem can always retreat
into an elaboration of the tropical scene
mentioned before, and time is passing
for all of us – isn't it?

Which island was it that the schooner
visited that year …

Dazzle

the dazzle of the New
– its own great and unique beauty –
(her long black hair reflecting a summer morning)
like the fresh white liner at anchor
in the sparkling blue sound of this Pacific island

An equatorial republic asking for foreign aid –
the large ship at anchor; a new pipe-line
and harbour installations; the glossy black capstan
and tar melting on the roads.
So many excuses and subsequent apologies
for the numerous blunders and inefficiencies
of my native workers –
the covers and symbols of my own astonishment
and love for you

But still I can't stop this wonder
that dumbfounds me every time I see you,
or, when alone, ever come to a full realisation
of what's happened and is still happening
and will continue happening.

I just gape at you
and know how I must appear so crazy
all red faced and sweating in the ridiculous
general's uniform of my small republic.
I am weighed down with gold braid,
epaulettes, medals, swords and nonsense,
as you pass in a light summer dress.

Forestry work no. 1

Did I say that?
The prospect of such expanses still to be covered ...
hardly having set out   intimidated   so soon?
Up onto the ridge   the forest here like a cool grove of ash
with sunlight filtering down
Like a pilgrimage, maybe?
On the map there are a series of points   "The Procession"
Later playing with the children, it's quite natural ...
Your body gives   "The Acceptance"

I pick the wild flowers carefully
and take exactly one example of each species
"and with reeds and yellow marsh flowers in the clearing"
This conscious and essential "delicacy" in handling surroundings,
of course, flows out   takes in the
You understand this when we touch

In turn I slow my instincts   I know
to take in all the marvels as you give them me
So many pictures of "The Dreams"

Love in the organ loft

for Marian

The cathedral lay feeling rather damp among its trees
and lawns, lichen covering its white stone walls
near the ground that is still wet from a rain shower.
It is April – of course. (Why should songs have all
the good lines? – like "I love you", too.)

I'm beginning to wonder what I'm doing
and what is going on? All I know is that it's now
very late at night, or early in the morning …
You see, even this is disturbing and disordered.
Is someone weeping in the street outside?
It sounds like a man. It is 3.30 a.m.
But when I go to the window, I can see no one.
I might have asked him in to cry in the warm,
if he'd wanted. This isn't as stupid as it seems.
But everything on this (surface) level is so disjointed
that it can make even this possible act of kindness
appear to "THEM" as "foolishness" (if "they" feel patronising)
or "absurdity" (if "they" feel insecure that day).

At 5.00 a.m. I am still watching over my love
I love her more, so much more, than I've ever loved anyone,
even myself. In fact, this is a completely new
experience of *love*, like it is the first REAL time,
and love for real.
                    "My eyes hurt now, but birds begin
to sing outside anticipating the dawn – though I can find
no connection. Why should I? How absurd can I get
in this county town of the south-west province?
There appear to be no limits anywhere anymore."
"His lips were sealed." "What is going on now?
You needn't doubt that I'll just wait –
'Faites vos jeux' – until I get to the bottom of this."

The cathedral and its own lush green and garden,
and the comfortable and quietly rich church houses
with their private gardens that are set out
around the green – they are all peaceful and certain.

There is no question of escapism. (And it's about time
I woke up to this fact and appreciated the possible
sincerity of many such people and bodies.)

The birds masquerading as a "dawn chorus"
have now become quite deafening with their twitterings
– I am sending for a shot-gun sales catalogue.

But what can this mean? – that I should
sit here all night watching over my love
and at the same time I fix
more than double my usual intake
to feel without compassion by brain wince
under chemical blows.

I mean what is happening? – NOW!   Do you see
what I mean? – like does the cathedral nestle
in the sky's warm lap? OR   does the sky
respectfully arch over the cathedral's gothic
towers and roof, flying buttresses and pinnacles?
This parable can be used for most things – think of a river …

The belief that ignorance is usually cloaked
in pompous wordiness seems well proven
by everything put down so far. And, in fact,
anyone feeling the need to relieve his by now strong
resentment of me will be, when possible,
met in all humility. I accept my guilt
and am not surprised at these numerous "accidents"
that seem to follow my progress through this city,
like falling slates and flower pots.

But please, when you all feel relieved,
will someone tell me how it is I am
so blessed at last with a real love
– and this like I've never seen possessed by anyone?
But also …   and yet …

And yet I know I need no explanations
and, least of all, justifications. The fact that the woman
I love with such continual and intense joy
and find what was before always transitory

an eternal and unshakeable happiness. All this
is this is this is this …   I'm so happy;
and now as she turns in her sleep
her face's beauty fills me with a tenderness
and adoration that surprises even me, and fills my eyes with happy tears.

It's 6.00, and with the morning light
it seems my guard is over. No one comes
to relieve me – I couldn't stand rivals.
But why is the morbid masochism
of lines 46 to 47 still around? – Has it
no sense of decorum? All I want is to be able to
love as I'm loved and make my love happy.
Nobody here wants jack-boots,
or sleek vicious cars, or sleek vicious lovers,
or cocktail cabinets that play 'Jingle Bells'
every time you open the doors – "Oh boy!".
All we want is ourselves – and that *is* really great.

But, please, if anyone has any answers
to the little problem of diet, do tell me.
I must go to bed now, but messages
can always be safely left here. Goodnight.
Good morning.
                The cathedral is so pretty
here, especially in spring – so do visit.

Exeter. April 1967.

The nine death ships

1

"This isn't the Black Forest!" he cried. But the sky was *so* blue. "Do come in and put your revolver on the sideboard." And so, many days passed. It all became very neat and tidy. The house was swept clean and all the revolvers put in a drawer suitably labelled.
"I'm getting closer."
"You sure are."

2

The three men were very persistent, to the extent that they even became boring. The servants were appropriately informed. Only the dogs looked glum at the new situation.
"BANG!" – that changed it.
"My sweet, you see what I mean?"
The carriage continued ignoring the man who quietly read a news-paper.

3

Manhattan is not at all confusing if one appreciates logic. I do, for one.

4

The little house was so full of people that inevitably one of the walls gave way – but, surprisingly, nobody was injured or upset in the least.
"What a magnificent garden you have!"
We lolled the whole afternoon.

It was impossible to count the number of woodpeckers in the flock. But, unperturbed, they continued to wreck the country's entire telegraphic system.
The shot-gun blasted away.

5

"My eyes hurt from doing so much finely detailed clerical work in such a badly lit office."
That was how the report began.
Death was so near, it became a shy joke among the inmates.

6

There was a small black book on the well scrubbed table in the lighthouse. You could hear the sea pounding the walls outside. Inside the book were stuck several photographs of gravestones in wintery graveyards. It was late winter. There were also some postcards which portrayed the deaths of various characters. One was an obvious choice – "The Death of Chatterton" – painted by Henry Wallis. But the oval photo of Miller was not at all expected. The caption simply said "MILLER / Northfield Bank Robber / Killed on front of Bank, Sept. 1876." He lay naked and dead on the mortuary slab. The photo shows only his head, shoulders, chest and upper-arms. There were two obvious bullet holes – one low in his left shoulder, and the other high in the middle of his forehead. But it was only the first wound that had a stream of blood running from it.
The noise of the storm had by now grown quite deafening. It was impossible to hear what anyone said, no matter how loud they shouted. I was then further upset by the discovery that I was alone in the lighthouse. And it didn't look as though anyone would ever return. It was not even known if there had been anyone there to leave in the first place. It was all very confusing, and it seemed that I never would meet the owner of the small black book. For the while he certainly showed no intentions of returning for it.
I carried on whittling and putting ships in bottles.
Spring ploughing would be our next worry.

7

The houses were all yellow and the ladders green – such a conscious plan of life and its colours could only be described as "revolting", and that was being too kind by far.
The lush red of blood, though, and all its varying moods and hues was a continual source of surprise and joy.
"Don't worry."

8

"It was raining so hard and all the games had been played. There was nothing for it – we would just have to spend the afternoon watching the servants play leap frog. What a bore."

Luckily he never finished his memoirs.

9

It seemed that the worst was over. The iron black fleet had finally steamed out of the bay. There was no communication. But at dawn the horizon was still empty. The sea was slate grey. If only this had been "the worst" – but nobody can tell. The year was unsure – maybe it was 1900 or 1901.

The orchestra had to be slaughtered – they put everyone's nerves on edge. It was only through luck that Stravinsky escaped. That would be funnier if it was a joke. Insanity is always terrifying and illogical in its own logic.

As a distraction, let's not forget "the amusing woodpeckers" or "the surprising shot-gun" or "the confusing yet simple street map of Manhattan". They all serve some purpose – whatever that is.

The Sinking Colony

1968-1969

Linen

waking on the purple sheets whose softness
The streets heavy with summer   the night thick with green leaves
drifting into sleep we lay
The dazzle of morning   the hot pavements
fruit markets   "The Avenues"

"You and I are pretty as the morning"

on the beaches
machine-gunning the fleeing army
the fighters coming in low "at zero"
the sun behind them   and bombs falling all round
"Jah Jah"   CLICK CLICK   "Jah Jah"

the cheap pages crumbling already after so little time
St. Petersburg renamed the Soviet Printing House maybe

you leave the town   "the softness" like a banner
though where
In the countryside the trees bare and scrub bushes
scattered in useless fields
the darkness of a stand of larches
called "the dark woods" on no map

touching you   like the
and soft as
like the scent of flowers and
like an approaching festival
whose promise is failed through carelessness

Death of a pirate king

1
A small train quietly follows the coastline.
The sky is so blue over the boat-yards, and the sun is a blinding white.
Meteorology.

At dusk the fishermen climb aboard the train and clutter the carriages with their rods and baskets. At "two o'clock" it's as deserted as a shingle bar.
The green carriages. You're surprised. I can't explain *all* the echoes.
The lancers.

2
Ricochets make it dangerous for everyone in town, regardless of their, or any, involvements. On the horizon clouds of dust signal that the indians were tearing up the railroad again and cutting telegraph wires AS USUAL. This lack of imagination has something of the primitive in it. Alas. "N'est-ce pas?"

3
Banditry.

4
That ridiculous gun-shot. Outside it's raining, maybe. It's like the dream that is repeated so often that it comes true.

5
The window open, the curtains flapping, somehow suspended. It is the "softness" I'm talking about … Outside the countryside is seen in vague outline. It is "an obsession with the artificial". Make way for hills and the noise of people milling in the courtyard outside.
"Rolling."

The words

Clouds scattered across the sky   all so far away
and then the space between   this strange "distance"
What does "normal" mean, after all?   you move
toward the window   lights marking the headland
and the night becomes a milestone   though
I   the fog rolls up the hill from the sea
in waves   the town   *desperate*?
Whichever way we look   though so much at hand
only held back by obsessions
but "home" is so long ago   don't cry

the light's a very pale blue   then maybe   the next time too
a faint glimmer across the bay   neither moon
nor stars
and your letter making signs   concerning "understanding"
and "the magic tortoise"   what then?   or just tiredness

At each alternative   the colours in the sky
gradually changing   until you're lulled into believing
you've seen this before   but not quite
The wood-cut of a lone horseman
riding through a deathly countryside   raped

"You're very brave"   I clean the table-top
and you sat in that chair   two red poppies
in the garden below   at dawn
This apparent clumsiness is far from true

Cargo

As strange as the white cargo boat
heading east along the coast
two speed-boats named "Dark Red" and "Dark Blue" shooting off
in glorified arcs of spray   like you
naked again   beyond the Green Mountains' snow
licked clean   puzzled
running out of petrol smells

"Will the hostages ever be freed?"
there's no echo from the mountains
nor a messenger to be seen running in the distance towards us
There were many journeys …
But the dance-tune was not titled "The Chains"
– "How ridiculous!"

I reach forward and suddenly it's night again
and too dark for the jetty or the country walk
Such confinement is curious and absorbing
like an obscure scientific diagram   the combinations seem limitless
yet it is the same base that's returned to   for years?

Now you have dressed
and tidied yourself
– all is ready for "Departure"
and you manage skillfully
against such a background
and the sky this clean

Pullman

the train leaves   "goodbye"
crosses the river and heads south to the country
and that inevitable coast
" 'full stop' you say!"   but, well...
All towns have their problems,
atishoo and all that.
The champagne comes in and the night goes by
"Being a working girl isn't all stars"

"Let the teacup, painted with flowers, pheww.
Two rounds of toast neatly buttered, please."

We patter on

"What did you want, sir, toast?"

that's the way it goes – forgive me

The station. Goodbye. That question of consistency.
and this is only the summary
and the silly actions

(" Forgive me"?)

Animal days

1

"The polo season would start early in April
so there was no time to be wasted."

the night growing darker   the black plains
and below   the bright lights of the town

"knights on horses"?   "gentle ladies"?   "towers in the forest"?

it was as though your eyes filled with glass tears
crying some strange

there were peacocks on the high balconies
and a golden light   in fact "a heavenly rod"
came down from the heart of a clear blue sky
you see

2

"You're right, even though you won't accept it."

… with all the rifles brought back to safety
even the glimmer of polished metal

Buzzards, kestrels and hawks
circling high above the valley

the dust of the road   dazzling
with the white gates shut   do you understand
the garden so enclosed, and too green?

3

food is so very good

it is very black these days

the malevolence on the winter island

and what approaches in the darkness

beyond all knowledge   "the endurance"
surviving the fear

"but we're all so afraid"

and the children?

the indian chiefs
what are the wounds, anyway, and their cost?

In the morning everything is white
low clouds trail across the upper pastures
and the valley is thick with mist

"sometimes their canoes only hollowed-out tree trunks"

4

standing in the shadows or maybe in the distance
he   Like a long arcade or cloister
It was far from the grim scenes of the north
In his red tunic

The morning spent loading cord-wood onto a trailer

five young foxes in the bean-field waiting for the wood-pigeons

in the beech woods up on the ridge – the bark
still green and wet, the" sticks" just felled.

It's reduced to a violent struggle
with heavy machinery, and boredom

the castle crumbling sedately   "damn fool!"
the gilding already flaking off

Cutting it up into "blocks "on the saw-bench
The forest floor all torn up with bulldozer tracks
the soil a bright red   exposed below
the white shale backbone of the ridge

the sun sinking lower
the whole forest dripping moisture and green

the old railway station

5

holding a young rabbit in my hands
walking across the stubble in the late afternoon

soft fur   shocking like the heart-beat

the dark river   and angry knights milling
in the courtyard

setting it free in a hawthorn thicket
safe from the dogs

at night the land so bare   "rustles"

"They have no tradition of keeping their colonies neat."

"I care for that woman" the song began

6

squandered in a matter called "the heat of the moment"
not knowing what

" … at dusk the sound of church bells from the valley floor,
an owl flying low over a passing tractor."

white with rain

The corrugated-iron roof of the mission discoloured
with rust   the deep green of the jungle
in the humid gorge

Like oppressors   striking fear into people
with threats of pillage and "no quarter"

Inside the walls where
"No!"
too heavy   on evenings like this

in the courtyard
"the battlements"

The sinking colony

1

At the time being a young geologist with the British Raj in India I was somewhat limited in the actions I could take, you see

The expeditions into the foothills and mountains to the north with our mules strung out behind us along the mountain track

At the base camp

Back at the bungalow my young wife was wearing her long white dress. The dark mahogany rock specimen cases glowed in the half light of our bedroom

Standing on the verandah in each others arms, the first monsoon rains kicking up dust in the compound, the servants rushing excitedly to the stables

Though it was considered rather eccentric, we would, when we had sufficient funds, hire local musicians to play for us in the evenings. They would sit on the verandah while we would sit inside in the darkness. The servants *would* chatter, *noisily.*

2

The heavy iron gates were swung open revealing beyond
a rich countryside at dusk

"COME IN"

tentatively on the dirt path   ahead a dark cloud of purple
and unnerved by the sounds   the footsteps
brushing stones

Beyond in the mountains or rather the foothills it was harvest time

3 The ache?

There was a time of waiting while the rains lasted

It was cruel by nature of its very calculation, yet equally to judge this as coldness is a mistake, rather it was a form of preservation, a manufactured aim to allow time for some possible movement to come about

This is clumsy, but like a mould made to hold the final object and then be destroyed or forgotten once the real purpose was achieved – though such neatness in explanation is always suspect

There were complexities

4

To continue

The mansion was set in magnificent grounds
The trees were heavy with rain
and the fields of barley beaten down by summer storms

Haven't we been here before?
(sigh)   the impressive agricultural machinery
waiting for the dew to dry
You don't really need meters though to test moisture content

It seems so little is clear
The big house called "The Mansion"
and the cold damp

What are we expecting, after all?
The pain goes through its cycle alternating
with the sunny days
but can you look it "in the face"
and then continue skipping?

5 Canadian Days

The inventory seemed endless. Let's start again –
    Moose
    Snow shoes
    Tins
    Sap
    Maple juice buckets and cauldron
    Axe
    Spare whale bones
    Sledge.
I can't work it out

    "I was out in the bush felling timber at the time. I had my own
team of horses, a good one. Things looked good."
(We turn the page)
    "The maple tappers were passing through the district but no one
was expecting trouble."

    It was suddenly colder than anyone could ever remember.
Cracking noises all through the night.

6

They stumbled out into the clearing
We just stood there
Then everything was thrown into confusion
– someone fired a shot
the horses bolted and the dogs tied themselves in knots

The rusted iron gate at last fell from its hinges
– someone *had* been tampering with the padlock

What could we do with all this?

Somehow even in the dreams we all needed one another
though there was little comfort in this

The Big Chop

1969-1970

North

Snow on the furrows
and on the hilltop the black castle and cathedral
and the close city like an island
ringed by icy rivers
The days briefer, even darker

It is the small and isolated fortress
that lies to the north
where you are left
your nakedness on some white winter day

The snow cover
the gardens of ancient houses thick with it
and then the stars

you know
we shiver at the contortions
but have to perform
the desperate dreams
that we so carefully build
in the long weeks of loneliness

Too cold to even touch the flesh
yet driven on in the heat of the obsession
dazed almost when raising the head
and seeing beyond the window

Split down the middle – what's happening?
The unreality at the wrestling match
and then so much neater to avoid any analysis
with the picture books all ready and the warm fire
The clean white schooner's fascinating voyage

Night ferry

"The hotels in the narrow side streets…"
appears automatic
and all part of "the process" whatever that may be

and on the edges of town the sea
and some say the marshes
out of that deep tank of enthusiasm
we all admire so much

being cut in two
kissing round the borders of the hairs
and other reclining positions
back into the personal obscurity
of the obsession
Much grander sounding than when it
comes to crouching naked on all fours
"WOOF"
the animals range away happy as ever

It is the tortuous path threading between
the buildings

"WOOF" (again)

All leading to you and hunger
"I am obsessed with"

But

The travellers leave their bags at the station
and between trains visit the town briefly
It seemed worthless by virtue of its very shallowness
but how to reconcile their journey's necessities
with something nearing any real appreciation?
Can we say "service"?

Country Diary continued

"Ah, Hilda, my dear, you're so pretty." (in a German accent)

and the shooting?

I used to shoot a bit in Africa, get a duck or so for supper. But there seemed to be such a lot of killing going on. I felt I could not add to it. I gave up shooting then, except for a little target practice. Lost the taste for it somehow.

"his patrol was ambushed by Zulus"

Today

I tidy the room
it all becomes a notebook or an excuse

> "A bay seen through the window – it's a
> summer morning – the romantic coaster ploughs on
> leaving a smoky trail behind.
> At sea : 6 bells."

From the window : cluttered back-yards

It's now down to a matter of lists
that act as buttresses, even defences.
No? the same tired and selfish stories?

Out there...

There seems to be great activity
and everyone has been invited to collaborate
It's all very curious and useless
I mean "what body winds round what body?"
a poor excuse for "intellectual search"
or "a full and active life" –
though at times being "in love" is a life in itself

The floor is swept and all the ledges meticulously dusted
the room is then well aired by opening the window wide
I'm left standing in the middle of the room
holding a wet cloth

There are too many accounts of cruelties
but the other side always sounds slightly false
or is an expression of nostalgia
But what can ache more than repetition?

Cut into slices?
Stuck in *"the vertical"* – is that too obscure?

Shifrah... – Hebrew for "beautiful"

the night is soft
I give in   it is warm
you're not far away
but somehow suspended in the distance

I trail behind me many failings
that invade too much of what we are
"Forgive me" is very weak

The animals at the zoo were very grand
I admired them
and the gardens so heavy and green
You must see so much
that you let pass   to turn in welcome

Brooklyn

The city isn't necessary to our elegance
It's not a matter of going back
to the land
but *that kiss* on the forehead

The wind is so strong and yet soft
almost tender
At night on the ferry – the lights of passing tugs and
freighters
It is hard, I know, to live without this,
"out of love" as they say.
What can I say?   we kiss
with all the need and hope that
comes from this "lack"

You are beautiful   the whiteness of your breasts

We have this

"Inside the harm is a clearing..."

There were clouds   the sky was heavy
the rivers were heavy with flood
The line of hills the mud green usual
after the thaw
Through the middle the glint of steel rails
In the valley is a small market town
almost a village

***

In the morning her white body
(it being north european) and the black hairs
Your desire is revived

There comes this desire
to be clean
This involves distance
There comes this decision
of the necessity
in moving
at the right time
in the right way

***

There are many steamers moored in the busy estuary
"Come here"   we lean over the rail
The town is a whole scatter of colours
Our clothes are immaculate and white

The kaleidoscope of the tropics yet the simplicity
As I bend to kiss you my lips brush your hair
Somewhere in the clearing

***

164

The clutter   Above the ridge
the colours heavy   washed through
and he said then
"every man to his junk-shop"
not moving but fixed
in those same games of "identity"
Somehow a tight blue blanket
wraps us up
in the silly dreams
Your body

It's never like you dream it
turning this side and that

***

on the edge of town   the scattered houses
the Mill House roaring
people are walking through the water-meadows
it's a mild evening
we're taken in by the very aura
the famous cathedral
and the orchards on the hill-sides
this softness could be in any season

They're like running figures
seen as white flashes in the green distance
towards the rails

***

"Soon we'll be there   a few more days
you'll like it
the bungalow   the cool verandahs
and our walks in the evening
Naturally my work takes up most of the day
but it's only right that way"

We walk round the deck
the other passengers smile at us kindly
like accomplices in the dream
we all know

As we get under way
a cool breeze comes up river
and ruffles your hair

THE LONG BLACK VEIL :
a notebook 1970-72

*"things have ends (or scopes) and beginnings. To
know what precedes   and what* follows
will assist yr / comprehension of process"

Ezra Pound – *Canto 77*

*"In the Congo what joy could I take in gathering unknown flowers with no
one to whom to give them?"*

André Gide – *Journals, 31 March 1930*

Preface

How to accept
this drift

the move   not mapped
nor clear other than in
its existence

a year passed
I think of you
it's early on a sunny morning in June
and think of your thinking of me
possible

How do we live with this?
yet live with this

What have we *left*
from all *this*?

      "Concepts promise protection
from experience.
          The spirit does
not dwell in concepts. Oh Jung."
        (Joanne Kyger – *'Desecheo Notebook')*

two years passed "Oh Jung"
the cycle not repeated
only the insistence

The story is that, when a child, Borges used to come to his father. His father would have a number of coins that he would place on his desk one by one, one on top of the other. To be brief – the stack of coins is an image of how our memory distorts and simplifies events the farther we move from them. The first coin is the actual event, the next coin is the event recreated in the mind, the memory, the next coin is a recreation of the first recreation, etc., etc., …

But what of the essence of this? "Oh Jung's" insistences. The Sufi story of the famous River that tried to cross the desert, but only crossed the sands as water "in the arms of the wind", nameless but

Book One

the soft dawn   it's light
I mean your body   and how I ache now
yes, tremble
           the words?   how can they...

somehow the raven flying through endless skies
that ache too much   the unbearable distance
borne

Across the valley the sun catches the white silos
of these scattered farms
Up on the ridge

I mean following the creek …

As we lie in each other
dazed and hanging like birds on the wind

your body, yes   I'm talking about it
at last   I mean this *is* the discovery
Need I list the items?

On your way from the thorn tree to the house
you stop and half turn
to tell me...
that doesn't matter
but your look
and this picture I have
and at this distance

I have this now
I have what I have
         in my hands

dawn – light – body – words – raven – skies – ache – distance
– valley – sun – silos – farms – ridge – creek – each other –
birds – wind

The Flight – BA 591

Book Two

Baseball in Central Park.

Anti-war parade on 5th Avenue.

The Egyptian rooms in the Metropolitan.

Reading Gide's "Journals" in my room.

On the bus : the green Catskills. large black birds standing in the grass. wild blue iris in the swamps. two woodchucks. two rabbits. If other men's shoes fit, wear 'em.

We swim naked in the pool at night. The stars so bright. The hot night, the crickets and frogs singing. I hold you to me in a small room – the night air so heavy. Inside "the dream" …

A farm dog barks somewhere across the valley.

The bright greens of the woods, the sun streaming down through the branches. The crashings of a chicken hawk suddenly startled and flying up through the branches to the safety of the sky again. The rain that increases and

thunder in the distance
the air heavy
and the valley white with mist

our bodies wet

As dawn breaks
we wake
and make love
again
the sky grey outside
and the birds singing

The sun comes up
You rise and make coffee
The woods so green

We go back to bed and

I can hear your footsteps
going about the house
doing things
while I sit by the window
of this upstairs room

the birds singing
in the heavy afternoon
the muffled sounds of a t.v.
downstairs

that I want you
this is why

I will call anything that goes on in my head "a dream", whether it be
thoughts or imaginings, day-dreams or sleep dreams. They all give
pictures of "the possible", and that is exactly their value.

the two warships ploughed out to sea
waves flowed between them
as though dolphins lovingly touched each hull
in turn   No flecks of dust on the captain's
fine uniform   All the brass polished

Not the first   but one of many
such expeditions

Book Three

1:00pm, check into the hotel. It has two rooms and a bar. The town has two stores, three bars, a post office, church, gas station, fire station, and a small country library. People drive into town in their pick-up trucks, but it's not *that* "country".

Evening time out on the front porch step, smoking a cigar, watching the cars and people pass. Night bugs flying round the lights. Young men driving in pegs, putting up tents back of the fire station ready for the weekend "Fire Department Chicken Fry". The hot heavy night bringing the thunder and warm rain. Go to bed, the noise of passing trucks and the juke-box downstairs.

The fascination with *this* formality, *this* ritual.

Woken up early in the morning by the thunder, and rain beating on the tin roof of the porch. When I get up the air so soft and sweet. The square and hillsides a soft white with the fine mist. In the bar local farmers and workers from the nearby steel mills talking – "… a nigger wench, not a nigger woman..." As I leave the sun breaks through on to the lush greenness of this valley.

Walk up the ridge west of the town – the minnows darting in the creek. The rock bed, and the currents there. The smell of young ferns as I walk up the hill through the beech woods.

Go up to the wild strawberry patch again, squat down and eat some. Continue up along the road, the pine woods by the crest of the ridge "see for miles"

You walk through the door
No, now you stop your car in a small town square
I get up from the porch step and greet you
This is all "country manners"

There's no steamer bringing you to me
up-river at the hill-station
No long white dress on the verandah

It is …
I hold you.   Isn't this enough?

The feel of your breasts
        beneath your loose white shirt

"It was used by the commentator of the Himyarite Ode, either at first
hand or through the medium of Hamdani's *Iklil*. We may regard it, like
the commentary itself, as a historical romance in which most of the
characters and some of the events are real, adorned with fairy-tales,
fictitious verses, and such entertaining matter as a man of learning
and storyteller by trade might naturally be expected to introduce.
Among the few remaining Muhammadan authors who bestowed
special attention on the Pre-Islamic period of South Arabian history, I
shall mention here only Hamza of Isfahan, the eighth book of whose
Annals (finished in 961 A.D.) provides a useful sketch, with brief
chronological details, of the Tubba's or Himyarite kings of Yemen."
                    (R. A. Nicholson – '*A Literary History of The Arabs*')

The small town set in a valley winding between ridges,
the lush green, the white mist at dawn,
the creek bed almost dry,
white scattered boulders and the willows.
The meadows so deep, and floating on their surface
the yellow and orange flowers.
The cool beech woods on late afternoons.
You melt into this landscape
and this only a description of my love for you

At the hill-station   all the bearers fled

The delighted naturalist was left unconcerned
carefully placing his specimens in the black metal box

"… and when he spoke about it to his friends they smiled and said
they found the comparison odd, but they immediately dropped
the subject and went on to talk about something else. Hebdomeros
concluded from this that perhaps they had not really understood
what he meant, and he reflected on the difficulty of making oneself
understood when one's thoughts reached a certain height or depth.
'It's strange,' Hebdomeros was thinking, 'as for me, the very idea that
something had escaped my understanding would keep me awake at
nights, whereas people in general are not in the least perturbed when
they see or read or hear things they find completely obscure.'"
                    (Giorgio de Chirico – *Hebdomeros*)

Book Four

We choose our condition

the sun shines
the warmth and softness of your flesh
"belly to belly" (like the song says)

The air so clear up on the ridge
this light
and then looking down to the valley

"our condition chooses us"
she says

In the morning we go for a drive, buy cakes and
milk, and picnic by the creek. The afternoon
spent in the meadow. In the evening we make love
in the room.

the sun glittering   through the glass
scattering rainbows on the walls and ceiling
the soft turf beneath the trees outside
your room where we lie naked
with our love

the country music plays
the words sung
"Palms of victory, crowns of glory.
  Palms of victory I shall wear."

… felt so good this morning – as though I woke up beside you.

Book Five : Canadian Days

On the Northlands train from Toronto up to North Bay, Cochrane, and Kapuskasing. Then bus onto Hearst ("Moose Capital of the North"), and a jeep ride out to Jogues.
The night before the train full of drunks and bear hunters. Ridiculous. "No guffing".

And today early morning, the grey dawn. The "towns" we stop at just a collection of huts scattered at random around the rail halt and a dirt road. And then the bush again. Heavy streams and rivers, and the forest cluttered with dead and fallen trees. The occasional windswept meadow, a grey weathered farmhouse deserted, fallen apart. Nothing. The bleak empty plain, marsh, lakes, the crowded conifer woods, a single silver birch in the middle of this.

The Northlands. The watery sunlight on dirt roads. The dull green country. Hardly any flowers to be seen.

At night the stars brighter than I'd ever seen them, and the curtains of light, the Aurora Borealis. This brightness dazzling, but it's with you that I want it.

It is the surface
your eyes
The foresters tramp in weary
Driven into a corner (so to speak)
to say this
I hold your head between my hands
your eyes

In the morning sitting on the front step, everything so calm and still. The warm sun, and a total quiet only broken by the bark of the ravens. The vast blue sky, and the forest stretching off on all sides. The long straight white dirt roads with a line of telegraph poles along side, and then the forest enclosing them on either side.

Book Six

The questions of complexity

On Gide's death Mr. Forster said – "I realized more clearly how much he had got out of life, and had managed to transmit through his writings. Not life's greatness – greatness is a nineteenth century perquisite, a Goethean job. But life's complexity, and the delight, the difficulty, the duty of registering that complexity and of conveying it."

The distinctions

"Oh, Jung" (1875-1961) on "Marriage..." (1925)

The container *and* the contained
not *or*

one within the other
a continual shifting   and that both ways
– more a flow – from the simplicity to the complexity,
"unconscious" to conscious,
                              and then back again?
and the move always with difficulty, and pain   a pleasure

not so much a repetition
but a moving around a point, a line
– like a backbone – and that too moving
(on)

yang and yin
light and dark

An island set among islands
and that no answer
But the need there –
somehow to have all one's hopes there,
to see and touch, to be wholly in one place.
Yet over the horizon   as real as any...
the ghosts
and them always moving

BEFORE COMPLETION   Wei Chi / 64
But if the little fox, after nearly completing the crossing
Gets his tail in the water,
There is nothing that would further.

                    in the half light …
A minotaur? a cat? tiger?   Her face
a metamorphosis   seen   at once   many times.
Our powers generating ...
We touch, hold, and caress ourself

A bird flying high in the sky
above the clouds, and below them
an ocean, and a ship moving there.

"Such thoughts were very far from Julien's mind. His love was still
another name for ambition. It meant for him the joy of possessing so
beautiful a woman, when he himself was a poor, unhappy creature
whom men despised. His acts of adoration, and his rapture at the
sight of his mistress's charms, ended by reassuring Madame de Rênal
on the question of the difference in their ages. Had she possessed
a little of that practical knowledge of the world which in the most
civilized countries a woman of thirty has had at her disposal for a
number of years already, she might have trembled for the duration of
a love which apparently only existed on surprise and the transports of
gratified self-esteem."

(Stendhal – *Le rouge et le noir*)

Book Seven

My stomach   burns   Coming to you

How will...?

The peaceful and flowering public gardens,
the smell of the ocean again
So much tied in such sites
of past pleasures

Stepping into the new   always   with you

A low haze beyond the harbour's mouth

I am full and happy   now   at your side

... we finally begin to fall asleep as dawn comes,
as a single whippoorwill starts to sing ...

we wake, and make love. Outside a grey sea mist fills the woods.
Later, standing alone in these woods waiting for her, not knowing
how ... this journey today so far from

The tricks are pulled

                blue skies flash across the screen

The falsity when anything becomes a symbol

You are lowered   very gently
into the waiting boat alongside

Much later   ashore on this island
where tears rarely happen ...

You are away there on other continents
So hard – "It is hard to stand firm in the middle"
– waiting   for that lightness, that ease
of movement

The freighter was anchored in the middle of the bay with a full head
of steam up. As the launch approached

In the Museum of Fine Arts, Boston –

> *Mycerinus and his queen, Khamerernebty II*
> slate. fourth dynasty (2613-2494 B.C.)
> (The Pharaoh Mycerinus also known as Menkaure.)

In the Egyptian Museum, Cairo –

> *Mycerinus triad : Mycerinus, Hathor, and the*
> *personification of the "Dog" nome.*
> slate. fourth dynasty.
> (The personification of the "Dog" district
> (nome) is a woman.)

the tenderness. They stand facing us, she to his left, her right arm
around his waist, her left hand resting on his left upper arm.

Horus, Hathor, Anubis

Horus – the falcon headed god, the sun.

Hathor – the cow headed goddess, the sky.

Anubis – the jackal headed god, the guardian of the dead.

Horus, the rising sun, enters Hathor, the sky.
Obvious enough.

Doors flung open, a clear blue day outside, cactus, sage brush, and the yellow desert ochre, and the blue sky.   New Mexico.

Horus, son of Osiris, a falcon, whose two eyes are the sun and the moon, and whose breath is the cooling north wind.

Hathor, the cow, the sky goddess, stars on her belly, the sun between her horns, guardian of the Western Mountain, goddess of the copper mines of Sinai, of a woman's love and joy, of perfumes and spices, identified by the Greeks as Aphrodite. The mother who gives birth to Ra, the sun, at dawn. The destroyer on whose back Ra rides through the sky.

Anubis, the jackal, guardian of the desert cemeteries, master of embalmment, who oversees the weighing of each heart.

"a god is power personified ... In Egypt ..."

No godhead, no gospel, but "a multiplicity of approaches", each in its own right, each immanent in nature.

Book Eight : England

So much either side of the immediate
though at its height – the love ecstasy
of the "now" – it is only the immediate,
God's face.
(the Sufi poet, Ibn 'Arabi, writes of this)
God's face is the face of your lover.

I love you

the sky is full of wheeling gulls
Do I ask too much?
– the sea crashing white on the shingle –
that I'm torn apart each time you leave

the white buildings
the green sea and hills behind the town,
like some giant sandwich
and our love in the filling of it

You wheel above me

such whiteness

Christ, that I love you

how to deal with this?

I wait for you
not passively   but
I wait for you

My heart weeps

Who would ever have thought I'd write that?
"My heart weeps"?

"You must try, Psyche, to use up all your facility against an obstacle; face the granite, rouse yourself against it, and for a while despair. See your vain enthusiasms and your frustrated aims fall away. Perhaps you lack sufficient wisdom yet to prefer your will to your ease. You find that stone too hard, you dream of the softness of wax and the obedience of clay? Follow the path of your aroused thought and you will soon meet this infernal inscription: *There is nothing so beautiful as that which does not exist.*"

(Paul Valéry – 'Concerning Adonis')

Not a climbing, but a moving across the surface in a certain way, as though a soaking into the grain, what was there all the time, though never fully realised.

As though a monster haunts us – continually aroused at each "wrong" word, each "wrong" action, and roaring out from its darkness to terrorize us again. A giant and indestructible serpent filled with anger and venom, nightmare.

"Each single angel is terrifying." (Rilke)

Summer. The water meadows at dusk. The willows and long grass either side of the winding river, now only seen as a smooth black surface, the flow imperceptible. The buttercups indistinguishable in the growing darkness. Only the sound of your feet on the narrow gravel path. A cuckoo in a nearby spinney. The swallows out hunting. Across the fields the dim outline of the town – a clock strikes the hour, maybe in the church or the marketplace.

Book Nine

Today, lying on the grass in the park
by your house
                We were very close
Your husband, your children, you go
about your duties, you love
and care for them

Yes.

you there
me here

sometimes it's an ocean
spread between our bodies
sometimes only a matter of
yards across a carpeted room

you sit there
I sit here
there are people around us

the luxury
of setting eyes on you

You walk by my side through the park
what luxury
the

the cars the planes
the absurd mechanics
when all I want
is to walk up the hill to you

the silly girls clatter round
while you – the only woman I know,
the only woman I want –
are kept so securely from me
and at such a distance

a fierce wind tugs at the town
while I walk up the hill
and you on the other shore
while the sea bursts on this shore

there is a fine rain – I repeat myself –
it's night   there is a wind
To answer to …?
when our world turns in us
dazzling
That hand offered us when the clouds part

"No, it's real,
it's what I feel."
                    (by 'The Soft Machine')

The pride. Being with you, knowing very simply where I'm going, where I stand, of being able to put aside all the half-things and live with one sure knowledge of what matters, what is.

"… an ease in the air around us that we can spread into … and ideas are like stars instead of gravity – we're not held by them by their necessities."
                    (your letter)

Book Ten

The rain falling you could be driving a car now
somewhere

You drive the car and my hand rests on your shoulder
the radio is playing
the rain is beating on the car roof
and the road is a brilliant black

the honour of you
"I am honoured" someone says

that I should cry now

we all know what this means
and there's no need for any rich details

when John said "from egotistical to egocentric"
he was right about the process
there's no cause for shame

and the "honour"?

the word grows emptier the farther it moves
from the flesh
while *my* honour lives in your flesh

"You're your own train, you got your own track, and you can go
anywhere."

> (Fielding Dawson quoting Charles Olson in
> *'The Black Mountain Book'*)

But you the ground,
earth I want,
the place

the luxury of it
to hold my reality in my arms

the touch
of it
you
the feel of you
so much now

Book Eleven

Is it the Rilkean dream or "home" we come to?
At dusk the skyline obscure.
Yes and No.

Many pictures – the surface apparently the same.
A series of events, but the marks they leave varying.   Things
happen, have qualities.

And ahead?
The mountains, the wind, the sea   are there
we move through them, across their surfaces

like a moving hunter

On a "threshold"?   in the open
dazzled by the sunlight, and "nervous",

but moving – and that with care.
No end.

But the quality

The dreams do happen –
and there is no "home" we come to
– but on this earth, and open to its powers

A recognition of the ghosts that guide us. The dead watching over
us, surrounding us with a tenderness – as though they were gravity
– they hold us, their arms around us, however we move.

And Anubis guiding the dead through their journey.
Before the tribunal of Osiris, Anubis, the jackal-headed god, watches
over the weighing of the dead man's heart – the heart in one scale, and
in the other an ostrich feather, symbol of Ma'at, the goddess of truth.
And if the heart is truthful the dead man is led up to Osiris by Anubis
and becomes Osiris, god of the dead, of the under world – that is, of
the earth beneath our feet.

Book Twelve : California Journal

the eucalyptus groves on the mountain sides the road cuts
through – no – follows the contour obediently. The coast ...

the heat and wetness of us

later alone on the beach ...   the sandpipers rush about,
following each wave out, picking the sand. The gulls

... through the barrier. "That isn't pain, it's something else."

driving through the mountains. San Anselmo. San Rafael. the redwoods. The ease of walking in the hot sun in California down a dirt path laughing, ordering milk-shakes, and watching the traffic pass. Of being totally in one place. The dry mountains around us. Nowhere else

At night the smell of orange blossom at the post-office

In the bar I talked with this man passing through town about Union matters.

"... For Beauty's nothing
but the beginning of Terror we're still just able to bear,
and we adore it so because it serenely
disdains to destroy us. Each single angel is terrifying.

Ein jeder Engel ist schrecklich."

(Rilke – 'Duino Elegies' 1)

walk the length of the beach as far as the rocks watching the small and large sandpipers. Orange butterflies glide above the parking lot.

when we're together the time always so short. The minutes counted and noted down. And around these times the long hours of waiting.

that hot surface where our bodies meet, press together – "a melting spot".

she tells me of

the tearing

leaving

the only woman

We drive up into the mountains behind the beach. Muir Woods. Mount Tamalpais. The air so clear and sweet. On the short turf ... her laughing. She looks so beautiful.

In the evening in the room ...

Making love, the final blocks clear. My body taken into her body completely, and then her body into my body.

In that place the ease there

more beautiful than ever, her black hair so thick and rich

She anoints my wrists

the anointment a ritual like the sweetening of the body before burial, before our parting. My not realising the completeness of this until now.

In the distance the mountains – the dream echoed again and again in many parts, in many places. An antelope (not understanding this animal) lies down exhausted yet calm. Some form of quietness.

The ritual of – repeated again – No. We make love – to each other – in turn. The body glowing, dizzy, ... walking through clouds. The faces transformed again.

She accepts the objects – the stone, the orange blossom.
She gives the objects – the whittled twig, the dried seed pod

She puts the bead bracelet around my wrist

                                        lie naked upon the bed.

Qasida Island

1971-1972

Qasida

it's *that*
the quiet room
the window open, trees outside
"blowing" in the wind.
the colour is called green.
the sky.
the colour is called blue.
(sigh)   the crickets singing

windows open.   You move …
No, not so much a moving
but the artificiality of containment
in one skin. "No man an island" (ha-ha Buddha)
… lonesome, huh?

THE music, THE pictures
(go walkabout)
Small wavy lines on the horizon

somewhere over the distant horizon
the distant city (I hadn't thought of this,
but pull it in) and you

the children are sleeping
and you're probably sitting in the big chair
reading or sewing something
It's quarter past nine
I find you beautiful

* * *

the words come slowly. No…
your tongue   the lips moving
the words reach out –
crude symbols – the hieroglyphs
sounds, *not* pictures

196

the touching beyond this –
I touch you

in the water
as though I'm in you

that joy
and skipping in the street
the children hanging on our arms

***

You know... – the signals (on the horizon?)
"blocked off"   the ships at night
keep moving

these clear areas beyond the clutter
that clearing

on summer nights as we lie together …

there are green trees in the street
yes, there is the whole existence of
our bodies lying naked together
the two skins touching
the coolness of your breasts
the touch

The setting …
it doesn't really matter
We know
So much goes on around us

on the quay they're playing music
we'll eat and dance there,
when the wind gets cold
we'll put our sweaters on
it's that simple, really …

***

... the dry fields
Up on the mountain sides
white doves (of course) glide
on the air-currents   hang there

someone said tumble
"the sound of words as they tumble
from men's mouths" (or something like that)

there are these areas,
not to be filled, but ...

it's a bare canvas, but not empty –
all there under the surface

This is not about writing,
but the whole process
You step off the porch into the dry field
You're there
You see, you're *there*
Now, take it from there ...

One, Two, Three

An emperor gives a gift, stylishly,
and a Mughal miniature records it
(colour and gold on paper, height 7 3/16 inches)

we're dazzled   – all this art
and surprises   "Keeping the doors open"
Right?

Yes, I suppose, fascinated by the delicacy
of the piano part in the first movement
of Beethoven's "Ghost" Trio
("he sighed …"   but real enough,
aesthetic coat-trailing aside.
The delight beyond the technicalities
– not pursuing, but there
to be recognised

We can see this

 And all those private separations?

When "we" moves from the general
to the particular?

To talk of *you* now … ?
amongst all this "delight"
– moving into that other level –
the poverty of this, one without the other,
the delight more a refuge than any whole thing
when you're away

Up in the hills the court is assembled,
the gifts exchanged
From the balcony I see you cross a courtyard,
could almost touch you –
but the distance.
                    Be well.
the moonlight on your face
as you sleep now

***

hold me

outside the rain falling in the street
I hold you   your flesh so soft

to begin to say – "I love you …"?

the heat of your belly

away   the hills
(Fuck "the hills")

my mouth on your throat
my body smells of your body

***

There are many fields
and the fortresses are so far apart.
The troops stand in line on the parade ground
while the sun beats down on them
and their bored officers.

it's another day

meanwhile ...

                    there are many settings

A group of men can sit stiffly
for a regimental photo of the survivors of the disaster,
and then try to look neat and alert.

And their children ... ?
living in a calm beyond this knowledge?
It is not so much a question of guilt
on either side, but maybe some form of recognition
which rarely happens.

And the years pass until one generation dies
and their knowledge with them
leaving behind only feelings of confused longing
that quietly spread beyond any conscious resentment.

Now put it together.

Blue enamel letter J.

the dirt *is* good
Up on the hillsides rocks in the fields –
but ploughed, and sown, and the wheat grows.

At night there are shooting stars
and comets, the moon bright,
but only adding "weight" to this

We lie together

***

passing through the scattered villages
hill towns in the distance

the touch more than words

years pass   "slowly whittled down,
torn to shreds" – is that the process?
I don't think so, but

that instinct   Always dazzled by the new
and leaving behind something known "too well"
but not known

the avoidance of these "difficulties"
a constant despite the "changes"

The land is rich here,
the terraces of vines and olives

… unable to get this clear,
the process
to live on land the roots growing down
in one place   a movement, yes
but a constant – *that* simplicity

***

The clear blue sky over the mountains reflected
in an enamel miniature portraying exotic scenes with
ornate buildings – The Far East?
"Abandoned temples and palaces set deep in the jungle …"

"things" crowd in   (a fascination with the
forms of obscurity)   then move back
giving you that space around you

It is beyond any conscious decisions, but in the end
involves them
                    your kiss

some form of floating

High above the rock outcrops ravens, and hawks
circling   dwelling on one spot
below

New Year

for Shifrah Fram

a dark forest somewhere
with a chain of lakes
scattered between the mountains

no one for miles (literally)
except you   a white movement
among the trees   a "blur"

but more precise than that

maybe a long way off a railway
but I think not
nor a moored seaplane on
one of the lakes

even the possibility of dirt roads
now seems remote

it is all very still
(like) some form of memory
the outline of your breast
seen clothed
in a crowded room

there is the sound of the wind
in the tree tops above you
and your feet on the pine needles below

fading to
the white area in which the "blur" is lost

the journeys   moving
              "... trying,
to get it right"

that past *now* present
and then...
              we move

not circling but an
unknown progress

looking down the slope
through the trees to the lake
at times losing all sense of direction

now you enter a crowded store
in a large city

it is somehow impassive

"in control"   "our condition"

With a photo by John Walsh

1

On the maps the countries marked there
and the distances
that separate
the areas between
          ... called "land masses"

No matter what

You there at that distance
to be measured in miles?

a red truck parked in the dusty town square
here

a relentless and continuing series
of separations that by number grow unreal

left with   the place you're in now
(the word "you" variable)

From the window

2

the rooms empty   a haze of sunlight
"the dead" pass by?

outside   in the country
the land is rich and fruitful
people hold the harvest with an honest pride
smiling at the camera
the tenderness there of that smile

3

A vegetable market by the roadside
up there   to the north
The station-wagon parked on the gravel

In the room   the silence
dust   caught in a sunbeam
The place like nowhere in its suspension
but everywhere   Again and again

Clouds up over the mountains

"… part of the process …"

Five postcards to Alban Berg

1
waves break over the headland
the pain of closeness   / "to a lover"
The mountains
walk in the mountains
The lightness of touch
clear air

2
the blue sky
(pan to) spring ploughing
and cattle grazing on the (green) slopes
the wild flowers abundant and   many coloured
Can you see now?   can I …?
Many miles away…   Here

3
The dark night   / "close to your lover"
the rain and wind outside

4
in the evenings as the sun sets
red skies and the swimming

the insult of an image
when it's only what's here before you

5
the skies clear   (blue)
midday   the moon still there
sheep deep in the flowers   daisies and poppies
Off beyond the distance "you"
Minutes in the day when (maybe) the pictures cross
and focus
The island   firm
the mountains up into the sky   "beyond"

Boston to Brighton

Boston

1972-1973

Triangulation of points A, B, C.

A)

half moon up there
down here snow-shoes   walking through the forest
North Vermont   10 degrees at 10 a.m.

At the end of the pier ...
Thinking of you?
Who are you, anyway?

"Snow-shoes on two foot of snow"
                    and
"A photo taken at the end of Brighton pier."

B)

piano music on the radio –
no, not nostalgia
A crossed station coming through with details of commerce

cars driving through the streets
in the rain, snow on the ground

A helplessness in all this   (classic scenery)
the presence of the things, yes,
but in the face of their presence...?

What force anyway?   busy   maybe

But beyond the immediate...?

"All here, cap'n"

C) MAXIMS

old man, you talk like things are eternal,
    I mean fixed forever.   "No way."

                  Kung right.
       went against his own father

Image *is* the ultimate enemy

Ignorance the enemy

Boston Notebook : December 1972

in the park surrounded by apartment buildings,
art museums   in the kitchen
word for word   snow on the ground

to get something clear   mapping
how it really is now   (embarrassingly so?)
"I just want to tell you the truth"

In the sky we read of momentous changes
And chart them?

the small daily details
talk with people   what eaten   drunk

"peppermint cremes and champagne.
44 Joy Street, Boston, Massachusetts"

*

There's no pleasing some folks.

You pays your money
and you takes your choice.

*

the grey pyramids set on a flat desert plain

wild flowers and long grasses in springtime on some island
    to the south and east of here. Shall we say Mediterranean?

the well-known riders approach – not out of any nostalgia,
    but rather the fact of their very existence

Along the front of the porch   someone was walking up and
    down, and beyond him   the blue sky was set with fragments
    of white clouds

Some kind of bitterness held in foreign lands

Massachusetts *or*
On visiting Walden Pond, 1st January 1973

rain on the roof   cars in the street

in the pine woods   snow on the ground
the lake iced up   blue sky above
hot sun   one of those days
not even "wood smoke"

               climb back into the car
drive home to Boston

Pull a beer from the fridge

turn the radio on to – { the rock station
                      { the concert music station
then – { sit down in the chair
       { lie down on the bed

you know …

To put it on the line,
straight
The perfection, that precision
of movement

"I went down to the local bar
to have a drink or two
As I walked to the jukebox
my eyes fell on you

"Bartender said you're
               disengaged
and I saw you trying to look
                   my way

"I said now wait
stop a minute
I said now don't
hold the phone
'cos I really really really
got to
       have you"

Portraits : 1 - 4

Portrait : 1

rows of white houses leading down to ...
sun sparkling on the sea
and the white cliffs off to the left
                  the east (that is)
                  (looking south)

"south coast sea town I dream of"
title of this song

Portrait : 2

a dark forest covering a large area of land.
On its edges are flat ploughed fields
and further on you come to some crude peasant villages
– all quite small and somehow Russian looking.

On a Sunday (the time is summer)
the peasants gather at the centre of the village
to talk, to even dance, on occasions –
there being a church service earlier in the day
presumably

Portrait : 3

tree lined avenues – poplars in full summer leaf –
crossing flat grainlands – maybe France –
the golden cornfields north of the Loire,
(that's 15 years ago) – Tours – Chartres

Portrait : 4

the sailors' postcards sent from ports
far away and far apart   "off on manoeuvres"

the thoughts of "an easy home" somehow lost
amongst all this activity, though still nagging
in our more "uneasy" moments

Aboard the cruiser *H.M.S. King Alfred,* May 12th, 1905.
"We are just now out for a spin down the Firth & if all
is right we leave here for Portsmouth tomorrow morning
at 6 am, arriving there on Sunday night. I am enjoying
myself pretty fair. Feeding on coal dust & salt water.
Hoping you are all well I remain   Johnnie/"

The destruction of South Station, Boston

In front of the warehouses, trucks and buses driving by,
the red demolition crane and two yellow bulldozers

All the giants, massive

... on the sidewalk, lost amongst all this,
I can't understand what I'm doing
eating the hamburger plate ($1.35)
in the *Blue Diner* across the street.

South Station half pulled down
and beyond the tracks the docks
falling apart –
foreign steamship lines complaining at the
lack of facilities and dangerous conditions
– two diesel engines and a shunter
standing, their engines running,
at the end of the platform

Like is "it" taking over –
does the "massive" run the city, exclusively,
or do I run within the city, "exclusively"?

A small room looking into a cramped courtyard,
the music on the radio – a shell to keep off
the nakedness in a strange city, any city,
"home or away"   always foreign
moving through these

yet the whole affair lumbering on like an automaton
regardless ...   (the giant red machines)
though this too dramatic
a picture   everyone goes their way
strange pleasures inside it all

Nineteenth Century Poem

to say "on the edge of tears ..."
hard to define   the tears rarely happening

rather it is a state
the confinement of loneliness
walking the streets with such pain

"friendship"?
"a sharing of interests" not the same as "a mutual concern"
– any fool can talk books, one way or another

A clump of yellow crocus in the Victory Gardens
The bright morning turning dark
Rain clouds in the early afternoon

Your state a result of whether you've eaten or not.
It's that simple, brutal, often enough

To imagine, amongst all this flat language,
another place.

Boston Spring

Song of praise?
the strong wind cutting across the river
blowing grit in the eyes of the pedestrians crossing the bridge
after visiting an exhibition of Indian miniatures
from the little valley kingdom of Kangra in the Punjab Hills
(N.W. India) painted in the late 18th century
or early 19th century?   I think not.

*

1) Take a bath.
2) Drink some chocolate.
3) Go to bed.

What else ?

*

There are so many evasions
and the cunning fox knows all the
bolt holes and impenetrable thickets
in this particular patch of woodland.
Emergency Instructions by heart,
by rote, THAT IS
"*rote*, n. Mere habituation, knowledge got
by repetition, unintelligent memory."

1)
Paper place mat at "The Riverview" restaurant on Dock Square, Kennebunkport.

"KENNEBUNKPORT, the fifth oldest town in Maine, was settled in the part now called Cape Porpoise in 1629. Incorporated as Arundel in 1719, its name was changed to Kennebunkport in 1812. For many years sailing vessels brought the name of Kennebunkport to every civilized corner of the earth. Many vessels were built on the Kennebunk River coursing through this town. Later Kennebunkport was discovered as a summer resort and again became known the world over. It was here the late Booth Tarkington made his summer residence and Kenneth Roberts, the well-known novelist, had his permanent residence.

Cape Porpoise and Goose Rocks Beach, a part of Kennebunkport, was first sighted in 1603 by Martin Pring. It was on Stage Island in Cape Porpoise harbor that the first permanent settlement was made in 1629. The town was depopulated by Indians in 1690. Today, Kennebunkport is an artists' paradise and thousands of visitors come to enjoy its gleaming beaches, pine forests, quaint winding streets, beautiful colonial homes, famous Maine shore dinners and warm hospitality."

2)
Postcard.
"THE OLD SALT ALONG THE NEW ENGLAND COAST.
Many's the stories he could tell of years of sea wind and salt spray, summer's heat and winter's icy blast on the Atlantic Coast. Survivor of a past age, he still maintains his proud independence with dory, lobster trap, and net."

3)
Signs along the last 100 yards of the Port Road before its intersection with the Wells Road (Route 9), going toward town.

K'port Women's Exchange / Est. 1919 / Home cooked food / Bread is our speciality / Cakes Pies Donuts Rolls Brownies Cookies Jams Jellies or Birthday cake.

*

Eleanor Clough

*

Stop ahead

*

Rev. R.C. Hewitt

*

No parking

*

For Sale   Whitecap Realty   967-3055

*

      ↑ KENNEBUNK BEACH

      ← KENNEBUNKPORT

      WELLS →

*

Village Mini-Mall Bazaar

*

Sunoco

4)
Postcard.

Greetings from Maine

(Picture of a large lobster painted bright red collaged in the sky over a view of a Maine fishing town.)

MAINE "Pine Tree State".
CAPITAL : Augusta. AREA: 33,215 sq.mi. POPULATION: 969,265.
MOTTO: "Dirigo". I Guide. FLOWER: Pine Cone. BIRD: Chickadee.
TREE: Eastern White Pine. 23rd State admitted to the Union.

5)
3 gas stations, a library, post office, several churches, 2 general stores, a drug store, hardware store, and a large number of summer shops filled with 'artistic' bric-a-brac, and a couple of restaurants and hotels.

Take your choice.

Brighton

1973-1977

Brighton • October

a cloud passes by
the stuffed animals in the museum
  continue to stare straight ahead

at sea three freighters wait on the tide
  to enter the small port

load of timber
cargo of coal

a man walks along the edge of a park
beneath the trees that have just begun
to shed their leaves

I am thinking of the forms of peace,
or, rather, pure pleasure

CHÊN 震

one of those
        rare
                moments
       when

thoughts of death
strike

The desire to hang on
        to what
            I have

to not   lose
sight

     of
            what's held dear
the line of hills
           that edge
(the) coast

*

sometimes there is

the need

      to explain

make that mark

           clear

the clarity

      what believed

or rather   hoped for

*

              to be afraid   of

no action clear

        but

              sets of blocks

the hard rain at night
but with mornings
                      (so) clear

blue sky and sun
like spring   the winter

to move carefully
                  here

        but how
when so crowded
                  by those fears

*

Chên / the arousing (51)

"When a man has learned within his
heart what fear and trembling mean,
he is safeguarded against any terror
produced by outside influences."

"Six in the fifth place means:

Shock goes hither and thither.

Danger.

However, nothing at all is lost.

Yet there are things to be done."

*

fear, v.i. & t. : to be afraid of,
hesitate to do, shrink from doing;
revere.

*

"a long road"

                she said

"it's a long road"

fear of loss

the loss spreads   (as much)

through the future

            as in the past

Hauntings

      in the face of which

           we

survive somehow

"a long road"

Old Bosham Bird Watch

for Jud

1
out of nothing comes…

nothing comes out of nothing

cut   /   switch to

a small room, in a building of small rooms. "Enclosed thus." Outside there are bare trees groaning and twisting in the wind. A cold long road with houses either side that finally leads down hill to a railway station. The Exit.

2
Out on the estuary four people in a small dinghy at high tide. Canada geese and oyster catchers around. The pale winter sunlight and cold clear air. Onshore the village church contains the tomb of Canute's daughter, the black Sussex raven emblazoned on the stone. Small rooms.

3
Sat round a fire. The black Danish raven rampant.
In the dream.
Enclosed, I reach out. She moves in her ways that the facts of closeness, familiarity, obscure. Our not quite knowing one another in that sense of clear distance, that sense that comes with distance, like old photos making everything so set, clear, and easily understood – so we think. Face to face the changes flicking by second by second. Not the face fixed that yes I know her. Not the easy sum of qualities

4
How long since you've known who you are? How long? Why who you? Don't know. Long time. Only have old photos, old images, old ikons peeling. That man who lived at X, did Y, travelled to Z, and back, "The Lone Gent"?
Why, who was that masked man? Why, don't you know?
NO!

5

In the closeness that comes with shared actions. From keeping a room clean, keeping clothes clean, cooking a meal to be eaten by the both of us. In that closeness, maybe on the edge of losing something gaining something. Questions of clarity and recognitions.

6

We swing hard a-port then let the current take us, the ebb tide pulling us out towards the Channel. The birds about, the colours of the sky, the waters, all the different plants growing beside the estuary, and the heavy brown ploughed fields behind these banks. Here, more than anywhere else, every thing, all becomes beautiful and exciting – and the fact of being alive at such moments, being filled with this immense beauty, right, Rilke, "ecstasy", makes the fact of living immeasurably precious.

7

Enclosed by cold in the winter. The clear sharp days walking down hill looking out to sea, the wind up, the waves crashing on the shingle beaches. And the days of rain and harsh grey skies, coming home from work in the dark through the car lights and shop lights. The exit always there. I can't say I "know" you. But neither can I say what "knowing" is. We are here, and somehow it works, our being together.

8

The sky, the gulls wheeling and squawking above, the flint walls of these South Saxon churches, the yew trees branching up into that winter sky. I know these. But not what you're thinking, what anyone is thinking. I can never know that, only work with that – as it comes. Open arms open air come clear.

9

The dinghy is brought ashore. The people drag it up the bank and carry it to the cottage where they stow it neatly. Everything "ship shape". Out to sea the coasters head for Shoreham and Newhaven. Along the coast small blue trains rattle along through Chichester, Littlehampton, Worthing, and on to Brighton.
The fire is stoked up in the small room. The people in the cottage all eat dinner together, are happy in one another's company.
That I love you, we know this, parting the branches and ferns as we push on through the wood.

Green Summer Notebook

nearing mid-summer

sweet nights of light
                    and red skies

Venus appears in the pale air
the evening star
(delete whatever)

a warm stillness
a still warmth

rise from the couch and put the
tomato plants inside the house
"frost waits for no man"
someone should say

stuck in the basics of survival
rather than the trivial

the ground to work from

the light slowly failing, as
they say, so I can no longer
see this page clearly

stuck in the basements of survival
I reread this as mistakenly

* * *

Take notes. Make outlines out.

* * *

THE CENSOR LOOMS

back of all thoughts

and meanwhile back at the desk

eyes follow me from their pictures

> my father
> F. T. Prince as a young man
> Rembrandt
> Robert Louis Stevenson

their gaze follows me (like all "good" pictures),
penetrates, yet seems somehow indifferent,
almost looking above one's head, my head,
or just to one side of my head

> the evening is passing
> and something can't be shaken
> > free

There are dreams and actions and responsibilities

* * *

the darkness brushes your face
we float through it as though under water

To lie on these nights
beside the one you love

To hear piano music somewhere nearby
light from the neighbour houses cutting the room

To keep it *that* simple
the foundations built as you go

you know

Charles de Gaulle Airport – Roissy

for Jud

cool gliding corridors of steel and glass
hung in the air   —   that amazing
display of elegance   "city of the future"?

     (So this is what Futurism means??
     and this my first Futurist poem??)

         and yet amongst all this "comfort"
I only think of you,
of a plain wood table in the kitchen
sitting drinking coffee together
the small garden outside
the cats demanding as ever

I "wax pastoral" as they say
in my love for you and the life we make
but know what this means
and its value

Now   here   surrounded by these elegant machines
and graceful forms   —   buildings that
yes, men have built
         I cannot say
what   but that in no way
rejecting them   I have to live
by the simplicities I know

Portraits from my life

Page 1

Something passes before one's eyes, or even
at the edge of one's vision

There are swirls of light and crashings of sea water

Redon drew portraits of Bonnard and Vuillard

And the bottom right panel of Giotto's 'St. Francis receiving the stigmata'
shows St. Francis (plus companion)
feeding, or greeting, the birds
All – St. Francis, companion, birds, and lone (palm?) tree
– somehow floating on a cracked gold background.

Page 2

on the side of the lake a decaying boathouse
the whole landscape windblown

waves breaking on the granite boulders that form a
promontory beside the boathouse

Up through the trees
                    the log houses

MAPLE SYRUP
Grumiaux playing Bach's sonatas and partitas for violin
Fetch some logs in for the fire
GIN

"thank God for Culture"

Page 3

In a hotel room, that seems to be near
the railroad station, sunlight is reflected on
the worn and elderly furnishings and the
woman who sits in a pink slip by the large
round table.

In the suburbs a young girl in her early teens
stands naked before a mirror in an elegant and
large drawing room.

Page 4

O Princesse de Broglie

       "my body's falling apart, breaking down"

the sky blue silk gown slips off your shoulder
to eventually reveal your plump white body
as erotically delightful as your slow eyes.

Discreetly I leave the salon, O Princesse, and
the excellent company of the charming M. Ingres,
and return through winding night streets to
the bed of my own dear Madame d'Harwood
whose sweet darkness and well rounded form …

       "my body's falling apart, breaking down"

Page 5

The fruit is in the bowl,
       is in the white whicker basket,
       or lies artistically about the table top

The flowers are in the vase
The woman sits beside the vase thinking,
looking off across the room, somewhere, her
elbow resting on the table that's ruled by the flowers

"O girl musicians and dancers of ancient Egypt.
O hand maidens, O queens at the feast,
at the festival in Thebes.
The wall paintings whose reds and umbers…"

The sweet life with all in profusion
"The luncheon of the boating party" by Renoir
The brush drawing of a woman's head by Matisse

Lest we forget…

Page 6

To the south the warmth of easy afternoons, of talk,
of "food and wine", of the easy touch of bodies;
while to the north the chill rain and drizzle that
comes between the swimming and "bracing moorland walks"

Dear Matisse – you know.
                    Thank you.

Sea Journals

for Paul Evans

On the coast

1

there are so few words
to use   to say
what fills me

the sea

my family

walking on the hills

2

the sea

and that thin luminous strip on the horizon
where sea and sky meet, where they flow
into one another

at certain times

Off the coast

1

Mid afternoon in mid-May a ship lying off the coast, off Shoreham Harbour, waiting on the tide to enter port.

The sound of the waves slapping against the side, the black iron plates thick and heavy with many repaintings; the wind rattling the metal lines against the metal masts.

A clear bright day, the sun hot on your arms as you sit outside the galley taking a breather, the deck in front of you littered with potato peelings and a few egg shells. All the clutter of the stern. The smells of the galley, the deck, the ship.

The engines quiet, still.

The hot and clean fresh wind from the sou' west. Looking towards the shore, the houses and docks and the green hills behind them so clear you feel you could almost reach out and touch them.

On the coast

3

waking on April mornings
the town covered in, filled with, sea mist.
And then walking down hill to work,
the mist, and the sea stretching off
in front of you

4

though to resist the urge
                        when so struck dumb
to turn to the encyclopaedia, the text book,
where you can see "how things work"
(which *is* a little use,
even the optics of it but...

the exercise useless in the face of
the sea's presence
where the words once more melt,
are of no use to say
how it really works

5

this island

        the continents

floating

        ON THE WATERS

clinging to the planet's surface
a skin so thin
holding a ball of liquid fire
and water

6

vast green sea
   waves breaking far out from the shore
   bright midday
                of spring drizzle and strong westerlys

Off the coast

2.

Barnacle Bill the Sailor had a dream that night. He dreamt that Ibn 'Abdi Rabbihi[1], the much loved and respected Islamic poet and scholar, was one evening sitting to *sagg*[2]. On his knees he balanced a transistor radio tuned in to Radio Cairo. The radio was playing a continuous programme of Arab popular songs. The toilet window, which was open, overlooked a lush walled garden. And since it was dusk the garden seemed even the more lush with its dark foliage and plants still dripping with the rain from a recent thunder storm.

The humid evening's quiet was only broken by the wailing songs on the radio. And Ibn 'Abdi Rabbihi thought, as time drifted by, of the roses flowering in that garden, and considered the similarity of a rose to the sea. Of how since both were creations of his mind, ideas that eternally existed in his knowing and His knowing, that there really could be no difference between the two, despite their apparent individual beauties. He remembered those lines of Muhyi 'l-Din Ibnu 'l-'Arabi[3] in his poem Fusúsu 'l-Hikam:

    "How can He be independent when I help and aid
Him?
    For that cause God brought me into existence,
    And I know Him and bring Him into existence."

And also in the collection of odes, Tarjumánu 'l-Ashwaq, he'd written:

> "My heart is capable of every form,
> ……………………………………..
> Love is the faith I hold: wherever turn
> His camels, still the one true faith is mine."

On the same night Lawrence Hammond, 2nd mate on the steamship *Charterer* out of Lowestoft, was on the bridge on the middle watch. There was the usual yellow glow of light from the instruments and the sound of the engines he had known so many other nights as the *Charterer* ploughed its way up the Channel. There was a light squall and he could hear the hiss of the waves as they curled past the side. As he lent forward trying to look out at the night he noticed large drops of water on the outside of the glass screens of the bridge. The sight of them completely filled him and he remembered the droplets of water that sit on a rose after a summer shower. He was back in that summer day, the sea a thin band in the distance, and the skylarks twittering in the sky above.

---

[1] died 940 A.D.
[2] drop excrements.
[3] 1165-1240 A.D.

London To Brighton

on the late night train home

"kind gentle creature he was, died quite young"
heard from the next seat down
"quite diffident, and nervous"

"I shall have to answer at the Pearly Gates.
 He declared a passionate love to me,
 and I... " (the rest unheard – train noise)

now all that comes through
is noise of talk and small laughter,
but none coming through clear

"choreographer"   (of course(?))

In love with the man in one's life
or not, as the case may be

from Notes of a Post Office Clerk

for Harry Guest

> *"For the heart of another is a dark forest."*
> Ford Madox Ford – *'Ancient Lights'*, 1911

the faces blur, yes
but the actions carry through

Moving or not moving
the angle or degree matter little

except the realisation
of the powers
we all wield

are responsible

      for what   we do

the act   politic

Storms blowing from the sou' west.
In the square the trees bend,
and make noise.
Spring tides highest for 300 years

Believe me

.

*

Hollingbury

Above the earth fort

    a skylark   singing

     twittering

The stillness as

    the mists roll in

        from the sea

so clear

       the air

here

    the sun

     catching

the line of hills

     in the distance

*

For three years
my lady and me
have lived in one room

I'm sick of living in one room
I'm sick of being poor
I'm sick of the rich taking from the poor
(and them pretending to not even know it!)

I'm sick of the rich.

*

sun in the skies

you're laughing   crying

it's all there

the pain   and the quiet pleasure

trains in the night going to
set destinations
but the events still unknown

I move, but not so much a matter
of intention, but what happens

*

the sea is grey green

flat

with heavy clouds low on the horizon
                         "low in the sky"

   the piers are set in the sea
the cliffs an off-white

*

246

old men move

      walk by

      stand

      speak words

which we come

         to respect

that there is the trying

which we so love

that the words come
– through all the veils of *that*
 date or *that* class
but which come – through

to show, make the marks
that show

a man cared and thought

and that his cares and thoughts

touch us

now

and push

us further in the trying

*

The set area   (like a square)
where there is the time and space
– the "peace and ease" ?? –
given   and/or   taken
to make the marks
of words,   language

to say   the words mouthed silently
inside the head

to speak

beyond this

*

                              … little birds

the horizon at seven o'clock on a
summer's evening
the sou' west wind grown gentle
the sky red
and the sea grown "relatively" calm

maybe where the sky meets the sea
a lone freighter
silhouetted
maybe three freighters
with crews and cooks and captains
are silhouetted
are even clear out to sea
                              there

I point in front of my face

*

the soft mist over the town
　　　the sea a calm grey
these late summer days　　quiet

　　　and always the sea and the
　　　hills sloping down to the sea

the freighters trailing the coast
to Shoreham

the points and depths

*

What to feel ?　　　deadened ?　　　No, but tired from the
day's work so that no thoughts are clear, and, therefore,
obsessive. Left with a series of acts to be attended to, and
that with its own pleasure. Preparing food, eating, drinking,
listening to the radio, lighting a coal fire, playing with the
cats, maybe reading a little, then going to bed.
Day to day.
Job to be done to get the money. And in the end it's just the
job, day to day, and the necessity behind it almost forgotten.

The choices. Choice made ?　　　never that clear.
But a realisation of things to be done, passed through.

*

behind 'The Downs" the sheep in the fields

here on the coast the people around

work   job

causing the tiredness?   and neglect
of oneself,   one's friends,   one's love?
or something else the real cause,
                    "root of the trouble"?

the exhaustion, yes, and the anguish
that stokes in all our dreams of ambition,
the works that "could" be done, "should" be done, etc., etc.

"there are no answers" he said,   too easily

But the love?
    that drives our motors so well.
    We know all about this
and our continual failings
to make *that* work

*

the map of the town   Brighton

streets passed through   so many times
the seasons that have passed
the houses once lived in,
a trail of worlds still there
like dumb monuments, markers of the past

on bright winter mornings the sun
shining,   sea   blue

far out to sea the freighters just visible
on the horizon

the pain – yes – a knife hacks,
      stabs, and cuts deep
I know
but your sweet smiling face
              making all clear
                          and exciting

*

behind the bank of machines

                  (the drunk technician?)
       voices come
but what else?
             voices?   words?
nothing

I live on an island
I work on that island

there is no home
(and that the hardest to admit –
   that we're here naked, alone)

   the island part of a continent
      and that part of the world (obviously)

   Fly, float, drift, from place to place,
   land to land.

And where is the knife less sharp, sir?

*

Sussex shipping

SHOREHAM

Vessels in harbour: Marsh Lea, Arco Test, Windle Sky, Jens Wal, Merc Nordia, Lady Sylvia, Teesport, Bridgeman.

Due today: Ekpan, Chieftan (steel, Sussex) Tor Wallonia (general cargo, gasworks and Aldrington Basin); Highland (coal, power station); Alexandra S (timber and hardboard, Masonite).

Due tomorrow: Bencol (wine, Aldrington Basin); Petworth (oil, Lennards); Esso Caernarvon (oil, Esso); Apollo (timber, South Wharf); Klaus Buck (to load, Inner Lay-by).

NEWHAVEN

Vessels in harbour: Olna Firth, Makaria, Carmen Tinillos, Playa de Naos, Valencay, Senlac, Capitaine le Goff.

Due tomorrow: Valencay, Capitaine le Goff, Senlac.

the work   now in England 1975   the steps that could change this, that could be taken now, open a few doors and windows, start the change that would produce changes as yet unknown.

a list of simple, practical, and just acts,
moves towards a real "socialism".

*

totally   "out to sea"
                "gone to lunch"
the freighters out to sea "waiting on the tide to enter port"

                                Fact and Symbol

waiting   to enter

The continual pain of time past, occasions missed, spoilt –
that carelessness now a ghost haunting
all of one's life, awake or asleep, dreams and daydreams.

The pain is not a dwelling in the past
but a livid scar   warning   for those future actions
actions now

not denying the ghosts
but banding with them
– their existence our gravity –
the dead surround us,
hold us up, that is support us,
lovingly
            in the progress

Not to be "immobilised", continually in *that* state
            of waiting,
but somehow cutting through
            into
No, not *into*, out to

the possible – no bounds, except those we choose

Wine Tales : un roman devin

by Richard Caddel and Lee Harwood

Note: This book is a collaboration using the pictures on various wine labels as the starting points for our stories. All but two of the labels were written jointly, and of course the book as a whole was edited and revised by both of us.

Richard Caddel & Lee Harwood 1979-1981.

"A mirror in a square white frame
Stands in the street, reflecting all
That passes it, starting to be
Obscured by the mist which drifts
Slowly in to land from the sea."

Paul Evans

"Please to let me hear if my female
moose corresponds with that you saw".

Gilbert White

Le sanglier / The House in the Forest

It's dark in the woods where the boars roam. It was always daylight when I pictured the house from outside, but now I'm inside it's black night. From the casements I see the dark forms of leaves dancing on the lawn. Come in. Oh do come in. I can sense you, almost see your shape in the doorway, hoarfrost falling softly from your clothes.

I am so old, my story so old, to tell it can shame no one. At the age of nine my little Countess divided her affections between the Marquis de Foucault, twenty years her elder and already embarked on a brilliant political career, and her hunting dog Babeuf. Who can predict the outcome of such childish affections? Five years later the Marquis was killed by a boar in the forest.

Notes

1. One can only hope, for reasons of propriety if nothing else, that Babeuf, the slobbering hunting dog, died soon after the Marquis. Shame is a dreadful thing.
2. "But what does this really mean?" said the junior lecturer. "Are we to take this as the re-enactment of the old Luxembourg myth with all the acceptances embodied in such myths? What of the narrator himself?"
3. On the edge of the dark wood there is a tumult.
Thunder clouds race across the sky.
4. Corruption spreads like a fungus, but not like lichen.
5. The boar was the symbol, or should I say emblem, of purity in pre-Christian northern Europe. Shields and helmets, for example, were often decorated with boars. In *Beowulf* such helmets are mentioned:-

> "... Eofor-lic scionon
> ofer hleor-bergan ; gehroden golde
> fah ond fyr-heard, ferh-wearde heold :"
> (l.303-305)

> "... The boar-crests glittered
> above the helmets: adorned with gold,
> bright and well-tempered ; it* stood guard over men's lives."

(* – the figure of the boar)

Château de Marsan / A Small Route Of The Mind

After supper I went walking. I filled a pipe and set off across the fields, leaving the last shambling buildings of town behind me, neither encouraging nor resisting the babble of mundane thoughts crossing my mind.* The hedgerows were just waking into their late spring colours, a rush of rich greens with splashes and points of whites or yellows in it, and the birds – the light was already waning – going noisily to roost.

As I passed the gates of the big house I glanced up the leafy, shadowy drive and saw a wren bowl across it, a sudden flight as if it had been thrown (I was thinking about a new way of compiling indices at this time).

Soon I was down by the river, and lost, as ever, in her noise. This evening the song was louder than it had seemed in the heat of the day: she too was settling her thoughts.

A light breeze sprang up as I realised the last daylight had gone.

"Grey Monsters Gain the Day" **

In a small room at the back of the house a lamp was lit and a bottle opened. The quiet of the evening was such that it could almost be touched. The silence was like a gentle but persistent presence.

A man and a woman were sitting on either side of a table. They were neither young nor old. Written in their minds was the phrase "a thorough investigation", though no words were spoken. The only sounds to be heard now were the occasional chink of their glasses and the distant murmuring of an unseen river in the black velvet night.

* cf. S. Suzuki: "If something comes into your mind, let it come and let it go. It will not stay long...", in Zen *Mind, Beginner's Mind*, Weatherhill, 1970, p. 34.)

** from the libretto to John Blow's *Venus and Adonis*.

257

Château Naudonnet / Naudonnet Afternoon

Catherine MacLaren had been the English governess at Château Naudonnet for four months now, yet her position still seemed so strange. The daily life of the château seemed alien, when she remembered her own upbringing and home life. The letters from her friends came from not only another land but another world, one that daily seemed more a dream than reality to her. Though possibly it was the other way round, and the world of Edinburgh was the real one while she lived in some dream she couldn't as yet understand.

That afternoon she was sitting alone by the window of her room. A popular novel was lying unread in her lap while she stared out the window. Her right index finger kept her place half way through the book. They were the neat and firm hands one would expect of a young woman like Catherine. Outside rain dripped from the heavy drooping branches of the ancient larch tree. It seemed as though this cold late autumn drizzle had been falling for weeks, though it had not. Soon it would be time to go down once more and deal with the arrogant and precocious children of Monsieur Calva. At this moment the two of them were probably working their way through a book Catherine personally couldn't bear.

As though to avoid thoughts of the impending lesson, she let her mind wander to the subject of Monsieur Calva himself. When would he return from Bordeaux? When would she see him again? be alone in his company? What would they talk of? And, most of all, how close would their next meeting be to how she imagined it? The disappointments and shocks to one's vanity when the two didn't match were only too well known to her.

Going downstairs she remembered an afternoon soon after her arrival at Naudonnet. She'd been out walking and was returning to the house quite late. As she turned up the curving drive she noticed someone standing on the balcony, watching her intently. It was a girl, about her own age and build – and dressed exactly like her. In a moment she realised – she was watching herself. Her mind saw not only the girl on the balcony, but *from* the balcony it watched the girl on the drive, and each vision was tempered by a wary, hesitant intensity. The girl on the drive lifted her hand to her mouth and gasped, and saw the gasp with the eyes of the girl on the balcony. They stood for a moment, then Catherine saw her other half turn and walk inside. Her mind could follow her through the soft furnishings of the upper drawing room, follow her at every turn in the passages, and away down the back stairs, where it lost her.

I wonder where I am now, she thought.

Muscadet / The Good People of Brittany

"Where are we now?" she murmured sleepily.

"On the coast." Paul's voice came to her from the window, where he stood, his earnest, bespectacled face outlined by the morning. "We lie low here for a few weeks, then get one of those fishermen to take us across the channel."

She jumped out of bed and pulled his greatcoat round her shoulders, running to the window to see where he pointed. The open casement served cold air onto her face and she shivered, thrilled by the sight before her. In the small harbour a few fishing boats rode restlessly at their moorings. There was little swell on the sea's surface, for all the wind, and the gulls sauntered idly about their affairs. Along the horizon a strip of cloud like a bruise gathered, waiting for a storm.

"Come away from the window."

She was so happy with Paul: the escape from Paris and the desperate friendless dash across the country seemed far away, though they were still far from the safety of York Gate. She hoped they could have those weeks in which to "lie low" from the Gestapo - but at any moment the scene could shift, suddenly, violently, to Germany, perhaps, or Italy.

This beastly war. There seemed to be no end in sight, only further tragedy, and further horror. Their momentary happiness was like an oasis of sanity in the midst of a desert of unknowing cruelty. And even so the edges of that happiness were continually worried by doubts and fears. Continually her day-dreams went back to before the war when they were just good friends at university together. Their innocence then reflected in the world about them, or so they thought. And now that same innocence so out of place.

She remembered their visit to the church of Santa Maria Maggiore in Florence and the grave of Dante's teacher, Brunetto Latini, in the chapel to the left of the choir. They'd shyly asked the sacristan to open the curtains for them to view the large altar piece perhaps painted by Coppo di Marcovaldo in 1260 of the "Madonna and Child" surrounded by saints, angels and two scenes. When would they be there again? When would they again stand together on that moorland hill-top near Saint-Just and look down the sheer cliff to the lake below filled with water-lilies in flower?

As these thoughts flooded in she was close to tears, both of grief and joy. The world in chaos.

Claret

The large grey château isolated in the middle of lawns and pastures that extend beyond reason.

A large dark grey building put to the cruel uses its exterior already suggests.

A Gestapo Headquarters – interrogation rooms and cells – the top window on the left almost exactly half way between the end of the building and the main entrance.

Though this is in my imagination in a sun-filled kitchen in the early afternoon in September.

Where such interrogations could equally happen – husband and wife piling up cruelly logical absurdities, complaints, and accusations while the babies cry in the next room.

Monsters & Co.

The top window on the left of a slum tenement seen from a train window passing through east London – Bethnal Green, Stratford…

Stop the train. Step into that room. "Hello, I am Anthony Barnett, Norway's greatest jazz xylophone player. I saw you through the window. I saw you moving about your room, sitting watching t.v.. I had to come to say 'hello', to embrace you. We humans must stick together."

The film breaks at this point. Crackling noises and smoke pour from the improvised projection room. The village priest rushes out threatening the noisy audience to be quiet or else... If we sit quiet and still we will be allowed to see the rest of *Sabu the Elephant Boy* with French sub-titles.

Claret Commentary

World in chaos. The children show ingratitude to their father. You want to cover your ears, but a friend calls instead. "On your own day you are believed. Supreme success, furthering through perseverance. Remorse disappears." How far?

No-one expects you to be a saint – no-one but yourself, and when you don't you're through. I remember once I was in this fancy château for questioning. Above me on the ceiling was this huge religious scene, cherubs and saints in long robes. So as they twisted the wire tighter I looked up and saw this saint smiling down, softly, intensely, saying 'no-one expects you to be a saint...'

World in chaos. Ache of absence. Long silence as the film breaks.

Come here, come into the sun, where I can see you. Oh, how you've grown, and how smart you think yourself in uniform. You think that nobody has suffered as much as you – how you pity yourself, staring wildly into my dying eyes.

Look how the dying sun strikes fire from this young wine.

Franz Reh & Sohn Liebfraumilch

The twelfth meeting followed the pattern established in previous years.

Otto grabbed two glasses and stood up to give a speech.
Muller lined up three glasses and sat down to stare at them.
Klaus, swaying backwards and forwards, sang college songs, and *never touched* the wine before him.
Feuerbach just drank away from a seemingly endless secret supply.
I toyed with a single glass the whole night.
Heine was late (again).

We broke up soon after two o'clock. No message had arrived.

Entre Deux Mers /
I Still Hear The Squeak Of Your Axle

Between the two seas
we parted
years ago

now my children are grown
– and yours?

the bell on the church has rung
for years
unanswered

small insects
leap
from axle to vine
destroying the future

Rosé d'Anjou / Buff on Blue

All they were left with was a small fragment of glazed decorated pottery. No one could now tell whether it was from a plate, saucer, or bowl. The design – what there was of it – seemed to show a branch with an acorn. Other strands wove across the picture. Were they ribbons or serpents? One strand distinctly looked like a ribbon. Another so like a serpent, though it could well be the end of a broken branch.

The whole fragment measures roughly ½" by ⅜", and is drawn in black on a white background.

Such fragments, when found on a hot summer afternoon in the countryside, always seem mysterious, and, for some unknown reason, both beautiful and very sad. The double edge of passion. Love and rage. And a crude shift to even cruder symbols found in the fragment of beauty and destruction.

Step back from the edge of the field high on the hills. The skylarks sing and twitter above, and a cuckoo calls in the distant copse. An aeroplane circles the lovers deep in the wheatfield.

Civilised talk along a leafy path observed by curious cows and indifferent proud horses. Mr. Bremser approached carrying a worn black brief-case.

What race memories are brought to us, unrecognised, by birdsong? Every high, grassy place in England is redolent with that tireless, rolling music which, seldom copied by avian mimics*, must be rich in inherited message. I used to think, looking at the spine of Williamson's "Scribbling Lark" (which I hadn't read) that the title was a perfect description of the song: arcane calligraphy.

In the sunny courtyard of the farm Mr. Bremser showed us the finds:

This is very important: it is the earliest ceramic ware to be found in these parts. Rather crude, perhaps, for these were unsophisticated people – often barbaric and cruel to one another: but then, what will future generations say of us?

This, too, tells us much of the life of those times: some young lad may have given it to his sweetheart, and she thrown it away in disgust – certainly its imagery is direct, and primal.

And here is a fountain pen, Parker, black, still in working order. Who can say with what passion the poet flung it aside on these grassy slopes to listen, helplessly, to the skylark's song?

*Lemaire, F. (1979) in Ibis v. 121, pp 95-97.

XIIIe Exposition de Bordeaux, Prix d'Honneur

What is this naked youth doing sitting with, what appears to be, an elaborately decorated stick held in a (somewhat) suggestive manner? And then this full bosomed woman who now appears at my side waving a (?) palm leaf, or is it a rather frayed fern?

Hello sailor, indeed!

Château du Grand Abord / An Epic of Everyday Life

He staggered across the moonlit lawn towards the window, where her anxious, searching face stared out. Her slim body seemed inept and clumsy in the expensive clothes she wore, her fingers pulsing at the windowpane. He wanted to call out to her: It's me, Paul, I'm back. I'm sorry about last time, but I escaped, I'm free now. I've come back for you so that we can try again.

But the words died in his throat as her face, aged beyond belief, lit up in the joy of recognition.

> Dear Linda,
>   I just called to return the bike, and the Bloxom book, neither of which did quite what I'd hoped for me – we must discuss this sometime. Nobody was around except old Rusty, beating up the dust on the path with his tail, so I left them in the summer house with all those bits of old pots – hope you can find them!
>   love,
>   Catherine

Château du Grand Abord / rewind:

The fugitive was dragged from his bicycle by a fierce dog as he turned from the country lane into the drive. And miles east of here the deserter was left bound to a tree with barbed wire by the retreating army.

A young soldier, still a boy, lay in the ditch with his intestines sliding out of his shattered belly. He cried out for his mother as the officer stepped forward with his revolver to put the man out of his agony. The officer was in peace-time a teacher of mathematics and music in a small provincial town.

"Walk joyfully throughout all the world
and answer that of god in everyman."

An uniquely full and scented flavour particular to this region.

Boredom and drudgery are directed to the tradesmen's entrance.

Silvaner – Rhine Wine

The gloom of a rainy Sunday evening in North Wales was easily dismissed with a large gin and tonic. Laying aside my copy of Poucher's "Welsh Peaks" I leafed through a copy of 'The Countryman'. It seems that tweeds will be de rigueur in the Residents' Lounge of the Plas Teg Guest House this autumn. My fellow climbers and I then proceeded to the Dining Room where Major Hoover and his lady wife were already seated at their table and discussing the art critic Edward Lucie-Smith and Catholicism. I was not quite able to understand the connection.

We'd had a grand day climbing the Arans. After the steep haul up to Aran Fawddwy we'd negotiated our way over rock outcrops and snow patches along the windswept ridge to Aran Benllyn, the lesser of the two peaks. Later we'd descended by a more leisurely route following a diagonal path across the scree slopes into the Hengwin Valley. Beside the natural exultation that comes from such exercise we had also certainly worked up a good appetite.

The main course at dinner was ham baked in cider accompanied by a reasonable claret. We then decided to have a bottle of white wine with our dessert, two of us choosing the chocolate mousse while the other two worked their way through a rather limited cheese board. Our host recommended a certain Rhine wine none of us had tasted before. We were not disappointed by his charming suggestion.

During a lull in the conversation my attention was drawn to the scene portrayed in the wine's label. It was a scene of contrasts. In the foreground was a populous city that bristled with castle turrets and church spires. Behind the city was a plain of empty fields bordered by a large and impenetrable forest. Beyond the forest rose a long and bare mountain ridge.

Silvaner / Same Label, Different Table

Major H. was peeved that the party on the next table wasn't noisy enough to complain about.

He was also peeved to note that the same wine he'd found rather sickly with his lamb they were obviously enjoying as a dessert. Idly he stared at the label on the bottle before him and imagined himself in command of the rocket silos in those distant hills – scanning across the plain with fieldglasses towards where he (and, he supposed, the people on the next table) sat looking into the label.

For no reason his mind threw up the disquieting image of two sturdy youngsters in red and green striding off up the forest path with their satchels and correctly fitted footwear, and not a thought for anyone behind them.

"Hey, come back! Don't leave me!" he thought, then stared around with embarrassment.

"I wonder where they are now?" he thought.

Final Claret Label

Your mind is tossing on the ocean, you step through the picture frame and the spray hits you. The deck kicks under your feet and your heart soars. There is "much to be done" – What next, Captain?

Your life, or lives, the old griefs – very real at the time – what do they matter? Your rosebushes, snipped in the late sunlight – who'll tend them, or your memory of them?

Your mind is running nose-down on a sea of ideas, you have dreamed yourself into the real world – and that too is illusion.

"My ships have all miscarried"

There is no wound, no ache. O you, out there, approaching, you inside, sharing this window seat, sharing my life, for us there is no hurt.

Does a single white rose in a glass vase on a bare window ledge say everything? And outside that window a vast cobbled square stretches off to the water front. Grand buildings with elegant arcades border the remaining sides of the square. Ships at anchor sway with the tide and wind, and strain on their ropes like dogs.

At this point two cherubs appear in the sky at the corners of our vision puffing out their cheeks. An angel and a naked woman come forward carrying a large antique coat of arms. They're all preparing us for the voyage.

We're to leave our memories and head into invention, into the unknown or vaguely guessed at, the fruits of old rumours and stories.

But still in the cold sunlight of that room – sitting beside our bags, the steam rising from our small coffee cups – a memory of a land of box forests, yew and hazel, and the honeysuckle and daisies. A memory that could never be left. "Yes, we were now in that enchanted calm which they say lurks at the heart of every commotion."

All the wrong notes

1976-1983

Wish you were here : six postcards

for Antony Lopez

Preface

Great clouds of sadness and poverty cross the sky
shadowing the land below and the people's minds
The wind strong and bending the young trees

At the coast there is, yes, a brightness
the crashing of waves on the pebble beaches
the cliffs a dazzling white wall either side of the haven

The autumn with those weeks of white mist mornings
and afternoons where the light itself takes on a golden haze
All of this surrounding and filling us – the giant clouds and the
                                                            bright sea

The Walk, Abertillery Park

            to walk the paths where birds sing,
to at night see through the tree tops the whole scatter of stars

the humans and animals walk out in the darkness
night hunters while the birds sleep the planet turns

I can only talk of, at such times,
the wonder and the loneliness of this

Population figures fade in the apparently endless shelves of statistical
registers. Mr. Jamesson turned to close the small low gate behind him
then walked at a brisk pace down the road, fearful as ever of being late
for work. His telescope and bird books lay waiting in the front-room
for the weekend.

Tryst Road, Stenhousemuir

proud of watch and chain
proud of stone solid houses
proud of new coat and shoes
proud of being photographed in this cold bleak treeless street

a lump of tenderness sticks in our throat
while 'SENTIMENTALITY' flashes on the screen
but proud, all the same, of the continual struggle
of people
to survive and make despite

"I have always felt that I was living on the high seas, threatened, at the heart of a royal happiness," wrote Camus. And Stevenson too on his first long sea voyage spoke of being filled with a total happiness he'd not known before, his health and spirits being completely revived by the experience.

And wasn't it at a cottage in Stenhousemuir he started to write 'Treasure Island'? Maybe I confuse the names and the town was really called Braemar. But whichever – a bleak place.

Rue de la Pierre, Messines

Camus wrote of Gide:

"I had never met him before, and yet it was as if we had always known each other. Not that Gide ever received me very intimately. He had a horror, as I already knew, of that noisy promiscuity which takes the place of friendship in our world. But the smile with which he greeted me was simple and joyful and, when he was with me, I never saw him on his guard."*

and in Messines the grim peasantry stand around in the cold bright sunlight of this particular winter's day. The clear blue sky goes unremarked by the minor officials who are busy with their mean business. Hard and mean as a peasant's heart, someone might say, and these, their sons, continue the tradition even though decked out in uniforms and the occasional modest decoration.

In the picture rue de la Pierre goes straight ahead then disappears to the right. And out in the icy countryside an avenue of standing stones goes *its* own way straight across a stretch of bleak moorland radiating some other kind of strength and that wonder shut out elsewhere.

yet the coldness that grips one's whole body

Someone unseen opens the double doors within the apartment and the stranger steps through smiling. We are filled with his warmth, his face like the sun.

*Albert Camus, *Encounters with André Gide*

Maison Desgardin, Route de Gameches, Tours-En-Vimeu (Somme)

To make one song of praise,
even on a flat muddy plain,
in weary farmlands and hard factory towns
To praise those gentle and careful acts
people *do*

The family with a large dog that live in a small new house
on the edge of town
Each with their own distinction
The knowledges and unknown skills of *other* people
never to be taken for granted, ignored.
Each one

Rays of sun breaking through the slate grey clouds
and spot-lighting a gentle ridge of hills,
a clump of trees, two or three small fields
And in the air the bird song,
the clear music

Blick auf Grimselgebiet

I think of you
I think of the walk down through the pine woods to the village
I think of the questions of affection,
of those that were dear to me and
those that are dear to me

And at this point the quiet and loneliness of
a deserted hotel balcony overlooking an Alpine valley…

Yes, here in the mountains far from any sea,
snow on the peaks, the cool air of evening
scented with resin from the pines, early spring

A lengthy description merely buys time, can go on
filling many pages – the excuses
for failure and the inability to clear air in the midst of clear air,
rather sinking back into the luxury of refined loneliness,
of cultured thoughts and a general fascination with
the 'finer points'

Opening the book that he had earlier carefully placed on the white table cloth, he continued to read a collection of short stories by Bruno Schulz. The beginning of one story particularly struck him with its appropriateness to his present mood. It began: "'The Demiurge', said my father, 'has had no monopoly of creation, for creation is the privilege of all spirits. Matter has been given infinite fertility, inexhaustible vitality, and, at the same time, a seductive power of temptation which invites us to create as well'."

The air was so sweet. The white linen of the table cloth such a pleasure to his eyes and his touch. It seemed anything was possible when he had such a sure sense of where he was and what he was doing at this very moment. Everything would follow naturally from this. The word 'flow' is maybe more accurate than 'follow'. Everything would flow from this without the hindrance of nervous plans or plodding schemes. It would just flow, glide through the air like some amazingly beautiful and powerful bird of prey, like the buzzards that circled this valley.

Contrejour sur la Plage, Saint-Enogat

Two boys splash along the beach

the streaked sky of late afternoon
the grand mansion silhouetted on the headland

as though the sun stranger lay in wait
ready to burst forth   but not today

let it rest
              hugged in the arms of the sea
naked
in bird song sea sway

Entering a bookshop in the capital I buy a copy of de Montherlant's 'Textes sous une occupation, 1940-1944'. I obviously see this choice, because of my great affection for it, as somehow more than apt for my present situation. As though I continually feel that I too live besieged and threatened by 'dark and brutal forces', and yet strive in spite of this to be open and fresh to all the wonders that do finally triumph over the invaders.

This would be as good a place as any for me to start writing my biography, for anyone to start writing *their* biography.

Poem for an Edinburgh room : Sky

waking
        the clouds passing
                                outside your window
the room in the sky
a space – room   filled with peace
and the quiet passing of time
as though nothing exists outside the room,
below the room,
                except sky,
soft blue air,
                soft grey air

The town that does exist, but
for now is quiet, passive

The hills that embrace the town, and
the tall stone houses in that town
            (barnacle bill the sailor)
are there, set there.
                            greens and greys.
and above them all   over all,   the arc
of the sky   where
                    I'm now floating

Pikes Peak

Dismal car rides plagued with dust and heat
to admire the scenery

bare ridges of mountains
scrubland
battered pine forests

To reach out in the morning
to touch and kiss the one you love

"Take me to your leader, earthman"

Machines

1

In the darkness you could hear hooting noises, ahead? somewhere "out there". As though ships were passing in the nearby estuary. Or maybe a distant freight-yard. In such blackness the strings of yellow lights "illuminating the scene" could only be imagined. The stacks of timber and oil drums, the quiet of the night.

Across the field maybe the dark outline of a wood? That's another possibility.

Enclosed in such a state. The dark pressing in, felt brushing one's face and hands, "the soft fur of nights".

2

In the darkness of the cottage, midday, and the large stone fireplace filled with wood ash. Up behind the cottage the beech woods, below, the steep green slopes down to the valley. The trees and valley a soft grey white with the mist and drizzle of early autumn. In the darkness of the cottage...

"breaking down at the continual brutality of it all, and my failure, once again. The tears flow down my face. I bury my head in the arms of the woman I've also failed."

A mile and a quarter walk away a black farm raincoat lies neatly folded up beside a tall hedge with a sharpening stone and bill hook on top of it.

3

IMAGINE an elegant octagonal room with a high ceiling. The room is about 30 foot across and has french windows along the four sides of the room that face south. These windows look out over extensive lawns that finally end in a shrubbery and woods. It is a summer afternoon with clear blue skies as far as you can see. The time is about 2.30 pm.

The room itself feels pleasantly warm and airy. The walls are painted white and in their decoration and the matching mouldings on the ceiling show the house to be built in the 18th century in the Georgian neo-classical style. The floor is parquet and polished to a fine and rich glow. The only furnishings in the room, which is otherwise bare, are a Persian rug and a small table. The rug lies on the north side of the room and measures 10 foot by 6 foot. Its colours are generally lighter than usual and the abstract design less elaborate. The small oval table stands in the middle of the room.

On this table stands a machine of some sort, or maybe it could better be called a mechanism or instrument. The instrument is about 3 foot high and at its mahogany base measures one foot by one foot. The overall impression is that of a neat and complex arrangement of brass joints and mechanical parts, and shiny steel rods, all in motion that is both smooth and dignified. Atop the mechanism a steel foliot rod rotates slowly, the two brass balls at either end glinting as they turn. This escapement regulating, as they say, the transfer of energy from the spring to the various gears. The whole machine is a combination of many such correct regulations. Stepping back from it and closing your eyes you hear well oiled clicking noises against a background of the distant noises from the gardens outside. A blackbird singing and the sound of a small group of people approaching the house.

1a

"It's cold enough, tonight?"
"Oh yes, it is that."

2a

"How are you? OK?"
"Yes, fine. Right."

3a

"Well, of course facts must be true, but when it comes to it that's kind of irrelevant. I mean the story is where the work is done."

4a

Nikolaus Pevsner: "The English portrait conceals more than it reveals, and what it reveals it reveals with studied understatement."

5a

"Yes, well, that may well be so, but I still find it difficult to accept."

6a

... a startled blackbird winged up through the beech woods, finally disappearing into the delicately leafed tops, its cries echoing on long after
This isn't nature poetry.

In progress

...on the ground
above the deep cistern
No one at the gate

the sweetness
of naming the names   trees in blossom

        almond
        orange
        lemon
        fig
        mulberry
        pomegranate
        apricot
        bay

    the jasmin

flowers on the mountainside

        anemones
        narcissi
        asphodel
        orchid
        hyacinth

the green lush clover, chickweed, the short new grass

No one at the gate
the time granted

Text for an engraving

"In the wild end of a moorland parish, far out of the sight of any house, there stands a cairn among the heather, and a little by east of it, in the going down of the braeside, a monument with some verse half defaced. It was here that Claverhouse shot with his own hand the Praying Weaver of Balweary, and the chisel of Old Mortality had clinked on that lonely gravestone."*

For on 8th July 1853 Commodore Perry sailed into the Bay of Yedo with his squadron of 4 U.S. Navy ships, and established a base at Loo-Choo (Okinawa). And so one form of ritualised barbarism replaces another, I guess. The Japanese woodcuts portraying those four tall black ships have a beauty in their colouring that is a far cry from the probable ugliness of the incident.

Though these facts were so remote from her, she could certainly imagine 17th century Scotland or the establishment of western capitalism in Japan as she sat that afternoon in the top room. All around her were stacks of slightly worn and dusty furniture, piles of books, and large trunks filled with mementoes and "things that will come in useful some day". Outside the countryside and gardens were sodden. The rain soaked long grass bending over the swollen streams. Wet gusts of wind shaking the trees. In a late autumn such as this she could only sit, as though frozen, for afternoons that never seemed to know any progress. She imagined what it must have been like for Robert Louis Stevenson in the South Seas. How would his afternoon have gone at the Vailima estate on Samoa?

"…until about 2 when I turn in to work again till 4; fool from 4 to half past, tired out and waiting for the bath hour; 4.30 bath; 4.40, eat two heavenly mangoes on the verandah, and see the boys arrive with the pack-horses," he said.

*RL Stevenson – introductory to *Weir of Hermiston*

To be read very slowly

for Harry Guest

At two bells on the middle watch - unable to forget the cry of wounded creatures deep in the wood. The bridge in near darkness except for the yellow light glowing from the compass, the instruments.

Haunted by a strange dream of a wild and thick wooded country, a forested lowland with high bare ridges looking down on all this, walling it in. The possibility of ruined buildings made of stone lying somewhere within this forest, in fact such sites scattered like dying stars throughout the forest-land.

To wake from such dreams, sweating, and in a tangle of bedclothes. To wrench open the port-hole and fill your lungs with that clear sanity of sea air. To see the ocean again sparkling with moonlight, reassuring us, always there.

But when struck with that dark hard reality of death how the fear fills us again and again, whether awake or dreaming. Both at the loss of all we love and hold dear, the gardens, the sea coasts, our families, and the loss of our hopes and dreams, of what we still need to do, to find out, know. Always hungry in the face of such hauntings.

In the undergrowth of the wood small creatures go about their business. The moss and lichen, the small delicate ferns, flash and sparkle with their own movements in the night. Sleeping birds overhead.

As you enter Fishguard harbour a cargo ship sits on the bottom half-submerged, only the bows, bridge amidships, and the funnel and masts in the stern above water. Seaweed trails from the deck rails and rigging. Once ashore you climb up atop the giant granite cliffs, their edges rich with cowslips, thrift, and orchids in flower. The vast ocean in front of you. Gulls wheeling and squawking in the bright air. This is not a dream. A short distance inland you find standing stones set in small lush wheat fields.

"On certain mornings, as we turn a corner, an exquisite dew falls on our heart and then vanishes. But the freshness lingers, and this, always, is what the heart needs." (wrote Camus)*

*in *Return to Tipasa*.

The beginning of the story

1

The castle was built on a small hill overlooking the river. Probably it once commanded the whole valley – chose who could pass through the valley, who could come up river in boats, who could cross the river at the nearby ford. Now it stands empty and the surrounding lands are once more scrub and forest. The castle, after all, was only built by men and manned by men. And now it is just one more feature of the landscape, though maybe more passive than most.

2

Parting the leaves you look out onto a sunny meadow that slopes down to a small wood with a stream the other side.

A thick wood bordered the meadow with the beech trees' branches trailing the ground. The leaves of one tree slowly parted and a face appeared.

3

Blue objects flashed before the eyes of the face. As though a giant blue boulder dominated the foreground, and all else was only a haze. A rounded blue cylinder rising out of the earth, or descending from the heavens. There were obviously many explanations and interpretations for all these stunning phenomena.

4

Late in the morning on a mild and sunny autumn day I was in the kitchen. First I made a delicious chocolate blancmange, then prepared a bowl of stewed pears made even more fragrant by a touch of ground ginger added to the boiling syrup before introducing the segments of pear. The quiet happiness one feels with such domestic duties is perhaps one of the greatest joys of having a home.

The choice of dishes prepared will obviously signify something to a person looking for such things. Whether he's right or wrong is of little importance to me.

5

Threading its way along the valley was a string of pack horses. One could just make out the small figures of the accompanying traders.

Up here overlooking the valley...

Perhaps they're not traders, or not all traders. Perhaps one of them is a magician. How to imagine his clothes? that is if he dresses differently from his companions.

And whether he should be a wizard rather than a magician? And whether, rather than these people merely being on a journey or trading, there are more serious and more exotic matters in hand? Threats of dragons? Threats of invasions by harsh forces, or worse?? Threats of the moon disappearing, of tides growing wild and ravaging the shores, flooding the valleys?

6

The wind moans about the houses and the last yellowing leaves are stripped from the trees. The birds become more obvious and seemingly more active in their continual search for food.

Trim the wisteria, tie up the jasmin and honeysuckle, re-stake the chrysanthemums, beware the gales. Trim the house, all ship-shape. The winter almost upon us.

7

In his pouch the wizard had a small silver box. The box was beautifully engraved with curious designs and the suggested figures of birds, otters, foxes and wild boar. There was no apparent way of opening the box, though it could be opened by the wizard. Inside was a small flint blade and a flower that never faded.

8

A quiet and mild day in early winter. The sunlight in no way clear or bright but somehow there. The garden below my window is all wetness. The last damp yellowing leaves hang from the wisteria. A single half-dead pink rose is the only colour in the flower bed other than the dull browns and greens of the dying leaves surrounding it. On such mornings a similar lethargy fills us.

9

One clear night the wizard stood alone in a small meadow beside the river. The moon was almost full and clearly lit the whole landscape. He placed the silver box on the grass and stepped back a few paces. The box then slowly opened as though of its own accord and, once open, a bright silver light burnt over the whole surface of the box, inside and out. And at the same moment as the silver box opened a blue cylinder of light slowly appeared hovering a few feet above the box. The blue light, at first faint, as the box's own light was, gradually generated more and more power until it was a near-dazzling throbbing humming block of BLUE.

All this happened in silence, though somehow you sensed at the edge of your hearing a small and delicate music almost like the tinkling of glass wind chimes.

After a time that no one could measure or remember the blue cylinder of light began to fade until in the end it was the faintest of outlines, and then disappeared completely. And at the same time the silver box's light also faded and died, leaving the box an almost indistinguishable dark object set in the pale moon-lit grass.

10

A great sadness fills us.

Questions

i)
Does the man go mad?
Does he even commit suicide? (hence a well-rounded drama) or continue a life of quiet suburban despair? (so a well-rounded 'Modern' drama)

ii)
Is the wizard murdered soon after this event?
or several years later?
or does he lose his powers? slowly or quickly?
or, the reverse, does he go on to become truly prosperous and renowned for his skills, living to a fine old age?

iii)

Late on a summer evening we find ourselves in the leafy suburban streets of some small town whose name we don't as yet know. There is a velvet darkness that brushes our lips and cheeks with great sensuality. This darkness is only broken by the vague pyramids of white light around the rare street lamps, and the opaque yellow glow from some curtained windows where people are still about. The silence hisses and crackles, it is so near complete.

iv)

Shrieks of anguish are muffled in blankets.

v)

Do we pour chocolate blancmange over the wise wizard? explaining to him the while that it is a symbolic gesture attacking all he stands for, but that he shouldn't take it personally?

vi)

Are we denied peace?
Not the peace of answers, set ideas, and realised hopes, (stagnation), but the peace to do things we want to do for ourselves. To push on, unhindered by jobs, exhaustion, and 'the treacle of fears and evasions'!!??

vii)

The man closes his book. Out of his window he knows and sees the seasons change. His guarded optimism is justified by events.

viii)

Shrieking statues are suddenly muffled in the public gardens by council workmen. The flowers join in the horrified chorus. 'WHY ME? WHO ME? NOT ME?'

You essai. You o.k.

for Paul Evans

> "Once again, the philosophy of darkness
> will dissolve above the dazzling sea."
> Albert Camus 1948

1

a rock outcrop in the sea

a deserted car standing on the empty shore road

Gulls shriek in the air above the rock
while below thrift and small orchids flower
in that awesome hush between the waves breaking

The blue leather upholstery of the car is too hot to touch
the sun being that bright and strong today
A neat green cardboard box has been placed on the back seat

The scents of the sea and the coast join
somewhere up there in the sky –
                              A pyramid of light?

Or would you be bored by all this after the first day?
The ground too damp and civilisation too far away?
What if it rains and you have to trudge miles to the nearest shop or
pub or public transport to get away from all this, to have a few decent
'home comforts'?

2 /1900/

Hold the horses! It's Hotel Wolf!
or as they now say, in these modern times,
Wolf Hotel, and since then renamed The Sisson,
Saratoga, Wyoming.

Step inside
to the palm filled lounge and big easy chairs
and just the right soupçon of barbarism.

O cold blooded murderers,
the sweet-hearts and glory of this continent!

"Peaches! Fresh peaches!" cried the two gauchos,
and the little boy, lifting the canvas that covered their fruit cart,
saw only a heap of severed heads.

You do step into the bar, but are rightly nervous beneath your assured
and sporty manner. No tennis courts here, I'm sorry to say, only child-
like card-games played by unpleasant adults. I wouldn't stay long if I
were you, though I'm not.

3

I turn my back on all that and re-enter
the alchemist's dark chambers
A glass prism is set on the table top
beneath the window and scatters sunlight
in bands of colour 'a marvel to behold'

Books, equipment, and implements are
stacked about the room
all as aids to discover 'the wonders and secrets of nature'
through human invention and curiosity
godlike

a stuffed baby crocodile hangs from the ceiling
the retort glows gold with its fire

Dear Sir,
　　　　Your moods of deep depression can weigh heavily on you
for several days or more. I can really do very little for you or your
state. Such melancholy can take up to 6 years to fade from your heart
after the original emotional shock. I would suggest your taking long
walks in the countryside and that you try to mix socially as much as
is possible.
　　　　　　Signed,
　　　　　　　　a doctor.

4

TO SPELL IT OUT: the barbarity in all its forms,
in the face of which our blundering frailty,
our frail giant-steps.

"This book," wrote the French Resistance leader Colonel Georges,
"springs from a sadness and a certain amount of disgust at seeing
myths take so much precedence over history... Our truth has no need
of mirrors that would exaggerate it."*

And you, Anna, with your two fierce-looking sisters and, presumably,
stories of real hardships and dangers in the now placid Mid-West, or
even further west, Kansas maybe. It's different somehow, though I
can't explain.

Families on all sides of 'The Water', with their own strengths like
islands in the flood, us all sat on top of the roof like a bunch of
drenched chickens waiting for the waters to subside and then be
submerged again within the family.
It's difficult to explain, warming and frightening at the same time, the
love there.

There are the Grand Events, the 'dangerous times' when maybe more
than a rightness about a family is needed – though I can't say we live
in such times, and, even so, any such dramatic behaviour has to have
a base-camp somewhere, n'est-ce pas?   though maybe not

* Colonel Georges (Robert Noireau) - *Le Temps des Partisans*.

5

Paul, you must know it already, but how in the upper left margin of the first page of the manuscript score for *The Fourth of July,* Charles Ives wrote to his copyist—

> "Mr. Price: Please don't try to make things nice! All the wrong notes are right. Just copy as I have. I want it that way."

You walk by the sea on a grey February afternoon with your daughter Lucy and a grossly over-enthusiastic dog. On our meeting we remember, though don't talk of it, the obviously lucid and witty conversation we'd had the night before when (somewhat) the worse for drink!

The mistakes, the difficulties, ... these words almost used too much so that they become some sort of totem or excuse, but it all falling, and us too, every whichaway.

In a little frequented corner of the museum we find an old and heavily embroidered trade union banner on display. The gold silk on a dark red velvet background shows a motif of clasped hands, and all of this faded and somewhat the worse for wear too. I can't make out the motto, but it's probably something like "Strength in Unity" or...

Out in the street again we head back towards the beach. The sea really *is* magnificent, a vast sweep of silver-shot slate grey that fades off and up into the white grey of the sky. The chilling sea wind grips our bones.

Plato, Dante, Pound & Co. give up but try

for Rafe Harwood

That dumb paradise
                            beyond the words
that no one can write
                            from Plato down to now

"Now of the heaven which is above the heavens no earthly
poet has sung, or will ever sing in a worthy manner."

                    whoever – all those 'great men' –

no competition

only left with
                    "Let the wind speak
                                that is paradise."

and this
talking of the joys of children, the paradise of them,
            can only be known by those who have the children

you, my baby son, whether seeing your smile or hearing your laughter
or just the two of us hugging
it's *that*
                            no words beyond the bare account

***

It all breaks down
(which is as near meaningless as most such phrases)
but a general collapse of the words
(Mr. Jung forget your symbols)
beyond them

son of   son of   son of

that joy
your smile as I hold you
in my arms

***

my childhood –
                        no memory, only old photos

war on, father away, windows taped to reduce blast of splintered
glass from the bombings of said war

only old photos of this, no memory

only knowledge of what the fathers missed, what we kids missed
– the hugs and paradise of being together

***

But to tell it as a story, as though to someone else,
        the distance somehow hazing the sharpness
        of this knowledge.

It won't do

As evening draws in

for Jud

Weeks of waking in the early hours
to lie trapped in a half-dream
shuffling and ordering obscurely titled pages.

The failure of all attempts at exhaustion –
long moorland walks in the heat of summer,
reading heavy biographies, drinking.

Without you, without your company,
the talismans are powerless –
the long dark crow's feather,
the small cube of quartz and wedge of flint.

To wake in the morning's bright sunlight
our bodies entwined
before the arrival of the children
in our bed.

Afterwords to a poem by Jack Spicer

(in memory of Bill Butler)

"They've (the leaders of our country) have become involved in a
    network of lies.
We (the poets) have also become in network of lies by opposing
    them.
The B.A.R. which Stan said he shot is no longer used for the
    course. Something lighter more easy to handle and more
    automatic.
What we kill them with or they kill us with (maybe a squirrel
    rifle) isn't important.
What is important is what we don't kill each other with
And a loving hand reaches a loving hand.
The rest of it is
Power, guns, and bullets."*

        webs of lies upon webs of lies
a spreading mould of hate and viciousness
and death walking among us all

That mean spirits and the dishonest man now hold sway
        poison us all with their intrigue and venom
Where no hand of kindness reaches out to touch
        our lips as we pass
As though love were driven out of the town
        and only left alight in the quiet of a home

And you now gone 3 days with death
and now gone 3 days with death your big bear-hugs
your watch and chain, your self

We have no words to talk of you
to tell our loss
only the stuttered conversations on the phone
the broken phrases stood awkwardly round a kitchen
an empty cup in my hand

                *Jack Spicer – *Ten Poems for Downbeat* (poem 9)

At this distance I praise you as the days grow darker
and know the impossibility and uselessness of such
You walked (past tense) talked (past tense)
and with all the clutter we humans drag behind us
                                        were dear to us.

Just friends

Two men enter a Victorian house in Kensington and view a re-created Arab courtyard and a series of indifferent paintings.

Two men sit by Kensington Round Pond on a chilly autumn day and discuss the birds and animals to be found in cities.

Two men and a woman sit on the swaying top deck of a bus driving along the coast road from Newhaven to Brighton on a November afternoon.

Three men and two women stop to pick up large red-skinned potatoes that had fallen from a farm lorry, and then continue on their walk to see a tree full of herons and a lone kestrel perched on a footpath sign.

Two men walk on a summer evening through the leafy streets of west London and discuss renting a studio.

Two men stride along Hadrian's Wall in March and are met by earnest hikers in orange anoraks and woolly hats.

Two men walk by the sea at night.

Two men in the dark of a hide quietly lift the wooden flaps and observe the mud flats below them, the curlews, dunlins, grey plovers, cormorants, shell ducks, redshanks, and herons.

Two men in Essex study an ancient church door with graceful iron work said to be Viking in origin.

Two men wave to one another (figuratively) at a great distance (real) and slowly fade from each other's sight.

Two men write letters to each other and meet, ride a motorbike, drive in a hired car, and take long train journeys north.

Two men scramble over a recent cliff fall searching for flints and fossils, and then fade in the sea-mist.

One man... the lush parks and mute statues.

At this moment I feel close to tears.

A poem for writers

To finally pull the plug on the word machine,
to rise from the chair late one evening
and step back into the quiet and darkness?

The dull white lights of the control-room of
a large hydro-electric dam in Russia
a computer centre in Brighton
the bridge of a giant oil tanker in the Indian Ocean.
Subdued light that reaches every corner
with no variation, tone, or shadow.

To leave the warm desk-light's tent
and step out into the…
      "I am just going outside and may be some time, Scottie"

Trains rush through the night,
across country through suburbs past factories oil refineries dumps,
the lights from their windows quickly disturbing the dark fields and
                                                                   woods
or the railway clutter as they pass through town,
staring in at the bare rooms and kitchens
each lit with its own story that lasts for years and years.
A whole zig-zag path, and the words stumble and fidget
around what has happened.

To walk out one January morning across the Downs
a low mist on the hills and the furrows coated with frost,
the dew ponds iced up.
The cold dry air.
And the sudden excitement when a flock of partridges starts up
in front of you and whirrs off and down to the left,
skimming the freshly ploughed fields.

"O ma blessure" groan the trees
with the wounds of a multitude of small boys' penknives.

No, not that –
but the land, the musics, the books
always attendant

amongst the foolish rush and scramble for vainglory,
talk or noise for its own sake, a semblance of energy
but not necessity.

Throw your cap in the air, get on your bike, and pedal off
down hill – it's a joy with no need of chatter,
Hello Chris.

South Coast postcard

Big City screaming railway station jukebox
     pounding crowds drinking talking to them
     -selves   A whole hot wet blanket of racket
     pulled over our heads
In the middle of such
     to imagine a remote town and an anonymous
     and 'boring' life with little or no company
     except one's own quiet self-righteousness
Ahhck – twisted and tortured in these ropes
     harbour walls the iron sides pulling away
     silent screaming echoing all the other
     screaming and crazed racket
The blocks in   The blinkers on

* * * * * * * * * * * * * * * * * *

SIR JOHN CORDY BURROWS Knt.
THREE TIMES MAYOR OF BRIGHTON

ERECTED BY HIS FELLOW TOWNSMEN
AS A MARK OF THEIR ESTEEM

1878

Paralysis

THE TALKING HEAD SPOKE:

> 'Hid in the coarse grasses
>> bee orchids and pyramid orchids,
>> hare bells and   urrr ....(?)
> On the bare hills
>> overlooking the lush hedgerows
>> below .... (?)'

SPINE SNAPPED
BODY GONE LIMP LUMP
READ ME SCHOLARLY BOOKS
       "A History of Christianity"
       "The Journals of Eugene Delacroix"
IN THE TOWN – DON'T STOP – CROWD IN –
WORK WIPE OUT – STUMBLING DEPRESSION,
POVERTY AND ENVY, INSULTS AND EXPLOITATION,
AND OTHER ABSTRACT NOUNS, I. E. IDEAS
slide sideways down and across to:
FLEET SUNK. PLANTATION SMASHED,
OVERGROWN, RETURNED TO JUNGLE.
body lying there
dust gathering on the chess pieces
lying there in the still disorder of an open box,
the Baedeker guide to Florence undisturbed on the bookshelf

Midday the gulls squawking on the roof tops
       in the centre of town,
            their giant shadows covering the crowded
            streets below as they slide through a blue sky.
Midnight the wind along the cliff path, the sound
       of waves breaking on the shore, the distant
       white light of a flashing beacon that
       interrupts the soft darkness.

ONE BLINK OF MY EYELIDS MEANS 'YES'
TWO BLINKS OF MY EYELIDS MEANS 'NO'.
HEAD SWIVELLING IN GLASS CASE
ON MARBLE PEDESTAL
THE PHILOSOPHER'S STONE.

Bath-time

for Ted Kavanagh & Barry MacSweeney

A motor torpedo boat covered in giant bubbles silently appeared
through the early morning mists. It was only when it was almost
upon us that we could hear the muffled roar of its engines, and
then only faintly.

I have as much knowledge of myself as I do of why I was adrift in that
rubber dinghy in the Malay Straits.

All the books and maps and knowledge give us too little, leave large
blank spaces, 'terra incognita'.

"...citizens who work and find no peace in pain.
I am chains."

In chained numbness, not confusion, the war boat bears down on me
on us where Educated Summaries are not worth a spit in hell.
The Cambridge Marxists, with large houses, cars and incomes,
can shove it.

"Anarchist Fieldmarshals, Socialist Judges, Dialectic Fuzz, Switched-
on Hangmen, and all other benefits of Correct Revolutionary
Practice."

I don't need patronage I need something else.

The mists clear before the burning sun, the sea empty and flat as a
sheet of polished metal. The long day ahead

Claret

The large grey château isolated in the middle of lawns and pastures that extend beyond reason.

A large dark grey building put to the cruel uses its exterior already suggests.

A Gestapo Headquarters – interrogation rooms and cells – the top window on the left almost exactly half way between the end of the building and the main entrance.

Though this is in my imagination in a sun-filled kitchen in the early afternoon in September

where such interrogations could equally happen – husband and wife piling up cruelly logical absurdities, complaints, and accusations while the babies cry in the next room.

Monsters & Co.

The top window on the left of a slum tenement seen from a train window passing through east London – Bethnal Green, Stratford...

Stop the train. Step into that room. "Hello, I am Anthony Barnett, Norway's greatest jazz xylophone player. I saw you through the window. I saw you moving about your room, sitting watching t.v.. I had to come to say 'hello', to embrace you. We humans must stick together."

The film breaks at this point. Crackling noises and smoke pour from the improvised projection room. The village priest rushes out threatening the noisy audience to be quiet or else... If we sit quiet and still we will be allowed to see the rest of *Sabu the Elephant Boy* with French sub-titles.

Text for two posters by Ian Brown / Poster 1

It's the vase of tulips and a mirror trick, though this time the vase is not
    set between facing mirrors but between a mirror and a painting
    of a mirror with a vase of tulips, and this in turn photographed.

It's the beautifully printed exhibition note in front of a Korean
    bowl that has been placed on burnt umber hessian. It quotes
    Bernard Leach's praise of the "unselfconscious asymmetry" of
    Korean potters, and how nothing in nature is symmetrical, but
    everything is asymmetrical, a nose not perfectly straight, the eyes
    not perfectly level.

It's those dreams of perfection, 'the man of your dreams', 'woman of
    your dreams', 'the budgie of your dreams', 'your dreams come
    true' to a jarring chorus of cash registers and half-stifled moans.

Again and again and again and again, and the months and years glide
    by hardly noticed so heavy and dull is the obsession.

to raise your head for one moment clear of this

        skies and clouds ahead
        and the fields and cities below
        as you fly through the sunlight

And below, not looking up,
"Are you going to see the new gorillas?" he asked as we
    walked briskly towards the Jardin des Plantes.

A cold dry day in January with mist on the Downs,
    frost on the furrows and ice on the ponds.
A flock of partridges suddenly starting up in front of me,
    and whirring off to the left skimming the ploughed fields.

but André Gide wrote: "The strange mental cowardice which makes
us perpetually doubt whether future happiness can equal past
happiness is often our only cause for misery; we cling to the phantoms

of our bereavements, as if we were in duty bound to prove to others the reality of our sorrow. We search after memories and wreckage, we would like to live the past over again, and we want to reiterate our joys long after they are drained to the dregs.

I hate every form of sadness, and cannot understand why trust in the beauty of the future should not prevail over worship of the past."

/Poster 2

SLEEPERS AWAKE
from the 'sensible life' whose only passion is hatred

A red and black pagoda towers above the chestnut trees
in a Royal Botanic Garden
The lush greens of south London back-gardens
O summer nights when trembling with that ecstasy
our bodies sweat and flood one another's

Burst forth – sun streams forth – light –
all doors and windows magically thrown open
a hot lush meadow outside
with dark green woods at its edges

turn it another way
These are insistences not repetitions
or the repetitions are only the insistence on

and it all crowds in:

"Nostalgia for the life of others… Whereas ours, seen
from the inside, seems broken up. We are still chasing
after an illusion of unity."
"Separation is the rule. The rest is chance…"*

which way to step?

and the dull brutality of monsters as they grind the bones
"forbidden to delight one's body, to return to the truth of things"*

The clouds part, your hand reaches through – yes
the glow and light in us, our bodies

And below around us – the flint customs house at Shoreham,
the call of a cuckoo as we climb up-hill to the Stalldown stone row,
the wild moor about, and from its edges
the churches, cathedrals, ancient and beautiful things.

*Albert Camus – *Notebooks*

Talking to myself

The sweet qualities of our dreams without which...

How the wind blows and our hearts ache to follow
the hazardous route the winds follow

           6 million Russians
           6 million Jews
           2 million Poles
           1 million Serbs
           Gypsies and others

The fern cabinet

"in that enchanted calm which they say lurks
                    at the heart of every commotion"

the dream look on an angel's half turned face

a faint cloud passes and
the distant landscape is precise in every detail

 to hold to "a wide and hospitable mind", a generous spirit

to "walk joyfully throughout all the world
and answer that of god in everyman"

a keel set for all the storms
and onshore the carefully jointed and polished mahogany,
the small forest of delicate green plants trembling

we die alone, lie alone
                    ("nor be in bodies lost")

though "There are no impervious skins or membranes in nature, no
'outlines'. Nothing is ever quite isolate."

two flights of geese come in from the east, the sun behind them, flying
low over the sea and across the dunes to the moorland beyond and the
still water there. The sparkle of the sea with the wind rising, the sharp
marram grass, the purple heather.

"I still bathe me in eternal mildness of joy"

(Quotations from Herman Melville, J.L. Borges, George Fox, John Dryden,
Antony Lopez, and Herman Melville.)

Faded ribbons around the lost bundle now being devoured by moths

Homage to William Strang

Late on a hot summer's night in Central Park

> (At this point creaking noises are heard as a faded and flaking cloth backdrop is unrolled showing a star filled sky and crude silhouettes of palm trees – a touch incongruous, but…)

two adults skip through the planned woodland to the children's playground where they vigorously swing on the swings, laughing and talking all the time.

> (Various constellations of white stars are set on the midnight blue – graphic fictions of the bear, Orion the hunter, the ladle, the plough. A special effects machine is working hard in the wings pumping out a soft humid air to match the scene.)

After their games they amble somewhat aimlessly across the park towards the streets and buildings. Where next with the romantic rush? that will possibly end in dissatisfaction and second thoughts in a dishevelled bed in an airless apartment?

'Dawn approaches, the sky lightens appropriately' read the stage directions.

* * *

A clear sky suddenly appears when I close my eyes.
There are no clouds on this day.
A monoplane slowly crosses the sky, returns, circles,
then goes off on its way.

A woman enters in loose thin pants.
Clouds, small white clouds appear,
and cross from left to right.

A spin of the compasses that stride off
to Cologne, Hanover, and Berlin.

The dream on the close cropped turf of the chalk ridge
blurs, then fades into telephones and posted objects.

* * *

A 14th century Italian painter, who specialises in gold leaf, appears
at this point with his apprentices. There is much clattering of paint
pots. Trestles are set up, and pigments are ground in the mortars.
Bright sunlight streams through the high windows onto this scene of
noisy industry that, as the days progress, will subside into the sounds
of brush strokes and intermittent groans as men shift their cramped
bodies.

Days, months, even years, pass all for that day when the patron will
enter and gasp with wonder at the finished work.

Angels cluster and rustle just to the side of my vision.

Years later...

* * *

[Paros]

sun streams through the window
onto the table

there is fruit in the bowl on the table
and flowers in the vase

the bare white walls gleam
with that reflected sunlight

You open the window
The pleasure of summer days slides by
unnoticed –
as though timeless – the days mingling

The trees rustle and sigh
as the wind comes up

I touch your shoulder
with my lips
and you then turn to me smiling

The vines are doing well this year
The house stands firm, clear and fresh
as it was hoped
Our embraces seal the knot

* * *

The arrogant woman in the large red hat
and bright green dress stares out of her gilt frame,
a book held limply in her left hand.

LIBER GENERATIONIS IHESU CHRISTI FILII DAVID FILII ABRAHAM
son of David son of Abraham

A black crow's feather lies on the moor's coarse grass,
is picked up and carefully taken to a house many miles away.

A white and blue and red feathered archangel
tramples the dragon and opens the loving scroll

Children joyfully rush about gathering the short grey and
brown feathers they've discovered in the hill pasture
happily ignorant of history and the death involved

Her pale and flushed face aches with tension.
Anger and violence seethe like maggots
beneath her glazed refinement.
For one moment – to get up and stride about the room –
will she? No, she remains seated on a hard high-backed chair.
The question of where vanity and obsession meet or divide or…

"Suffer little children to come unto thee"

* * *

A starling's breast crowded with lustrous stars
set on a black varnished night
and the angels all a-flutter

And, washing the whitewash from our hands, we remember that
Henry the Third's "favourite decorative motif, in both his castles
and his palaces, was gold stars on a green background... Work, he
commands, must be *decens, pulcher, sumptuosus.*"

the sound of children laughing outside

Then gusts of rain and wind and
a blur of colours signals the arrival of the rainbow door
We step through into a meadow of long grass
scattered with dandelions and dog daisies

A 13th century ceiling meets Schubert meets
a glass of chilled white wine and a ripe peach

* * *

[The Progress of the Walk]

blackbird's song
skylark's trill
cuckoo's call

lush woodland
wheatfield
re-entering the trees

an aeroplane circling
naked lovers

a blue butterfly
a small fragment of decorated pottery
The End:

Sussex Downs

"I'm just in love with all these three,
The Weald an' the Marsh an' the Down countrie"
                    Rudyard Kipling

To fall in love with the countryside
and stay in that love
writing love poems

in one's head, one's eyes, one's fingers,
one's body   walking
through the hot July wheatfields
heady with the scent of camomile.

Poems beyond any words
of explanation
                    and only left with the notebooks
                    filled with lists and impressions:

'Delicate harebells trembling
above the white stars of the wild thyme
as I climb the ramparts of Cissbury Ring.'

'An electric-blue dragonfly
skims the dewpond near Chanctonbury Ring
where the beeches rustle in the sou'-west wind
and the Isle of Wight appears
like a huge misty whale on the horizon.'

As though all my life I've been approaching
this,
earlier carelessness behind me now,
being of that age
settled
        and eager to see what lives outside me:
the Downs that "swell and heave their broad backs
into the sky".

There are no ghosts here
but as though we lived forever,
all of history and ourselves alive in this one moment
in one place with no wish to be elsewhere.

A child's view of railways

for Rowan Harwood

The railway station is shut for the night.
The trains stand silent beside the dark platforms.
The train drivers have all gone home
   and are now asleep in their beds.
The gates are locked against a burglar
   who might steal chocolate cake
   and lemons from the buffet,
   or tickets from the ticket office.
The small shed is also padlocked
   where all the parcels and letters are kept
   ready for the morning trains.
Another shed has been kindly provided for passengers
   to sleep in while they wait for trains,
   and this too has been locked against the same
   possible burglar.
Though the railway policewoman will go and get
   the lemon back from the burglar – at night.

The lost children wander amongst the heavy
   railway clutter talking in their sleep.
A magic black cat will solve all the problems
   and then they can build a new world
   and begin a new story.
Tea and coffee will be served to all the animals.

Williamine

for Carlos de Llano

Giant pears, the size of cart-horses,
erratically roll towards the castle and village.

Who could resist such invasions
no matter how stout the hearts of the citizenry?

The marvellous colours – yellow turning to orange
across the dappled and shining skin.

Prostrate as a Swiss lake I lie waiting.

St. Michael's Place

for Shifrah Fram

Dumb monuments
talk then go silent
or maybe hum to themselves

The darkened top floor window
where you used to live
where we used to live
that I now walk past

You've been gone years now
and I too have wandered
Yet suddenly on turning into a street
one remembers a moment that happened
years ago

Small ghosts haunt the unwary

For the photographer Kurt Hutton

The dreadful loneliness
that cuts short all talk, all words.
Men and women walking the night streets,
snow on the lawns and ice in the gutters.
And one person walks from one point to another,
then, after a brief stay, back again
walled in by the cold, the heart, the tongue.

The white hills are criss-crossed
with tracks – animals, birds, and humans.
Such clear marks of time and existence.
And in the hollow the makings of sad posies
– old man's beard, rosehip, and yarrow.

As though planets of ice roll through space
in slow motion while the fathers of previous years
lie under frozen soil, bereft of that warmth so dear to us.

Monster masks

Masked monsters stalk the land

Grey Monsters Gain the Day

"Trust me" said the monster. Who should, why should anyone
trust the monster? as he delicately and handsomely
dances the steps of his greedy desire. A personal tango
(with complications).

"stroke my fur, sniff my scent"

Running naked in the rain
Running round in pulsing circles
in the clearing

touch me touch me don't touch me don't touch me touch me touch me
don't touch me don't touch me touch me touch me don't touch me
don't touch me

In a bare and spacious room
filled with light – the windows
opening onto early summer
The quiet, and clarity of thought.
Descartes and the 18th century meet
the wolf boy of Aveyron (c1800),
the Noble "Savage of Aveyron".

From a narrow window the minotaur gazes down on the lights of the
city. On such evenings the loneliness almost overwhelms him, trapped
and hidden in his labyrinth. The maze as much a protection for him as a
trap for his victim.

The beast within

aped by cheap comedians and actors,
nervous commercial ventures, on a fine knife edge,
feed some need

Beauty and the Beast.

Alpine mastiffs reanimating a distressed traveller*

When you step through the rainbow door do you find yourself
on a bare mountain slope with the first winter snow falling?
possibly even in the middle of a blizzard crouching
behind a rock face for shelter?   Or is it
into a deep meadow scattered with flowers and birdsong?
Not so much a matter of heaven and hell, but...

Civilised pursuits are abandoned in the busy rush.
The heaven of playing chess, of country walks and
mountain climbing, of good company and food and drink,
music and books. The true heaven of being loved and loving.
But the "Busy Rush" rules, and "Tenderness" is shown the door.
As these abstract nouns lumber by we head into the ice.

But the distressed traveller, dusting snow from his fur mittens,
struggles free from this particular avalanche, patting the heads
of the helpful and friendly mastiffs. The Tyrolean monks approach
and once more the wolf pelt covering on his gloves has proved its
                                                        efficacy.
At such times, like a gleaming ikon before his eyes, he imagines
walking along a seashore late in the afternoon with his loved one.

(* title courtesy of Sir Edwin Landseer's 1820 painting)

320

Dream Quilt

30 assorted stories
1983-1984

I was a giant great and still
That sits upon the pillow-hill,
And sees before him, dale and plain,
The pleasant land of counterpane.

Robert Louis Stevenson

1. Nautical Business.

Growing up in that south coast town in the 1920s and '30s – there was really little choice for the boy. At the age of 14 he joined the Royal Navy. After the tough and rigorous training at Portsmouth he was sent to sea. His first ship was on patrol in the Yangtse River. The young sailor's duty was to keep watch at night in the bows. He was there with a long pole to push the bodies that floated down-stream away from the ship.

When a very young child he had accompanied his grandfather, who was a shepherd, for whole days on the Downs. As far as the eye could see the hills were speckled white with the flocks.

2. Sotto Voce.

Hugo the giant emerged from the forest rending his beard. Down below in the village the peasants trembled in their clogs.

CLOMP-CLOMP   CLOMP-CLOMP

He strode down the hillside.

His brain was in a state of extreme anguish, troubled as he was with the problem of comprehending advanced science and high technology, computers and electric kitchen equipment. "See how his lips quiver," whispered the magistrate's clerk.

A giant-size red car drew up and the chauffeur got out. He respectfully tipped his cap as Hugo approached. Hugo the giant got in the car and was driven north on a giant road. It took them three days to reach their destination. It was a house set in the middle of a bare moor. The only sounds were the wind and the short barks of a raven.

3. Booth's Bird Museum.

The long grasses and reeds at the edge of the marsh thrashed and sighed as the wind got up.

A duck punt silently slid out onto the mere. The hunter lay prone on the punt's bottom, his breath white in the winter air. Small white clouds puffed into the dawn.

The deafening explosion of the punt gun brought a rain of fowls that flopped into the water. Expertly gathered by the dogs the birds were hurried to the museum to be stuffed and placed in a naturalistic setting.

The smell of highly polished linoleum and slowly leaking radiators.

4. Lans-en-Vercors flashback.

Surrounded by forest the upper pastures seemed untouched, yet years before some people must have briefly waded through those meadows.

Cycles of snow, rain, and sunshine were endlessly repeated while pairs of large black crows circled above.

Stood still? Hardly so.

5. Fairy tale.

There was a deep rocky inlet on that coast. In other places it might almost have been called a fjord.

The sea snaked its way inland, crowded by bare mountains. In the distance, further up the valley, a scatter of lakes glittered amongst the dark greens of the forests.

As the sailboat rounded the point the malicious dwarfs swarmed out from hiding. The young people in the boat bombarded them with heavy volumes of the Children's Encyclopaedia and drove off their attack. These books were but one of the trophies the children had acquired on their long adventure.

6. Mosquito nets.

He had passed through the jungle and left the river region far behind. The expedition was now camped close to a native village out on the grasslands. The veldt stretched off flat and endless whichever way he looked. Here and there an odd stunted scrubby tree survived somehow.

The other members of the expedition searched for insects and small mammals. His own contribution was to make a study of the ways of the village and the language of this hitherto remote tribe. He found that he had to continually reconsider all the assumptions he'd made about the native customs and habits. It was both a stimulating and a troubling experience for him.

Under his mosquito nets the explorer dreamed that night of his young children sleeping, sprawled in their beds at "home".

7. Ode on Large Trees.

After the long and laborious climb up that giant Monterey cypress

> – digging the spurs[1] in, hitching up your cord, digging the spurs in again, hitching the cord, adjusting the climbing line, then again the next step up, digging in the spurs, embracing the tree hitching up your cord, digging the spurs in... –

the quick ease
and bliss of rappelling straight down to the ground.

O, the miracle of the monkey knot!
The beautiful simplicity and strength of a bowline tied to your harness!

8. Vacuumed Eggs.

Crowded streets, houses, trains; haunted by memories of wars. Forty years later the ruins still there, and people rushing in all directions. It's grotesque and frightening, the power of such memories.

Mea culpa mea culpa mea maxima culpa.

Not even there. A stunned child onlooker. American GI's coming to the house at Christmas bringing Coca-Cola and for me an eggcup filled with sugar.

How is the switch flipped?
A giant vacuum-cleaner to appear from the sky and suck up all that past dust and debris.

---

[1] spurs: an essential piece of tree climbing equipment – metal spikes on steel shanks that are strapped to the climber's boots and lower inside leg.

9. Family tree.

"My great grandfather (that is my father's mother's father) sailed from Devon to New Zealand. He set up a small import-export business there on the south island.

One year he and two friends made a large profit from selling wool. They decided to treat themselves to a trip back to England.

During his stay he met a 'fashion buyer' in London, a woman who would be called a 'fashion model' today. My great grandfather, when their romance blossomed, decided to stay on in England. His own wife, as he'd discovered on their wedding night, was a chronic alcoholic. She had already been confined for some years to a sanatorium in New Zealand.

The arrangement eventually settled on by my great grandfather was as follows. He bought a small inn called 'The Swan' in the Thames-side town of Chertsey. The fashion-buyer became the manageress and himself the permanent guest.

In 1908 he sent for his youngest daughter, my grandmother. On the long voyage to England she passed the time sewing buttons on the captain's jacket amongst other things."

10. Woolly rhinoceros.

In the August of 1833 Charles Darwin arranged to leave *The Beagle* at El Carmen in Patagonia and ride overland to Buenos Aires where he would rejoin the ship. During his crossing of the Pampas he had to visit the camp of the notorious General Rosas and his army of gauchos. It was necessary for Darwin to obtain a pass from the General to allow him to safely continue his journey. Rosas was at that time embarked on a campaign of genocide against the region's Indians. It was later that he became the bloody dictator of the Argentine.

It is curious that in none of his stories does Borges mention this chance meeting of the great theoretician and a ruthless practitioner of the theory of survival of the fittest.

11. Dream bed.

The two athletes were running side by side across the countryside in perfect unison. It looked almost as if they were loping rather that running. Maybe they were ballet dancers and this a rigorous training session for all the "grands jetés" in *L'après-midi d'un faune*. When they reached the narrow plank footbridge across a wide stream – this was somewhere near Winchester – they reluctantly had to run one behind the other. On the other side of the stream stood a small potting-shed in the midst of some trees. Someone had foolishly shelled the two hard-boiled eggs clutched by the runner. When they were placed in the coarse lunch sack in the shed there was no way they could avoid being coated with dirt and hairs.

"Very interesting," said the doctor after a significant pause.

12. Purple sheets.

Low clouds trailed across the mountain slopes, obscuring the ridge and peaks above. It was late one afternoon in December. At this hour the forests appeared a dull black and the sea below a smoky light grey. As dusk approached you could see the regular flash of the lighthouse on the distant headland of Point Reyes.

At this time there were two lighthouse keepers on duty. The head-keeper was a solitary man. He had never married, and with his father dead the only family he had left was a mother who lived in a far away country town. In a way his present life on these lonely cliffs perfectly suited his temperament. The assistant-keeper was an equable and happily married man. He and his wife lived in a snug cottage that sheltered in a hollow behind the lighthouse. Each night they slept in each other's arms. Their bed had purple flannel sheets with dark blue pillows, but that's another story.

13. The choice.

It was like visiting some remote stone ruins in northern Europe. An atmosphere of sadness and failure accompanied the chill. The damp beech woods on the ridge stood bare and silent beneath a cold grey sky.

It was prehistoric in the loosest sense. Poking with a stick amongst the embers, looking for... the past so undeniably far away, dead and gone.

"You see it's all a question of choice really. It would be a matter of balance, but since any sort of balance – I mean physical balance – is impossible now its down to the either/or question. The sailor's life. At home or at sea. No other way."

14. Another Brighton boy.

There was a strong south-westerly blowing as they ran the hogboat down the beach and out into the sea. The olive green waves heaving and crashing around them. The creamy surf whipping up the shingle. After a few stokes on the oars they hauled up the sail and were under way. When they were about eight miles out from the shore they let down their nets, joking and talking quietly amongst themselves. The bright winter sun warming the deck and rousing the fish smells of the boat and themselves.

Ashore, in a tall grey house near the station, Master Beardsley was contemplating exquisite sex while his mother, a local beauty known as 'the bottomless Pitt'[2], went about her rounds of Brighton.

---

[2] Ellen Beardsley, née Ellen Pitt.

15. Hommage à Beatrix Potter.

"Show   no mercy," purred the ginger cat. "That's the way   it goes."

"But … but…" stammered the bewildered pet lover. "Are you sure? I mean… well…"

His question was interrupted by the sharp noise of two mice hacking the plaster food in the doll's house.

The brandishing of a poker doesn't solve it.

Maybe painting watercolours of mushrooms or breeding prize sheep solves it.

But pokers, rolling-pins, sticks, flower-pots, and even sharp teeth don't solve it, frightening though they may be at that moment.

The onions fall from my large pocket handkerchief and roll down the garden path.

16. Moules à la béarnaise.

Early each morning the chef of the only restaurant in Saint-Jacut-sur-Mer would drive into nearby Dinard. His small blue van sped along the narrow lanes, *"La Terrible Menagerie"* emblazoned on its sides in red and gold paint. Whatever was fresh and best at the market would decide that day's menu.

He always put so much thought and care into preparing his dishes at the restaurant. The best meats, fresh local fish and seafood, herbs picked that morning in the restaurant's own garden, glowing vegetables and dusky fruits brought that day from Dinard. It was a matter of true artistry in his case, as possibly is the case with all good cooks.

The poplars whizzed by as his van approached Dinard. Then just on the edge of town he slowed down and stopped opposite a track that led up to the Lacolley farm. As he'd hoped, he could see Madeleine, the farmer's eldest daughter, crossing the farmyard to and from the milking sheds.

"One day..." he thought, as he reluctantly started the motor again and continued on into town.

Madeleine Lacolley was a tall, lean, strong young woman with a fair complexion. Rosy cheeked with long auburn hair half-way down her back, her rich brown eyes had a look that at once seduced you yet told you nothing.

(Imagine all of the above.)

17. Rafe's stories.

One day 2 cats was sitting on a seat in the park that were sleepy so they fell asleep on the seat and they saw a cat playing an accordion and he played it very good and then he went away and then they fell asleep again and they kept sleeping for ever.

Once upon a time there was a park a magic park so whenever somebody went in the park the person got killed that is why it is a magic park and do you know how the magic got there somebody put it there an old witch put it there with her cauldron she had red and blue and green bottles.

One day I saw a flying violin with a bow and I said "Look Rowan there's a flying violin" "He he he he" said Rowan "Ho ho ho ho" said mommy. It is so funny, I am going to catch it so I did then I gave it to Rowan and she played it and that is the end. And then the violin turned into a rocket and then I went to the moon and the man in the rocket found a very precious moon rock and it was so precious I had to put it in the museum and it is still there now.

Rafe Harwood

18. Climbing Party.

Sheltering in a jagged rock outcrop near the summit of Glyder Fawr Mr. Evans and Mr. Harwood snorted with irritation. Below them – on the saddle of the ridge between Glyder Fach and Glyder Fawr – their companions floundered like beached seals.

"What's the matter with them?"

"Why don't they get a move on? No back bone!"

These and similar disparaging and irritable remarks were muttered at the slowness and general lack of effort and determination by their friends.

Little did Evans and Harwood realise, or want to realise, that Mr. Bailey and the Davies brothers were in fact pinned to the bare rocky ground by the force of the gale. Their negligence in not being properly equipped with crampons and ice-axes was now painfully obvious.

Eventually, by traversing the wild boulders and scree beside and below the Devil's Kitchen, the party was able to descend from the heights just as dusk was falling. They made it down just in time and were certainly lucky in meeting a lone climber who'd shown them the last part of the route.

Later, as they walked in the moonlight along the shores of Llyn Ogwen, Evans remembered that 1765 journal entry of Thomas Gray's:

> "The mountains are ecstatic, and ought to
> be visited in pilgrimage once a year. None
> but those monstrous creatures of God
> know how to join so much beauty with so
> much horror."

Once back at the cars the party divided – the Davies brothers leaving for Bala, and Evans, Harwood and Bailey returning to Waunfawr.

That evening in the near deserted dining room of the Royal Hotel, Caernarfon, after several gin and tonics, after a reasonable dinner and two bottles of Mouton Cadet, after eyeing the young waitresses and remarking on the same, the three gentlemen – approaching their middle years – rose from the table. All that remained on that sharp January night was the habitual negotiations as to who should have the unique hot-water bottle in their rented cottage. Such are the subtle pleasures and true exhilarations of life.

"A man without faults is like a mountain without crevasses. He doesn't interest me,"[3] thought Harwood that night in bed as he clutched the hot-water bottle.

"Most enjoyable," said Bailey sleepily.

[3] René Char – *Feuillets d'Hypnos*.

19. Goblin tales.

Once upon a time there were two goblins, Scowlmean and Sourgrump. They lived in the roots of a giant tree that grew beside a village. They hoarded gold and precious stones and were thoroughly unpleasant. Some might think they were really gnomes, but they weren't.

They lived their whole long life in this manner.

OR IF YOU PREFER IT : 19a.

Once upon a time there were two goblins, Scowlmean and Sourgrump. They lived in the roots of a giant tree that grew beside a village. They hoarded gold and precious stones and were thoroughly unpleasant. Whenever they could they would cause trouble in the village by doing mean things. The lives of the village people were made wretched by all the hurting and pinching, breaking and stealing, and all the other evil tricks played by the goblins.

So the village people went to ask Hugo the giant what to do. Hugo was a very kind hearted and friendly giant. He knew exactly what to do. He took hold of the tree and shook it and shook it and shook it – and Scowlmean and Sourgrump were bounced around their house inside the tree roots like two peas in a pot. Hugo kept shaking, and Scowlmean and Sourgrump kept bouncing around their house.

When Hugo finally stopped shaking the tree the two goblins were so dizzy and battered they didn't know whether it was Monday or Friday. The staggered out of their house and off over the hill, and were never seen again.

20. A Rangoon Creeper : Certhia Rangoona.

"I'm madly keen to entertain the troops," she cried. "Darling, I just adore khaki. The scent of army tents drives me to distraction. I can't control myself. I have to admit it."

"Oh, absolutely splendid!" chortled Brigadier Tench, rubbing his hands vigorously together. "Splendid! Don't worry about a thing. The padre and Captain Caddel will arrange everything. Simply splendid!"

At this juncture the brigadier's batman, an ex-regimental boxing champion, entered humming 'Comin' in on a wing and a prayer' and carrying a drinks tray.

"That will be all, Robinson," snapped the brigadier.

On the deserted parade ground the wind whipped up clouds of dust that then drifted off and away to settle on the freshly whitewashed stones. A bored sergeant swatted flies in the Orderly Room with a battered copy of *Bugle Blast*.

21. Birthday Boy.

Many years ago Bill Butler said that your birthday was the one day in the year when you should do exactly as you like. I immediately took this advice to heart, realising the pure pleasure and sanity of having one completely selfish day free from all obligation to others.

Today, the 6th of June, 1984, is my 45th birthday. The sequence of my pleasures:

> Waking into a fine summer morning with the sun shining and blue skies over Brighton. A cup of coffee and lying in bed reading Jocelyn Brooke's book of poems *The elements of death*.

> A long walk on the South Downs between Berwick and Eastbourne, taking the most roundabout and charming route, botanising and idling on the way.[4]

> A telephone call from my son Rafe to wish me a happy birthday.

> Dinner.[5]

> A concert by the Chilingirian Quartet in which they played Bartók's wild, witty, yet very moving duos for two violins, as well as two very pleasant Mozart pieces – the trio in E flat for clarinet, viola and piano, and the piano quartet in G minor. The quartet was joined for these last two pieces by Andrew "suitably dishevelled" Marriner (clarinet) and Clifford "elegant to a fault" Benson (piano).

> The day finishes with an agreeable late night conversation and glass of scotch with Adrian Kendon. And so to bed.

It would have been nice to have shared some of these pleasures with another person, but such are my circumstances that this was not possible or, rather, not the case.

* * *

[4] How to describe a summer's day in the Sussex countryside? Such an account, it seems, can't help but appear wayward and dull, the whole pleasure being somehow "low key" and near indescribable. And yet that pleasure is one of the most acute and important in my life. I'm not just talking about the vague

delights of "Nature" and "the countryside", but about a very particular countryside, that of south east England, something very special for me. But even so, how real can such a subtle obsession and love be for those who don't know this landscape?

I take the train from Brighton to Berwick. It's a lovely bright sunny morning with a soft warm breeze and small white clouds flying through the skies. From Berwick Station I turn south and follow the lane for a mile or so down into Berwick village. Along the banks and hedgerows – blue shepherd's purse, tall rich yellow buttercups, purple clover, pink and white campions, herb robert, and the dirty white lace of cowparsley. And behind the hedges – the lush greens of the meadows and wheatfields. And above – the repeated cries and warbles of a scatter of skylarks.

At Berwick village I stop for a beer and sandwich in the garden of the Cricketer's Arms. Surrounded by flowers how strange that one's eyes focus on one thing – the white paper doily on the plate – that triggers memories of past private worlds. No, not Jocelyn Brooke's bar of transparent green soap nor Proust's madeleine, but a paper doily.

In Berwick church – a mainly Saxon building sited on a prehistoric mound – I'm surprised to find paintings by Duncan Grant and Vanessa Bell. The walls, rood screen, altar and even the pulpit are decorated with their work. A nativity scene is but one of the many subjects chosen. A virgin surrounded by Sussex shepherds and young boys with 1940s haircuts, a view of the Downs as a background. I'm doubly surprised as the paintings are quite good and not the usual mess of pastel colours and poor draughtsmanship I've come to expect from, for example, Duncan Grant.

I continue south towards Alfriston, walking along a narrow path down through a field of wheat then up through barley on the opposite slope of this shallow valley. My hands brush the ears of corn as I walk, but I'm absurdly distracted by imagining Alfriston will be crowded with coach parties of Midlanders. All of this appears completely foolish as, when I do walk through Alfriston, all I meet are a handful of elderly tourists, all quite innocent and well-meaning. Fear and snobbery obviously go hand in hand in my case.

Once beyond the village I take the path south-east across the fields and then up onto the ridge of the Downs just above *The Long Man of Wilmington*. The glaring white of the chalk track and the call of the cuckoo in the spinneys below. I then walk east along the ridge across the short-cropped turf, pausing at the barrow above the *Man* to admire the pale blue flowers of the wild thyme. Suddenly two army helicopters roar overhead. It's the "D-Day" anniversary. I'd forgotten.

I then descend from the ridge across the steep pastures towards Folkington to visit my orchid track. It's become almost a ritual. Each birthday I come here to visit this secret and magic place. But everything is disappointingly late this year. The cowslips are still in flower and I can only find five common spotted

337

orchids, and them barely pink with their flowers not yet open. I lie back in the long grass and close my eyes. The warmth of the sun on my face, a blackbird singing in a nearby hawthorn bush, the rustle of the leaves in the breeze. Pure heaven with a few erotic trimmings.

Eventually I have to leave and take the path south to Jevington, then up Willingdon Hill onto the bare high Downs again. The long sweeping views – the thick green Weald to the north, the cliff-tops and sea to the south. The sweep of the coast east to Hastings. Reluctantly I continue across the tops and down into Eastbourne and the inevitable late afternoon train back to Brighton.

[5] Dinner was a slight disappointment. Not the hoped for meal that would combine excellent French cooking with good wines, but egg and chips at the Lewes Road Diner. A slight blot, but...

22. John Butler to the rescue.

Greater generosity hath no man than to let a friend row his dory.

Not for me "the stream of consciousness ramblings of an agitated mind" that Mr. Berkson's reviewer comments on. Rather the civilised delights of gliding across the water in a truly elegant skiff or dory. To pull on a fine pair of oars and effortlessly slide through the water. To have them sweep clear of the water and swing back sweetly dripping ready for the next stroke. To dip them in the water and pull again on towards the small sandy island, the haunt of seals and herons.

Such a range of pleasures. *John Biglin in a Single Scull*, that rosy-cheeked determined gentleman portrayed by Thomas Eakins; or Monet's lazy and sociable driftings down the Seine; or the satanic Alfred Jarry in his racing shell. What need of a nobler lineage?

These summer pleasures – so distant from the wintry past. Almost forgotten the low mist over the frozen river and the ice encrusted willows on the opposite bank. A man in a long black coat crossing over as though dancing to the irregular reports of the cracking ice. A secret messenger or a fleeing refugee? A host of possible stories. And further south, with the thaw well on its way, the night ferry chugs across the estuary. The distracted lover or an anguished spy walks the rail, blankly staring at the lights of passing freighters.

No, this is long past and summer is truly here. In the immaculate lifeboat station the coxwain John Butler can untie his cork life-jacket and go home to his family.

Almost blinded by the sunlight he steps from the building and gazes at the surrounding mountains that slide into a glittering sea.

23. Rowan's stories.

One day a cat was walking in a park and he found a precious stone and it was a piece of gold and his friend came and said that his piece of gold was a very precious stone and his friend took him home and they had a cake.

One night a wicked witch and her friend were mixing a spell that made people disappear and then a person came and another and another and BANG!! the people disappeared.

One day a little bird was looking for some food and he found some and it was a piece of apple so he took it to his babies and he left one for himself and then their mummy taught them to fly and they liked it.

Rowan Harwood

24. Domino Champion.

"My grandfather – that is my mother's father – suddenly dropped dead late one summer in his garden. He was over 80 and had had no previous illnesses. There could really be no better way to die. To suddenly be struck down in the middle of all those roses and dahlias that he loved and treasured so much.

From this distance he can be said to have had a hard but happy life. As a young man he worked in a boot and shoe factory – one of the few choices a working man living in the Midlands had in those days, that or the mines. Intent on "getting on" and learning his trade, once a week after finishing work he used to walk the ten miles to Leicester to attend evening classes on the leather trade and shoe design.

Eventually he and his cousin started their own shoe factory in a small terrace house. In the two rooms upstairs the "clickers" worked cutting out the leather uppers and the women machining them together. In the downstairs the leather soles were stamped out and then nailed and sewn to the uppers. The "office" consisted of a 6 foot by 4 foot cubicle at the head of the stairs. Everyone in the family worked in the factory.

During the 1930s the factory made boots and shoes for the big shoe shops, and by the late 40s had expanded into the next door house, using the back garden for storing the hides. By the time his sons and daughters took over the factory it was truly prospering. My grandfather, though, never retired. Right up to his death he would light the factory boilers early each morning, tend them and potter round the finishing room for the rest of the day.

My "Uncle" Ernest, who had a larger factory a few streets away, was even more successful. He had married my grandfather's sister, Hannah, and even in the 30s he was doing well. But despite his success he was regarded by the rest of the family as a disgrace. His "crime" had been making boots with cardboard soles for the Republican Government during the Spanish Civil War. The disgrace was probably more to do with ideas of honesty and good craftsmanship than anything political.

My mother and I used to visit Aunt Hannah, even though such visits were disapproved of by my grandparents. I remember the front-room with its cabinet of Uncle Ernest's ivory curios. The strings of elephants, of course, and a series of balls, one inside another, all carved from one piece of ivory. But most of all I remember an ivory pagoda about two foot high that stood on a table, I think, the other side of the room. It had little doors you could open, and inside the bottom door was a carved statue of the Buddha. It was beautiful and, for me at the age of five or six, a magical thing.

I've no idea where it is now nor who owns it – but I still think about it. Just as I still think about my grandfather fifteen years after his death. A dear man whose great joys were the prize roses and dahlias he grew in the summer, the magnificent chrysanthemums in the autumn, and the vine he tended in a small hothouse. A gentle man who during the war used to send us each year a bunch of black grapes in a shoe box."

25. Announcement: Swallows don't hibernate in mud at the bottom of ponds.

On the 12th of February, 1778, the first truly scientific British naturalist, Gilbert White, wrote to his friend Daines Barrington:

"Besides, it does not appear from experiment that bees are in any way capable of being affected by sounds: for I have often tried my own with a large speaking-trumpet held close to their hives, and with such an exertion of voice as would have hailed a ship at the distance of a mile, and still these insects pursued their various employments undisturbed, and without showing the least sensibility or resentment."

The all-hearing bees happily ignored the Rev. White, just as the runner-beans ignored Darwin's trombone playing. The bees kept buzzing and the beans growing while navigators and neighbours were alarmed by strange unexplained sounds drifting over the horizon.[6]

A group of ladies passed along a narrow footpath the other side of the hedge, chattering loudly. The scent of honeysuckle and roses sweetening the air. They entered the garden and went into the house for tea. Bursts of talk and laughter floating through the open windows long after.

---

[6] It is curious how often those we cherish most have such foibles, even pure wrong-headedness. The strange racial theories about the peasantry, for example, to be found amongst all the excellent writings on the countryside by W. H. Hudson.

26. Malaysia Dreaming.

The minesweeper was anchored close to the shore. With the war over the crew couldn't see why they should continue patrolling these waters. It was therefore up to the captain to keep their minds off such dangerous thoughts. The result was that days were filled with busy and pointless tasks. Discipline was tightened. Some sailors, who had dived into the sea to cool off, were even threatened with court-martial for desertion. And that was no idle threat. Lieutenant Mortimer Cat had his orders and resolutely intended to carry them out, correctly and efficiently.

The lieutenant, who strangely was to become a professor of literature in later years, gazed at the shore. The green palms swayed in an offshore breeze. The white beach was near dazzling in the mid-afternoon brightness. Of course he'd heard rumours there was some new "show" afoot, but that was all too far from his immediate concerns. When orders came they came. Not that one didn't have one's opinions but...

No, if anywhere his thoughts strayed back to H.M.S. King Alfred, the shore base where he'd done his officer training, and Showell Styles, that curious gunnery officer he'd met there. Recent gossip had it that Lieutenant-Commander Styles had been excelling in his eccentricity. The latest was that, while outfitting armed merchant navy vessels (D.E.M.S.[7]) in the port of Haifa in Palestine, Styles had climbed Mount Jebel Kafr Manda in full dress whites along with sword, medals, and all. This costume was apparently in deference to the local Arab etiquette that one dressed according to one's rank. That was all very well, thought Cat, but just not on, a bit off in fact.

He was roused from his reverie by the strong smell of oil rags and the clunk of boots on the iron rungs of a companionway as the chief petty officer emerged from the engine-room. But these immediate surroundings faded only too quickly as he drifted again into memories of that wintry seaside town. The black statues of dead queens staring out to sea at dusk and the lights coming on in the top floor windows of those long white terraces. Obscure members of exiled royal families in their overheated and cluttered rooms. The shouts of greengrocers dismantling their displays at the end of the

[7] Defensively Equipped Merchant Ships.

day. Beautifully arranged pyramids of apples, oranges and pears, cauliflowers and leeks, all edged with a line of those red string bags of assorted nuts. And always around the corner the worn boarding houses in small dark squares.

And then? Years ahead an overgrown tombstone in Lewes Road Cemetery? A stained marble cross and anchor inscribed:

"Faithful below he did his duty,
And now he's gone aloft!"

27. Rocky Road.

The clergyman clung to his panama and easel as he clambered over the rocks. A small boy trailed behind carrying a paintbox. The day was to be spent with the Rev. Edward Step painting picturesque seascapes and Arthur, the boy, exploring the tidepools.

All along the bright coast small sandy coves sat slung between rocky headlands. The Rev. Step and Arthur had the entire beach to themselves. They were quickly absorbed by their own private pursuits. The Rev. Step set up his easel in a suitable spot, scanned the horizon, and started preparing his palette. Arthur, an orphan taken on holiday by the kindly clergyman, began his exploration of the ferocious world of a rockpool. Starfish enveloping weary limpets. Sea anemones trapping displaced mussels. Crabs battling over territory. It was both horrifying and fascinating for such a tender hearted child.

Their peace was interrupted by a voice from above. Leaning over the cliff top was a pale bespectacled face that waved an arm.

"Hello vicar!"

"Ah, good morning Mr. Carding," the Rev. Step reluctantly replied with as much civility as he could muster.

"Doing a spot of painting, eh? Lovely weather for it…"

"Er, yes, lovely weather."

Mr. Carding's voice droned and fretted on oblivious of the clergyman's obvious coolness.

"Dear Lord, may a ferret attack the seat of his trousers and let this cup pass from me," the Rev. Step prayed, but to no avail. A firmer approach was therefore unavoidable.

"You must excuse me Mr. Carding, but I really must get on with my picture before the light goes. I know you'll understand."

"Oh, of course, of course. Terribly sorry. Do excuse me. Well, see you later!"

The head bobbed around several more times and then disappeared.

It took some time for the Rev. Step to regain his composure and to start on his painting. He was nagged by a stream of thoughts and sentences that continually tried to drag him away from his immediate surroundings. A sudden sense of the strangeness of his choice of career. The forced politeness in the face of the blatant hypocrisy of the well-fed 'pillars of the church'. He did not suffer fools gladly, the incompetent and crippled, yet had to. The tangled thicket of accusations, declarations, and bound with that the self-accusations and guilt. Like a neat puppet performing its set role. All the loneliness and dreams. The undeliverable sermons.

Eventually the Rev. Step calmed and began to lay the colours on his small canvas. The rest of the afternoon passed peacefully. The warm sun and a gentle sea breeze caressing his cheeks. At about five o'clock the Rev. Step and Arthur packed up their things and began to walk back to the seaside town. One more day of their holiday had passed.

28. Once more to dream.

There were two very small water-snakes. When held up by the throat they sang strange piping songs. There was also another marine creature that was somehow part of this freaks orchestra. An unnerving event.

There was also a woman who seemed to love me dearly and I felt this same love and tenderness for her. There was also another woman who somehow threatened me, us, in this maze of streets and passages. Fleeing circus acrobats?

A circuit was established that involved the orchestra's music, passing through a variety of doors, and meeting the women. It was not far, in fact and colours, from a "Fun House" exploded into the world of total fantasy from some provincial amusement arcade.

Maybe the story becomes too obscure and personal at this point and hence boring for the reader. Dreams cling to all of us as we wake and then move into the day. Are shaken off into our private drawers and left there like pet snakes maybe. A private taste.

Out of the house into the sunshine. Down the hill to the sea. On with the business. But nagged all the way.

"No, don't call that 'seaweed'. It's 'marine algae'."

29. Tofu in Carolina.

The story was meant to begin with two dragons lazily flying south from their mountain home. They were to have been passing over Tremadoc Bay on their way to Harlech when a witch appeared. The story revolved around the little known fact that when dragons open their wings at a full moon gold dust falls out. The witch was to be intent on capturing the dragons to brush their gold from them.

But this tale is interrupted by visions of people who die before their time or suffer long and painful illnesses. Though all this seems equally remote to the healthy and vigorous souls. Whatever it is happens out there, is beyond real belief.

One of the dragons was called Bronwyn and the other Paul, her young brother. The witch was known as Rita of Talsarnau. That the story couldn't be told disappointed all these characters, especially as they all had rather exciting parts. Paul was to have been caught in a dark net by Rita. Bronwyn tried to rescue him by various means, but failed. She then would have called in her friend Hugo the giant and together, using a number of disguises, they would have tried again. Maybe they would have been successful; or maybe all three would have had to be rescued from a black cave by Mr. Bailey and a party of his students out sketching rocks and trees. There are so many possible endings. But one way or another they all finish with the death of Rita the witch of Talsernau.

It's grim in ways you don't expect. Dogged by all the obvious pain and fears – yet you shut them out. The stories, if you suspend you disbelief, are not lulling.

"No," she said, driving fast down the winding mountain road, "that mode is basically uninteresting. It lacks real energy."

But beyond the immediate? What's over that horizon? or around the curve? Such dreamy questions have an edge to them, a hard bone below the soft fur. And the wonder. The gold dust falling from the sky like a gentle snow. An older woman taking two steps in a hospital ward.

30. The Land of Counterpane.

The toys were all ready. The faded but resolute general, the mounty with movable arms, the nurse, and the three sheep. They all set off along the maze of narrow rounded valleys that criss-crossed the green and mauve eiderdown. Their journey was not to be without adventure – the sick child was sure of that as he spoke out loud their conversations. The sheep with three legs kept falling over so had to be propped between the other two sheep or set against a suitable slope. The path was like those that wind from the crest of the Downs south to the sea. Bare hills and small copses set deep in the combes.

They bravely struggled on. They would fulfill their vague and continually changing mission and then return home. When dusk overtook them they started to make camp. They soon fell asleep around the campfire, but were suddenly awakened by a giant hand that descended from the sky. Though plucked from their world they soon settled into their new home, a box on the bedside table. The curtains were drawn and the child was soon asleep.

In the next-door house the child's two friends were also asleep. The boy, who is King of the Birds, can understand everything they say, lies curled up clutching his blue blanket. The girl, who is Queen of the Insects, sprawls in her bed, her arms and legs thrown out, fearless. One of their parents enters the bedroom and stands watching them as they sleep. It's as though he's trying to make time stand still, to somehow fix forever this scene in his memory. As tenuous as trying to engrave the colours of the sky in one's mind. The silver and gold over the sea seen late one afternoon looking from the Roman Steps west across to Bardsey. Moments that go beyond joy or tenderness into some other land that's beyond any words.

> "I was a giant great and still
> That sits upon the pillow-hill,
> And sees before him, dale and plain,
> The pleasant land of counterpane."[8]

---

[8] Robert Louis Stevenson - A *Child's Garden of Verses*.

Rope Boy to the Rescue

1983-1987

Places before, and you

1. Brighton

Alone in an upstairs room –
the sound of the wind,
a train in the distance,
and, faintly, the sea breaking
on the shingle beach.

In a dream I imagine you enter the room
and lie beside me.
The lamp light shines on
one side of your face.

2. Norwich

A world of contrasts that giddily swing between
inside and outside, joy and despair, but at least
knowing one is alive, knowing *I* am alive
knowing *you* are alive on this spinning earth.

The snow storm whirling around the ancient cathedral
inside which is such calm and quiet, and the air
and light made even more luminous by the snow outside.
Alone in a kitchen I sing for joy like a loony.

3. Kew

Fleeing the freezing east wind – January in a Royal Botanic Garden – I
shelter in the hot houses, a 19th century jungle fantasy, a reverse oasis
of palms and giant ferns, banana trees and bamboo.
"I'd like to slide into a forest where the plants press and close behind
us, a forest many centuries old, but it's still to be planted."[*]

I lean forward to smell the jasmin, its scent a rare almost overpowering
luxury in these grey winter days.

[*] René Char – *Lettera amorosa*

Further along the path a bush with small white flowers in scattered clusters with long yellow-tipped pistils. The scent as though far away yet very close at the same time, like jasmin though not like jasmin. *Osteomeles Schwerinae, China.*

As I leave I notice this particular hot house is called the Temperate House. How right this surprising allegory of our love – far away yet close, an oasis.
I want to hug Heine for writing such words as:

> "I love you because I must love you;
> I love you because I can't do anything else"

4. Chanctonbury Ring

Walking up the steep track through the beech woods
A bright, clear and sunny January day

The only sounds:

> the wind in the trees
> the bird song
> my own footsteps

Bare woods with soft olive green trunks
and bright green cushions of moss

Up on the ridge
the flint scattered fields of winter wheat
A strong south-west wind tugging at me
Yet a sense of stillness here
as though I'd always been here like this
fixed at this moment

Yet, no – months pass and spring comes.
You will come to shake my stillness and winter.
What a warm joy that shakes such foolishness.

5. Bolinas

The ghost across the bay has finally gone,
is near dead though
now and then a hand half-heartedly rises
above the waves and waves.

The price of this heaven in my heart.

Lying in your arms all night,
warm and so dearly loved,
my hand resting on your breast
held there by your hand.
Moonlight cutting down through the eucalyptus.

"A cloud of bright angels to carry me"

Desert phone

My heart melts at the sound of your voice,
at the sight of your words.

Our long history on small scraps of paper.

We cross the river and then, in the willow grove beyond,
prepare for the next stage,
go straight on even, our clothes still dripping with water.

And later
as though lost on the plain,
scrub bushes, canyons, the hot flat desert
with rolling blonde hills on its edges
and the arid mountains beyond.

How did we get here? we ask ourselves,
too hot to cling to each other for safety
and instead, dazed, seem to wander in circles.

No wise words, only a vague hope and trust
that waves like a mirage, falters
with the light breeze at evening time.

I can talk of your nakedness or your fire
but I won't.

What is the thin green line on the horizon?
Tree tops that line a cool steep valley?
another river?

The beams in the house are rotting, need replacing.
Too much weight? The burning blue
sky pressing down.

"Foolish Pride"

The sound of the wind blowing against the house
late in the evening

A decayed city imagined

The walls soaked in diffidence
(meaningless image)

biscuits diffidence

A sure knowledge of what doesn't exist, though.
Obsessive energy, even rage.

Over the skyline.

Instead a dithering weakness that claws together
some wool armour.

Can *that* continue?

As your "foolish pride" jets off
I woollily slump

A nervous need to continue talking
as I fend off what happens
"It can't happen" but does

O,O,O,....Northern California

O, rarely fingered jade sat on your blue velvet cushion
in the museum showcase.
O, handsome writing book half-bound in crimson leather
with beautifully marbled edges
sat on your exquisite and highly polished desk.
O, world of unused beauties.

Kick a stone, walk along the beach, kick the sea.
The dapper panama hat gathers dust on the cupboard's top shelf.
Dreams and more dreams. Brightly flowered vines
and the heady scent of eucalyptus trees that
with time is taken for granted and passes unnoticed.

To decorate one's life with sprays of leaves and vases of flowers.
I prepare the vase for you on the marble top of a chest of drawers.
It's just right. Will it please you? Will you notice it?
You did. Returning from your long journey
you enter the house, striding in with deeds done
and love.

That picture fades as the outside world crowds in
now. And your business continues.
My business continues.
The bright clear sunlight illuminates the headland.
A dusty pickup-truck stops outside the village store
and the dogs leap out as the driver enters.
People at the bar across the street watch this
with their usual bemused curiosity.

Someone in crisp clothing drives past on their way
out of town with their radio playing.
Through the open car window
fine phrases from an opera float out:
        "What new delights!
            What sweet sufferings!"

The dream fades. A rustling of the dry grasses
that edge the lagoon. We lost it.
And the business continues,
the daily life downtown "business as usual".

St. Emilion

for Richard Cupidi

On the table hidden behind the wine bottles
a prospect of mountains.
The peaks that thrill the hearts
of those who know them.
No, not a heartiness that would go amiss
in Château Bellevue or Château Fonplégade.

The organised gardens and vineyards
– especially of Château Fonplégade –
seem so far from the rugged heights,
the sweat, and careful placing of foot and fingers.
But not really.

Within their quiet rooms a bag can be
packed for the next expedition, dinner taken,
and the wine duly appreciated. The books will sit
on the shelf gathering a little dust maybe,
but all in its place.

When the rain drifts across this scene
memories rise in the heart in a greying room.
Grandmothers stand in photos waist deep
in tomato plants, immigrant streets of America
outside the walls.

"Mother I am far away from everything"
spoken by an apparent innocent
on the silver screen in a provincial cinema.
Tears streaming down one's face
at this.

The windows can be opened, even thrown open.
The countryside and vineyard are still there,
and in the far distance the mountains.
Clambering the heights how the joy
fills us, edged by exhaustion and
vague dreams of achievement, whatever that is.

Coat of arms on wall in ancient city

Bears dance to the music, slowly, awkwardly
in the grand piazza.
A thin but sufficient chain keeps them in place.

Grotesque beasts look on,
beasts cobbled together from various spare parts
and men's strange imaginations.
Is that a crocodile or an eroded dragon?
A winged lion or a sphinx?
All the world's plunder cobbled together.

Mists coat the lagoon this evening
as the ferry passes a low barge,
a pleasure launch and a small naval landing craft
on the flat waters.

In the palazzo an evening of decadence
is about to begin and the end is expectantly planned
for systematic and cold debauchery,
whips and black undergarments,
a series of calculated and delightful humiliations,
pains and pleasures.

Has the icon, looted from Cyprus, seen it all before?
The resigned virgin with child
cluttered with necklaces and improbable crowns.
A look of indifference is all we see.
She may sternly pity our fate, or
not even know it. Tough luck!
We'll get by.

We board the throbbing steamer.
Here come the bears hurrying from their last
evening performance and just in time.
"All aboard" someone shouts in Italian.
The splendours fade behind us as
we're cloaked in a sweet velvet darkness.
Ahead is the unseen landing stage,
the sound of crickets and frogs
and a bored bus driver calling to a friend.

The bears troop off and disappear into the night.
Their plans remain ambiguous.

Picture postcards and an object

for John Giorno

The grey ochre building seen vaguely
in sunlight. Trees in foreground.
Mediterranean even. Calm warm surface
with the tremble of nerves, hysteria, beneath.

To rush into the palm filled lounge to
wicker chairs and tables, and cool tiles underfoot
– hotels with strutting peacocks screeching in the grounds –
and then stop, twisting and turning, and out.

No, the calmly worried look of the madonna
in a cracked fresco doesn't help. She's
more resigned than knowing. You know?
Can strit-strut whichever whichaway but "no likee".

The sages can plod up their ivory mountain
– a few tricky bits where a piton wouldn't go amiss –
to another day on the heights.
But another day on the heights.

Late night who cares. You know?
The buildings obscure in the darkness and
the music folds out. I kiss your sweating cheek.
No servants to summon. No bells to ring.

I like your black boots, but this isn't a love song.
Your shirt soaked in sweat as you "lay it down",
tell "them" "how it is", or poke their assumption.
Poke what matters, dear man, if then.

But all these blocks of stuff get moved around
and we swagger out into the night
fired with the thoughts and the heat of it all.
And the anger and mirrors feed each other somehow,
feel clear for a moment.

Fairy flash

The deer descend from a dark grove
into the sunlit garden

Some form of stone giant lumbers forward
screeching and moaning

The startled deer bound off through the undergrowth
while the giant stands swaying as though dazed

Butterflies and small birds flutter round his head
haunted by memories

Dreams of children fill his heart
He crashes off into the trees

The price of happiness

Evasive action
/ like an enclosed courtyard by Crivelli

In this painting of the early Italian Renaissance
(a wood panel measuring 11⅛ by 9½ inches)
savage actions are portrayed
that go on around some children
who play peacefully in a garden.
Stabbing, knifing and other cuts,
verbal and real.
The young boy clings to the man, his father,
desperately weeping at the inevitable separation
that approaches.

Shall we have some blood
artistically scattered in the foreground?
Touches of crimson against a yellow ochre
background maybe?

At this distance how can we know
all the obvious facts behind this disturbing scene?

Hand from an Exeter cloud

Yes, now the night closes in. Yes, now the fireworks display over the cathedral has ended.
What now? The single bed in the 'guest room', the copies of Jules Laforgue's *Oeuvres complètes* at your head, distant traffic on the nearby main road?

"Is this something new?" asks the clerk
sarcastically.
Not exactly...

Dreams of children's voices heard the other side of a thicket. Dark green tunnels through the bushes and undergrowth. And later the next day leafing through an exhibition catalogue of Elizabethan miniatures – the sudden shock and recognition in seeing one titled "Man clasping a hand from a cloud".

Winter journey

Friday

The perfect word on the perfect page
doesn't happen.
The perfect pen and page rest immaculate
while the words stumble around
the animal noises and signals
that welcome or warn.

A journey begins
passing by brambles, bushes, trees and long grasses,
all white with frost along the railway embankments.
But then pushed sweating into the
crowded hysteria of airports, planes, and Immigration lines.
That time near endless –
only to emerge hours later
into the open air and you.
All worth it. All perfect. Page.

Saturday

Walking in the rain through the city
policemen standing on corners in their black raincoats,
the traffic hissing by, people hurrying
with folded newspapers over their heads.
Under the stoop an obscure door opens
into an artist's studio.
The quiet inside where works are admired.
Naked bodies cavorting around vases,
plates, and across lines of tiles.

Back in the apartment the quiet continues
while the White Rabbit rushes by outside,
his umbrella up, his watch in hand.

Sunday

Late to rise from a loving bed.
Orange juice, coffee, bagel and cream cheese.
And out the door into the wintry streets
to get Art.

The museum luxury of Turner and Rembrandt.
And the ponds in Central Park covered in ice
as we sit in the half empty café.
To walk at dusk across the wet earth
amongst bare trees to a bus stop
and the long ride downtown
of lights, signs, and crowds.
To ponder displays of vegetables and oriental teas,
to ponder your loving and beauty.

Monday

The ferry buffeted by winds ploughs on
towards the distant island,
passing ships at anchor, purposeful tugs and launches,
and giant statues, symbols to nations
where the words have blurred into nothing.

The icy spray glitters in a winter's sunlight
as we shelter but stare amazed.

On the main island are crowded streets
where the signs and language don't "mean"
what you hope for, but mysteriously grip.

The spicy soup a mere hors d'oeuvre.
And the ecstatic dessert to the day
a song cycle by Hindemith
that tears the heart in its silences.

Tuesday

The old man on the bus talks too much,
relieved to finally have found an enthusiastic listener,
though grows vague when pin-pointing
the best blintzes in town.

Words and music fill the evening
with a nervous warmth, but no blintzes.

Wednesday

Suddenly the wind changes
from the side, catches us unawares, turns us around.
And
we find ourselves falling into that old conflict,
not realising it but then realising it,
and somehow unable or unwilling to stop.
The argument rolls out with a violence
we can't understand.
It doesn't matter, it's not to do with us
in our daily lives, but belongs to theory and attitudes,
yet we can't stop
as though helpless we keep saying things
and feel the pain and distance grow
as we look on at this war.

As though a thick glass wall separates us
that should be shattered but we don't know how.
"The next goal in your future shall be accomplished"
said the motto in the fortune cookie. Is this it?
No, maybe it's the other motto that said
"Be more adventurous in your methods".

But the past catches us again,
catches up with us, too much.

Thursday

A calm and elegance away from

To walk with a springy step along streets,
feeling young and loved

In a world where things are done
and valued

Friday

A melancholy slides into the day
with the dawn awakening
The knowledge of journeys and changes

A list of questions is drawn up
and decisions demanded.
Can one ever live up to such
rigorous expectations? The day muddles on
with household jobs and delayed pleasures.

Two people walk up and down the freezing avenue
talking talking
as the wind cuts lips and eyes.

Saturday

The Patriarchs and Mothers' Boys march
into the room to a melody by Hindemith.
They *all* fail.
The fast car on the crowded road
weaves through the traffic towards the airport
leaving behind the room, its warmth and quarrels.
Out in the air lost as ever.

The "Don" takes a bow, but his voice betrays him,
tense and shocked when answering
an ordinary phone call "Can you join us for dinner?"

"I think you're a jerk not to accept me"
she rightly said.
He stands on a snow covered slope by
the edge of a wood as
children and noisy adults toboggan by.

She walks down a decayed and cluttered street
deep in the city music in her head,
but a numb hurt in her heart.

György Kurtág meets Sandy Berrigan

A song cycle

1

A listless evening sprawls out.
We hardly touch.
Through the half-pulled blinds
lights appear in the apartments opposite.

Slumped in our room
we leaf through books and music.
Neither here nor there.
A heavy heat in the apartment but ice in the streets.

You turn and look at me

2

That thin divide
between courage and stupidity.
To have acted and gained
heaven or a relentless hell;
or to have withdrawn and be
haunted by futile regrets.

The dizzying thoughts that
cut into a daily routine.
"What am I doing here, when...?"
But we grasp the "known",
the silent days, sat by the kitchen window
staring out across the rooftops at the sea.

Alone in my rooms I have my place,
solitary and silent,   and in the mirror
a face that's mine, self-absorbed
and lost in its mirrors.

3

In a remote village the snow
lies heavy around your cabin,
weighs down the trees' branches.

You dream of spring,
of the orchards in blossom,
of the scent of crushed grass.
You dream of

and the cabin door
groans with the wind

4

Despite it all spring comes
and summer follows.   Now
in amongst dark full trees
your cabin stands dry and open.
The white curtains sway in the breeze.

You lie there alone on your bed
listening to the birdsong outside
and the wind rustling the leaves,
a photograph and a star map beside you.

Some miles away the ochre cliffs and dark blue sea.

5

From capitals to small towns to villages
to remote stretches of countryside or coast.
We fly back and forth like trapped birds.

On the hill tops edging the sea
flocks of birds swirl up in clouds
then descend again into the fields and long grass
then up again and at some unknown signal
suddenly fly south across the sea on their way.

The autumn to be filled with such disappearances,
so much to be packed away.

6

In a winter dream "I fly to you".
The wells in the villages are frozen.
The pipes in the apartments are frozen.
Naked heart to heart could warm us,
yet my fears, our fears, freeze us.

7

The full moon heavy and oppressive
over the village. The dusty dreamland
above peopled with letters and imaginings.

I talk to you crowded by my own lies
and our mutual foolishness that gives
glimpses of the heavens.
But in love with being in love,
with feeling precious.

8

At dusk
you stand by the well dreaming.
At dusk
an owl slowly flaps into the yew trees.

You return and quietly work in your room.
You lean into the lamplight to thread a needle.

Above the dark outline of the hills
the full moon rises, mottled, orange,
heavy as our dreams where we talk.
A glimmer of its light runs across the sea
and meadows.

The Heart and Hand, North Road, Brighton.

for Ann Clark

And they took Brân's head to the royal hall at Gwales. Eighty years they spent at Gwales and they could not remember having spent a happier or more joyful time. But one day Heilyn son of Gwynn opened the door "we must not open" and looked out at the Bristol Channel and Cornwall, and as he did so they all became conscious of every loss, of every ill that had befallen them, as if it had all just happened.*

And then shift to...? shift to opera? why not? King Priam, Hector and Paris bathing their hands in the blood of Patroclus' hacked body. Erotic corpse fondling. Gnawed.
(Courtesy of M. Tippett.)

Then side step to Byron clawing the heart from Shelley's burning body.

All this, and then one night running through the rain along the narrow streets. I stumble into a pub and see you there, an "old friend". The evening keeps rolling, onto and into the drinking club, to lying in bed with you, us sleeping like precocious children in a room overlooking the city's centre.

Such accidents or the gods again.

And at dawn walking back through the deserted streets – the relief of having shared such tenderness, to be chosen. The silky colours of the morning's sky, pale greens and blues. And the street cleaners quietly talking as they start their work.

But yes, I love my elegant footwear, neat haircuts, a good tweed jacket and tight jeans (aging poet turned artistic country gent?), a black knit tie and light blue shirt. Robin Blaser, you honey.

My heart leaps into your hands. "Those years the happiest they'd known." How many of us left? It's all out there falling around and us too. And didn't someone say somewhere, the sexual act is the "nearest" we can get to feeling completely secure, to being totally alive, timeless.

* see the story 'Branwen Daughter of Llŷr' in *The Mabinogion*.

French flash

In memory of Alfred Miles

The room was square and white. It was filled with light. Had large windows on two, maybe three sides. Yes, white and light. It must have had two beds, some chairs. The floor? Polished boards maybe. Yes, must have been polished boards with a worn and faded small carpet here or there. And me eight years old, could be nine.

Each morning, hanging out the window. The fields all around the house and a dusty road leading into the village. Where then? Along into the village, small square, for café au lait and fresh bread. Bare knee post-war ration business. What was that? Lean out the window and... A strong sunlight on the fields. Lines of dark green leaves. Beans? In the distance the village, raggedy summer trees, and glimpses of the sea. Wake up and then... can't remember. My uncle was there, the window open, the sun and fields.

We stepped out. Must have. Down to the village, for food at least. Lunch or dinner. A piece of toast coated with thick pink stuff. "Mussels", they said. I don't remember any other food, but there must have been. Mussels, milky coffee in bowls, and large bright lollies sold by an old woman as you walked down the cut to the beach. A beach of fine white sand and small shells never seen before. Pockets full of shells, uncle and me. Exploring each cove, walking the surf.

Small secret coves. The large light room. No cars anywhere, only the distant cries of people going somewhere or doing something.

We went somewhere, made an expedition en famille. Several of such expeditions. But one time along the footpath to the next village, the path following the coast. Short springy turf. We reached an estuary, a bend in the river. "The Echoing Rocks" I was told. Lumpish black boulders set in a shallow wide river with a high bank behind. Small echo as small boys yelled. But no pause. The family moved on. Reached a ruined ivy covered castle. Was that the point of it all? Blank sequel. We must have returned on foot or bus. Home to that room, to that village and its restaurant. Stuck there – no – but that room. Away from the family home. The seashells in my pocket and fine sand under foot. Sunlight and the room wide as ever, windows to dream from.

What was it for you? A pleasure? A respite? Like a circling hawk or gliding jackdaw I hang around that old landscape, the fading dream.

Windowsill

The village lay in ruins.

The railway station, the small cottages nearby, even the big house, were all bowled over.

The village and the surrounding hills and mountains seemed deserted. The wreckage of a crashed light plane was heaped in the middle of the village square gathering dust. We will never know if it was the flying doctor or a German businessman. The breeze occasionally stirred the shreds of the fuselage. A door banged lazily in one of the houses.

A nervous silence, suddenly broken by snorts and crashings as, clambering over the massive boulders that lay around the village, the dinosaurs and monsters approached. The ground trembled.

The giant brown rabbit crouched at the entrance to her shell-lined grotto on the edge of the village. She did nothing. As though petrified. She didn't move to our aid.

The monsters were coming closer and closer. We could only guess at their purpose.

All at once before anything else could happen rockets screamed down. Red and orange flashes. White light. The creatures reared up and writhed horribly at this fierce intrusion into the Alpine scene.

"You are condemned to many years labour as a menial clerk in a minor government office. You will not stagger through the ruined village. You will always be up before dawn and follow a prescribed routine and route. You will NOT arm-wrestle dinosaurs, lie on flowery hillsides, pull something out of the debris."

This curt voice came from a black tape recorder disturbed and then promptly splintered by a passing monster's foot.

Summer solstice

Farm boys tramp home aching from the fields.
They know where they're going, though don't
as they plod past the decaying mansion
overhung with dark trees and surrounded by damp undergrowth.
Two more miles to go and then the familiar lit rooms,
the drawers of known possessions, the familiar smells.
They will wash, eat, and go about their evening business.
But it's all far from being that simple and innocent.
Small heaps of possessions litter the landscape.
Funerals are strategically placed throughout the years.
Even rushes of vague but powerful emotions, dumb love
and feelings that cut mazes in the heart.
They pass the darkening hedges and copses
too tired from their labours to care or notice whatever,
though the next morning it could be changed possibly.
In the spacious rooms of the mansion the wind sighs
under the doors along the staircases
from the stone flagged kitchen to the cramped attics.
"Long ago and far away" a story could begin
but leaves the listeners somehow dissatisfied,
nervous on the edge of their chairs leaning forward
in contorted positions.   Waking up one day
they could set off in another direction, fresh and foreign.
They could but seldom do, so cluttered are they
and rightly distrustful of such snap solutions.
                              The farm boys proceed
to the fields, again, or turn to the factory towns.
There are glimpses caught in the dusky woods
or on a fresh summer dawn of unknown skies,
unforgettable and dazzling in their beauty. But then
the long day stretches ahead. The stirred dreams settle down
with the dust, beyond grasp or understanding.
The unseen night birds calling calling

Seaside Suite

for Shifrah

1. Early August, Brighton Beach.

The sea a rich dark blue and the sky a clear light blue; the mottled colours of the shingle beach; the white buildings inland. Closing your eyes you hear the sound of the waves falling and dragging the shingle, the call of a gull, the wing beat of a pigeon, the sound of a distant family arguing "What have I done? What have I done?" sobs a small boy, almost hysterical.
Three small clouds pass in line to the west above Worthing.

2. Late summer

What does one hope for, after all?
Over the beach the smudge of orange sun
low in the sky early on a September evening.
The sea calm and almost clear like
that green glass slab for sharpening razorblades.
Not back that far, but here, and now.
A golden misty light as we swim
through the waters, bobbing and surging.
You really are the most charming and witty
company I could wish for.

3. Early autumn

A bar of bright gold sinks slowly
behind the wavering line of clouds,
their tops a pale pink and their bellies
a dove grey that slides down into the
sea's horizon.

As the day ends we remember the glitter
of the waves on a crisp afternoon.
As though for ever, not still but there.
But now you depart again,
like the seasons your coming and going.

The cold days ahead, icy days
walking the beach inspecting the debris
cast up by the storms and tides.
"Jetsam" is the correct term.

Moon Suite

1

Haunted by the moon.
The clouds part and you slightly appear,
your left side amongst the smokey greys.
The sky shifts again and you disappear
but I know,
your presence luminous behind those barriers,
smoke screens and soft airy diversions.
The night goes on but you're embedded in my heart.
The empty street, lamp lit trees,
and silent buildings crammed with unknown doings,
that world engulfed by you
so that near helpless I stand
or sit or lie obsessed by your presence,
whatever "you" may be.

2

Night after night the full moon bears down...
overwhelms me, as though hypnotised.
What is this moon madness?
I'm not a Chinese poet by any "stroke of the imagination".

3

By day face muscles tighten
bound by the dreams that
don't match the world

but
as the night progresses
the body relaxes
like liquid, flowing, easy
the tides drawn by the moon
in their fullness

4

Not an allegory
nor symbols for the near indescribable,
but an unknown quality,
imprecise and wandering.
Such vague feelings whose strength is
faced by the clear indifferent skies,
the regular phases of a moon
whose power is complete.

5

Watching a dull night sky
stood by my kitchen window – one's hopes
wretchedly and rightly projected out there
into the world. Mean creatures
near hopeless – but these moments
of stillness, near awe as
you emerge glorious from the clouds,
radiant anew, illuminating the clouds below,
the sea sparkling with your light.

The unfinished opera for Marian

Overture

In a remote grove in Kansas you sit
on the deck before your home.

The gramophone is wound up and through the hiss
of the old record a rich bass sings
Don Quichotte's dying words to Sancho Panza:

> "I promised you an island once,
> now all I give you
> is an island of dreams."

You get up from the deck and go indoors.

I walk through the long grass in my dreams
towards your grove to visit,
to even introduce this ancient gramophone
you don't possess
and play an old opera record
you may not like.

The sky reddens as dusk approaches,
a vast magnificent sky ceiling your grove
that I now enter. Name the names.
A spacious grove of walnut trees, hackberry,
elm, red elm, locust, pin oak, bur oak,
hickory, ash, and osage that now
fades into the coming night.

Leaning against a tree trunk I watch you
move from room to room.
In your lit home   out in the darkness
my face against the bark   you raise a hand to your face.

Not as a ghost or wandering spirit I come
but as a dreamer
whose love surrounds you
like the Egyptian dead that walk beside you.

The day's heat still radiates from the earth
as darkness finally overcomes the day
and a young moon appears in the sky
with Venus glittering below, the heart's pole star.

The curtain falls in dark red folds
and faded gold tassels. The orchestra pauses.

Act 1, Scene I

The curtain rises on a grove in Kansas.
It is mid-afternoon.
The dreamer lies down in the long soft grass
beneath the trees.
He at first stares up through the leaves
into the clear blue of the sky,
but soon drifts into sleep.

Cunning stage machinery now hides the grove and dreamer
behind gauze curtains and we are transported to
a piazza in Venice,
or is this the town square of Baldwin?
No, it must be Venice, and the story begins.
The orchestra, after playing quietly during these changes,
boldly strikes up the new theme.

In this the dreamer's dream –

It is evening in the piazza. Don Evano enters leading his
pet pangolin on a green ribbon. The Don, a vigorous blade, noted
connoisseur and melancholic in his middle years, takes a seat at an
outdoor café. He orders a dish of milk for the pangolin and a chilled
glass of wine for himself. The whole recitative is performed in a fine
baritone voice.

At the next table sits a lady clearly in a distressed state. It is Donna
Corazon, a noted actress and patron of the arts. She engages him in
conversation after the usual banter. He warms to the task after his
initial reluctance. Donna Corazon is in love with the Duke Nuvola
di Venti, a wild adventurer who has been away in the New World
seeking his fortune for many years. She is also secretly in love with
Don Evano. Don Evano is not sure who he is in love with.

Their conversation is interrupted by a religious procession, a military band, and a variety of street vendors with appropriate songs.

At the end of this noisy diversion the orchestra quietens and we hear again the strains of the small café orchestra playing a simple popular ballad. Two figures now enter the piazza. It is the lovers Leopoldo and Marianna. They are engrossed in each other's company and sing a tender duet, "Love is my destiny". Marianna has the wit of a Countess Almaviva and the stunning beauty of a Marianna. Leopoldo is a somewhat paler figure. The couple are then greeted by Donna Corazon and Don Evano. They all four join to sing of the trials of love.

The piazza once again fills with people and the whole populace, it seems, join to sing of the trials of love, and yet its joys. The scene ends on a nervously buoyant note.

Act 1, Scene II

It is the next morning. The piazza is nearly deserted as Leopoldo and Marianna enter. They have just been told that they must leave Venice immediately. Marianna is to go to Spain to be married to her exceedingly rich but stupid cousin, while Leopoldo has been commanded to join the Imperial Austrian Army.

Leopoldo, a fair tenor, sings of his inconsolable grief at their parting. Death would be kinder if this were to be forever. He swears his eternal love for her.

After a long last embrace and duet Leopoldo leaves for Austria.

Marianna is left alone. She sings a faultless aria of her woes and fears, and yet the hope that one day they will be reunited.
As she finishes we have tears in our eyes.
We stand and applaud her singing,
we applaud her beauty,
we applaud the very conception of the whole opera.

Act 1, Scenes III & IV.

There now follow two lengthy scenes filled with intrigue and misunderstandings. Beset by Albanian hussars on her journey Marianna is imprisoned, but escapes thanks to the machinations of Don Evano. Leopoldo near death on the battlefield is saved by the sudden ministrations of Donna Corazon. Various dwarfs and a few mythical beasts thread their way through the story here. An old crone appears warning one and all that "the path of love is like a bridge of hair over a chasm of fire".

The confusions and trials seem endless. Who is behind that locked door? Who leapt from the window as the baritone approached? Who has seemingly left with another?

As the curtain finally falls we feel totally exhausted.

Interval

Waking in the late afternoon amongst birdsong
I leave the grove,
walk towards your home.
A long dirt road comes from over the ridge.
A hawk circles then settles on a fence post,
flicks its wings, preening itself.
I'm without words to tell you…
And as I approach your dogs rush out
barking.

The dream takes me no further.
I stand for now only with memories and hopes
so intense they're near unbearable.

Your eyes glitter as we lie in the half light
in so close an embrace that
our breath and lips and limbs are one.
That one day we should walk across
this yard, talking, laughing, extending that embrace
into a fullness of days without limit.

You cross your new room – I can see this –
to place a blue and white vase
on a shelf, a picture on a wall,
to look at the treetops from your round window,
to smell the scent of new wood floors and walls.

Soon you will go downstairs,
get in your car and drive the 12 miles into town.
A cloud of dust will follow your path
on the country roads as the sun sets
in a fiery red then pink then mauve sky.

A clear crisp new moon rises,
a pure silver white awesome in its power.
I gasp at this as at our love.

Centuries ago an emperor sang
    "To the storms in my heart
           may she bring stillness".
That stillness and fullness we both seek.

People crowd in again, bells to perform
routine habits and lose sight of the heart.
The theatre too darkens and in the subsequent hush
the curtain slowly rises again.

Act 2, Scene I

The scene once again is an early evening in the piazza, but many years later. Donna Corazon and Don Evano walk together towards the café. The music is light and lilting and reworks some of the earlier melodies.

Leopoldo enters. He has finally been released from the Austrian army due to the intercession of Donna Corazon. He is greeted joyfully by Don Evano and Donna Corazon and all three then sing of the delights of Venice and the carefree life. Don Evano sings the aria "I love to live, I live to love." But Leopoldo is immediately downcast at these words as he remembers Marianna.

Don Evano and Donna Corazon decide not to prolong his agony. The Don announces that that very evening Marianna is expected in Venice free at last.

In ecstasy Leopoldo sings:

> "Che ascolto? E ver saria?
> Celeste abrezza!
> Io dunque, in braccio all'idol mio,
> Novella vita d'amor vivrei?"

> "What do I hear? And is it true?
> Oh, heavenly rapture!
> And shall I thus, in my beloved's arms,
> Begin a happy loving life anew?"

The piazza fills with people – the chorus – who join with the three in rejoicing at Marianna's return. They sing of the virtues of harmony, of the tender and constant heart.

Marianna enters

Suddenly I drop the curtain on this scene.
I stand in front of the red velvet, the toy theatre,
this elaborate allegory of our story.

We are face to face.
I look into your face, into your eyes,
through your eyes into that clear landscape
which is like an empty plain bathed in a warm sunlight.

I love you. I have loved you for twenty stumbling years.
No one ever in my life has that "power" you always have,
a force even greater than love
that makes me shudder at your touch,
so much more than passion.
The "perfection" and "paradise" of such moments
as your kiss brushes my lips

as we fall asleep in each other's arms
as we walk through a crowded market
as we stand together anywhere dazed and marvelling
at what is happening between us
in a miraculous daily life,
in the skies above and on the warm earth.
That the doors should be this open…

There are scuffling and muttering noises behind us. The curtain parts as Don Evano and Donna Corazon and other members of the cast emerge, not forgetting the pangolin, to protest at this selfish interruption of their performance.

We step into the wings our arms around each other.
The curtains are once again opened
and the opera continues

In the Mists

mountain poems

1988-1993

Waunfawr and after/
"The collar work begins"

Ferocious gales sweep up the valley.
Heavy snow on the hills and fields.
Water flooding the roads, gushing across.
Sheets of rain slanting over the bleak
moorland, the scree slopes,
the small village post office.

I want nowhere else
but to he here,
whether crouching in a stone windbreak
on a cloud bound summit,
or coming off the slopes battered and soaked
into a dark soft tunnel of forest.
(A strange form of pleasure you may say.)

But just to be here in this place.
The deserted remote valleys
dotted with ruined farms,
hawthorn and rowan growing in their hearths.
Climbing higher to the empty cwm
with its small slashed black lake.
And on up the slopes to the bare rock ridge
and the summits again.
Nowhere else.
It's that simple, almost.

The Rowan Tree

for my daughter Rowan Harwood

Once upon a time…

A climber's grip on wet smooth rock slips and he falls
to be saved by a small rowan tree bent across a gully,
                    "falls into your arms", "held in your arms";
and he was duly grateful and praised the tree and its spirits.
The rowan always a tree of protection
keeping "vipers and venomous beasts" at bay,
keeping witches and fairies, evil spirits away,
keeping the dead from rising,
keeping the milk from turning,
keeping the barns and stables and sheepfolds safe.

A beautiful tree, a powerful tree,
a tree of protection.
The care tree, the quickbeam tree, the wiggan,
the shepherd's friend, witchbeam, rowan tree.
And he falls into your branches.
Your magic works again.

But this is what this has all been leading to —
        The girl of the rowan tree stands on the battlements of
        Dolwyddelan castle, her long hair streaming behind her in
        the cold wind. A narrow remote castle with one tall keep
        from whose walls King Crystal, and the girl, can see a small
        dark lake backed by cliffs, patches of black forest, red ochre
        moorland, and the greying mountains. The air feels like snow
        on your face, fills your dreams and spirits with stories and
        magics.
        The girl of the rowan could become the tabby cat in the one
        farm down the hill, or she could become…
        At such moments the world is yours, your hair streaming
        behind you in the winter wind as you stare into the air and
        land and your dreams.
        Who cares what the rule-books say? that inane logic? when
        faced with this.
        The blast of the wind battering and lifting your heart,
        our hearts, into the skies.

And you save by your magics not knowing how,
or knowing but not caring how, like a tree.
The story could go anywhere
you like.

You stay free and clear, but with a caring
for the creatures whose soft fur or silk wings
warm the heart. Tender as
the touch of coarse skin or plants even.

So hang rowan twigs about the house,
nailed over the door, tied to the churn,
hung above the hearth, above the well.
Stir the cream with a rowan stick,
drive the oxen and horses with it.
Make the yoke pins of rowan.
Inlay the coffins with rowan.
A rowan walking-stick as power against "fascinations".
A piece in your pocket against ill-wishing.

When he thinks of it
it's the near silent rain and
the noise of water
cascading down the gully,
the feel of wet rock
like grease as he shifts his body,
the wind that pushes him
into the rock and rushes across the mountains
to your castle through the bare tree's branches.

Snowdon seen from Capel Curig

for Harry Guest

God's creation the mountains
silhouetted on a summer evening
soft matt greys
cut into a pink white sky
with bands of softer grey and cream white,
curled clouds in strands above,
and higher above.

An intake of breath? Beyond words at this
– the fading mountains
where one is as close to heaven
as ever possible.

(Snowdon - Yr Wyddfa)

Brecon Cathedral

for Harry Guest

Early on a Sunday morning
                    heavy frost whitening the ground
          ice crusted grass
an eggshell blue sky with stripes of pink low down
and on high a line of small rosy clouds
          strung above the small town
the boxed cathedral

A small congregation stands
          in the chill empty space then

half way through the Eucharist
          the bright sun rises
enough to light the upper half
          of the stained glass windows
                              behind the altar

that is to the east
                    I can't forget that
                    moment nor the powers there

***

But to praise God is a strange deed.
God or the gods need no praise,
only some thanks now and then
maybe,
whether a respectful nod
or wine poured on the ground.

***

The hills and mountains are oblivious
                    to all this stuff (maybe)
the heaven and hell the gods
                    in each of us

The sun melts the frost by mid-morning
but in the hills the pools are thick ice
A powder of snow on the north walls
of a bare amphitheatre of mountains
with red rust lines of scree cutting down into
the pale green and ochres of the moorland
Strong winds batter the empty tops
And the small sunlit town below
goes about its Sunday business

***

But it nags

talking to myself, I know, but

with or without *the* love.

A book is held open to us
studded with words
the fingers held in blessing
A clear calm smile on His face
No nonsense
It's clear enough

clear as the mountains
clear as the light shafting through the windows

***

'out of the blue'
the child asks "Do you believe in God?"
To which a faltering adult answer
goes nowhere near satisfying the simple question.

Saint David's Day on the Lleyn

for Harry Guest &
Brenda Chamberlain

A cool sunlight across the soft green fields,
across purple hills topped with grey scree.
A rust of dead bracken dappling the headland
on your day, Dewi, on our day.

Like hopeful pilgrims on our way
to or from – no matter which – but
the journey and the time right, blessed
by lean flowers and moss covered rocks.

A wall of cliffs, then over the channel,
a rip of currents and tides circling,
wind tugged waves, the spray flying,
the wedge-cut island of twenty thousand saints.

Saint Celynin and his great company on Bardsey;
and here Saint Beuno in the airy calm of Clynnog Fawr;
and you, Dewi, far to the south tucked in Dyfed
– all long safe and scattered in the welcoming ground.

A glint in the sharp spring air
as a young girl wearing her best clothes
walks alone along an empty country lane
clasping a bunch of bright daffodils.

(Bardsey - Ynys Enlli)

September dusk
by Nant Y Geuallt

The scent – bog myrtle
pressed between fingers,
even brushed through when
walking across this empty valley
fenced by crags.

A flat moor – the colours muted
as dusk closes in
the red rust of grasses and bracken.

A sense of calm almost,
the silence.
No bird nor beast.

"In a remote land far from here…"
No, not that far
the mountains and bogs.

As though in a dream,
as though in an underworld
suspended between "life and death"
wondering
"Is this what it's like?
it feels so good."

But no, here and awake.

The minutes pass as
silk air wraps itself
around my head.

May my children feel this touch

one day.

The artful

for Anne Stevenson

A house by a lake surrounded by woods
all reflected in that lake.
Like a small round painting, like a brooch
pinned to a woman's jacket.

This picture – the miniature scene, and
the woman's soft blue tweed lapel.

Mists close in until you can see
nothing but shifting white and grey.

The air brightens and it begins to clear
into sunlight, clear you imagine
of cunning traps and the games that divert
somewhere else other than. And in the sunlight
on a bright hillside, boulders and bracken,
the mottled white crags above, the lakes below
in the distance. Not shaken free
of imagined, but been there, real as
it can be. A copper tint to the land.
Haze. Feel good, moist-eyed, opened up.
As though time suspended, almost. Red gold.

The unknown woman puts on her jacket
and strolls out of the house to the lakeside.
Autumn. No harm done.
The sun catching the polished surface
of her brooch – blue-john or brown agate.

A shepherd checks his sheep as dusk settles
in the mountains. Obscure silhouettes
that act as possible guides to get home,
to touch familiar things, never taken for granted.

Bonsoir, Monsieur Bailey

A white bull stands amongst the black cows
at the end of a farm track high in the mountains.
All around and above the dark silhouettes
of massy peaks and ridges.
And below, down a narrow valley,
the rare yellow lights of scattered farms.

As dusk turns to night a cigarette glows
to signal your appearance out of the gloom.
Rope Boy wasn't needed as you safely return
from the wild mountain paths and barren summits,
nor Rusty the too faithful mountain dog.

Such rare moments of being where one is,
nowhere else, possible. An immense quiet.
Everything present, not skidding sideways and off.
As solid as Courbet. As intense as a
clear full white moon over Llyn Ogwen.

And other days... At dawn climbing
up a ridge through thick cloud only
to emerge – as through a trapdoor – suddenly
into sunlight and onto the jagged pinnacles,
small hot brown islands stuck up in a dazzling white sea.

Or an early afternoon as we kick steps up
a steep snow covered slope - the "collar work" begun.
You stoutly persevere, despite a few second thoughts,
on up beside the bristly ridge to the icy plateau.
And eventually, battered and chilled, we descend
to the valley, ourselves, and feasting to excess.

(Is this too remote for you, dear reader?
Too much "horrid and fearful craggs and tracts"?
Too much "What a scene! how awful! how sublime!",
"the roaring cataract and the sullen murmurs of the wind"?
Too much of scaling Mont Blanc, our skirts hoisted
around us, lugging mattresses, firewood and laughable tents?

Would you rather that a mummy jumped out of its case
and scared the small boy in the museum storeroom?
You can have that too, if you like.
"I see Nature bothers him" Maddox Brown noted of Rossetti.
But there *are* these other days, no matter what,
and I *will* praise the mountains and Mr. Bailey.)

Those times and pleasures. And once again
as we cling to a narrow ledge high on the arête
two buzzards mew below as they circle
and a raven honks and flips sideways and down and along.
Lines of mountains step away to the horizon
their silhouettes all the tints from blue to the palest grey.
And this not China but Gwynedd.

Who could ask for more? Rusty wags his tail
and even Rope Boy seems at peace as
he retrieves the last piece of litter
and chastises the last ill-mannered climber.
To the west the sea turns silver and gold
with a soft grey smudge of islands and headlands.

"A short troublesome bit of snow-work followed…
Bailey courteously allowed me to unrope and pass him
…I hauled myself up onto the flat sloping summit."

Visits to the mountains : a colour chart

1. *Winter climb : Chasm Gully and beyond*

It's the quality of light that goes beyond description,
amazes. Half way up the gully. The cloud descended. A soft
pearly brightness in the mist. A colour as though lit by
the surrounding snows.

Belayed. Looking down the gully. A world of ice and snow.
The colours – blue-grey, grey, white. All shades of white –
dirty white, a dim white, a cold clear white. And with dark
fingers and blocks of rock sticking up through the snows
and mists. And the drop that fades into a grey-white. A
luminous light. The only contrast ourselves and the dull
red of the rope snaking through the snow and down. As though
no time in this near silence, but…

We push on and work our way to the ridge top. Working away,
zigzagging. All the holds coated in thick ice and the ledges
in deep snow. And then at the top, exulted and exhausted.
Stepping into knee-deep snow, hail showers, and a fierce
wind tugging us about.

We head east and down, missing our path, but finding another.
And finally back again at the lakeside. Llyn Ogwen a steely
black flecked with wave crests.

As night closes in the dark grey of clouds silhouetting the
mountains. A misty half-moon over Tryfan.

2. *Night ascent of Cadair Idris, 1st June 1990*

The last light of the setting sun, like a thin wedge of
pale luminous jade, caught between a line of dark clouds
and the black horizon.

When night finally comes we turn and start off. The sweet
scent of may blossom as we climb the lower slopes in
fading moonlight. An owl calling somewhere below us.

In the darkness the lights of distant villages and towns
along the coast, and the lighthouses on Bardsey Island
and, we wonder, Strumble Head.

The faint silvery light gradually dying and leaving us
in complete darkness and an unexpected storm once on the
ridge. Desperately searching for the way by torchlight.

1.30 a.m. – on the summit – huddled behind a cairn,
eventually dozing, only to wake into a grey drizzling
dawn.

Someone once said there was a legend – if you spent the
night on Cadair the next day you came down a madman or a
poet. Maybe we came down both. Or maybe the legend belongs
to another mountain. But for days after as though floating
with these memories.

3. *Arenig Fach : Messiaen in the mountains*

A hot summer's day. The call of a cuckoo down by the ruined farm. Up on the hill, the mountain, we wade through heather and bilberries to the bare summit. In the distance all the mountains in silhouette, in receding shades of slatey greys and blues. Like a Chinese landscape painting – a whole scroll unrolled – but here.

Later by the small lake - sat with our backs against a boulder in the warm sunshine – listening to the birds – ravens, wheatears, skylarks, gulls. And looking east beyond the lake – a loose swirl of gulls high over the moor. Lingering there, as though we wanted such a time to last forever.

As I think of that day, I remember your unspoken pleasure in being there but also an underlying sadness and tiredness. This all cuts down deep into the memory. And now listening to Messiaen's "Quartet for the end of time".

4. *If you think this is just descriptions, it isn't*

Picture of a lead grey lake with snow falling, hurled
across one's vision.

Ice like large feathers laid beside and across each other
covering the water.

Shostakovich – 8th String Quartet, 1st Movement

Slabs of grey rock   sliding to black
ledges and holds   ice   watch that
a wrong move   sometimes just by luck
and stupid confidence   on up the cleft
and swing over onto   brush the snow out
the way   beside your face snow crystals studding
the ice glazed rock   hardly noticeable
the dull glimmer of it
The air   a diffuse grey glow   below
a lace of snow fidgeting on the small frozen lake
down there   through this glittering space
a strange stillness   a pause in the search
through a maze   choices upwards   a slanting crack
a vertical line   move one after the other
up blocks of rock   off   how   the hand grips
and the shoulders heave   a castle of sorts
a prize of sorts
On my knees now   staring in disbelief
praying
a snow flurry over a horizon of black spikes
an empty untouched snowfield ahead   steeply slanting
pitched off into air

On the ledge

a scratched rock wall.
falling out of life
through glaring light,
no, through dark smudges,
white and grey, snow and ice,
rock.   cold air.   flashings.

a final thudding stillness.

your body stretched out in a snow patch
beside a long black boulder.

alone on the rock
in this silence.   I.   then
clawed ice of a continued ascent
weeping shouting alone on the rock.

and you gone silently   down
through grey winter air
the mountains we loved

For Paul/
Coming out of winter

On a bright winter morning
sunlight catching the tops of white buildings
a tree outlined against the sea
a wall of flints

To be able to stop and see this
the luxury   of being alive
when the waves crash on the shore
and a fresh wind streams up the narrow streets
A moment like this lightens the darkness
a little, lifts the heart until
you can walk down the hill near careless

How can that be?   suddenly slammed up
against a wall by memories of the dead
loved ones completely gone from
this place

Shafts of sunlight cutting through the clouds
onto the everchanging sea below

How many times we discussed the sea's colours
all beyond description   words a mere hint
of what's before our eyes   then and now

Cwm Uchaf

In Brighton someone yells from a window
        down into the dark street and…

On the moon in a vast barren crater
        a rock very slowly crumbles into a fine dust

A fuzz of stars sweeps across the world
        partly known and unknown dark and light

across a table top across crowded grey cells
        in a fragile bone sphere cracked and shaky

tumbling down though never that elegant or controlled
        the stumbling descent through the days' maze

Jerked back by the stars the night sky
        pinning us to the ground in glad surrender

The absurd joke painful as a rock blow
        sleep though more prolonged sweeps on and over

There is a silence you can almost touch
        its pulse lick its fingers though

never complete always a faint ringing in
        the darkness

A sighing wind the noise of distant waves
        raking a seashore

All put in a box in this cave the
        star arms remote embrace

The soft fur of an animal stepping
        out of the cave two paces four paws

Then beginning to back back

Under the stars white dots drops
        of rich red blood drip onto the floor

In unknown halls bare and functional
        as a thick orange bag on a hospital trolley

The faint glitter of the rocks mica the sky
        catching the eye stood still almost

The dust the waves going nowhere in particular
        a gradual leaking away

Y Garn, Glyderau

In memory of Paul Evans

On a cloud bound summit
you don't stride out of the mists
across the rocks and dirt,
as I felt you might,
maybe cursing,
as I just stood there.

Instead
I plod on,
reach the familiar cairn.
No one there except the silence
and a heaviness.
The tugging winds and squalls
died down into this grey calm.

We've sat here before
on clear days – winter and summer
– "the world" spread out below us.
Everything possible, limitless.
But today shut in, blanketed.
I crouch amongst the rocks listening.
No "roaring boys" tripping by.
What would we have talked about?
Or just hugged and laughed?

Later when I continue west
along the ridge a breeze comes up,
and clears the cloud. The sun comes out.
A golden day as I come down
from the mountains, through the heather
and the shining tipping slate heaps
to meet my son under an oak tree.

Remembering the Easter hymn:
"The shades of death are pierced
                    his laws undone,
And trembling chaos flees
                    the rising sun."
If only… If only…

Sandy Berrigan in Sussex

In memory of Kate Berrigan and Paul Evans

High on the hills   a late afternoon
sun low in the winter sky
catching an endless net of spiders' webs
that silver and gild the grass fields.

That scene now a memory that
lives for years after you left
a country where I still walk
a land that cloaks me.

Today the warm sunlight of early spring,
mist in the valleys and along the seacoast,
the scent of flowers again - it seems possible,
days ahead, whatever, sea and sun, pleasure,
soft summer evenings, soft winter days,
soft and silken as your skin.

We push on into the mist not knowing,
miles apart, stumbling through the losses,
hoping, not even knowing why,
for such golden moments that make the
deaths part of us but warmly so,
not as a heavy grief or dark drowning.

You sit at a table or walk through a garden
or along a country road or city street.
You...   It isn't that simple
or clear. The weight of what's happened
is always there in our shadows,
dreams and daily memories.

Chinese thoughts on procedure

the first ice of winter
appears on the ponds, along the river banks
clear thin ice   a delicate glass
that thickens as the days follow

the first step out onto

not knowing

the small fox poised on the ice
listening listening for the telling crack

across the river the frozen willows
set in a depthless mist

Morning Light

1989-1996

Gilded White

for Sandy Berrigan

the snow is deep and soft on the steps
the temple roof thickly cloaked in snow
trees heavy with it
the gold carvings and red beams
luminous in the muted winter light

I look down on this from a high window
beside the window stands a tall grey feather
trimmed with charms   your gift
hung with small bells and beads and a moon
softly wrapped in wool

the day may turn   a soft dull light
to a brightness   a yellow glitter in the snow
a white cloud in a corner of the window
the ghost of a half moon in the sky

a table, a lamp, some books, a radio,
the sound of the sea in the background.
a quiet day. a cup of coffee.

on the snow covered path
or a street in a city miles away
a stillness. a middle aged woman pauses by the arch
and knocks snow from her shoes
an old man stands erect at the entrance to Via Orfeo
his cheap shirt washed ironed and neatly buttoned

Japan is a long way away   Italy is a long way away
California is a long way away   Sussex is a long way away
but all gently wrapped together in this moment
your gift

Homage to Albert Ryder and Bill Corbett 1990

A full moon behind a moving veil of clouds
in a silver black marbled sky.
And below –
the yellow lights from a few windows,
people noisily walking home,
talking loudly, laughing,
but all in a near silence that envelops
a clock's tick, a passing car,
a telephone ringing in the next building.

The moon darkens as the clouds mass.

*

In my room a flickering candle
illuminates the ikon,
the Christ in silver,
his mother and saints in gold.
A thick soft darkness.

*

Then the moon comes almost clear
illuminating the sky, giving a pale
ochre tint to the surrounding clouds,
silvering the wave crests out across the sea,
and the still ponds in dark fields.

As though a crazed skin covers our eyes
beyond which we see some form of stillness.

October night

"asleep among appearances"
Octavio Paz

Strange world.
The warbling and ringing of car and shop alarms
                                        in the street,
shadows on the ceiling.
A large mauve head appearing in an ochre background.
As though a dream landscape but not.
As though a painting but not.

Eyes shut
"you were in another day"
off in the distant mountains
where the darkness breathes
and the black silhouette of a hillside
edges a charcoal grey sky.
A seeming solidity, though thin as paper.

A near astonishment at the "facts",
the surrounding sounds and sights.
The "what is this?", "who is...?"
No step back possible

But a step towards?   out?

Behind your grey eyes...   These surfaces

A watchfulness, the distance between,
all words probing towards this puzzle.
The possible bridges?   in a clash of dreams –
though that too poetic and abstract to grasp,
shake with your hands.

A past "real", memories haunting amongst reality;
the present so... ?   dazed?   startled?

The colours of the dim light
projected through blinds onto a ceiling,
the feel of a cotton pillowcase on my cheek
And beyond that?

Not avoiding thought by a fence of questions,
but somehow unable...   to move

Clinging onto the rock face
The rain beating on the skylight
Clipped on
Floating like a sleeping angel
who then wakes touching the softness below

The old question

for Ben Watkins

The stillness,
is that what it's about?
The glint of light in a glass
set on a round wood table?
Sun streaming in from the window
onto some papers, a moving hand,
a man's knee.
That moment, stood still it seems,
a small heaven,
but outside as surely the wind
tugs at a tree, people walk by in the street
going various places.
What to do with this?
Take it while it's there, but… ?
"Moving through time" an unreal phrase,
but with an edge to it.
Stumbling often enough,
clasping such precious minutes
like icons to our breasts.
Somehow to…   What?
Somehow to negotiate or navigate or
just steer clear headed
through the days?
I don't know. I get up
and walk across the room,
turn and

Days and nights : accidental sightings
A bundle of 50 sticks for Joseph Cornell and others

a wire bent round a corner

*

So many pebbles on the beach, uncountable.

*

a silver fish reeled in from the sea. the sun glinting.

*

the line that says nothing. A chair creaks.

*

cut wood. walk the streets at night. rock'n'roll.

*

the wind.

*

fierce gusts of rain following into the night.

*

wind whistling and moaning around the house

*

stuck in the fact of absence

*

the air lightens – suddenly a blue sky, small white clouds masking the sun.

*

the pale ochre, wheat white grass as autumn clears its way and
the rust red patches on the moor

*

In the town…

*

Making the bridges

*

…walking upstairs carrying a basket of wet clothes…

*

the wind ruffling the water of a small pond

*

the clarity of sunlight, the calm it brings, inside not outside.

*

on the cliff top

*

… warm from a bath… scented… simple luxuries…
in the night

*

a clock ticks. a silence of sorts.

*

late afternoon – coming round a corner, down a hill – the sudden
sight of a grey silk sea shining

*

towards dusk two kingfishers skimming the river
walk on and back to a town

*

that's it

*

And now..

*

(space)

*

Watching clouds through a barred window passing from the west.
White clouds   blue sky.

*

always in the present?   ing   ing

*

Where else?   or some lack of imagination?

*

a lot of anger.   a lot of death-wish.

*

"Our beards stiff with ice" – that's a memory.
(I live in a version of the past as well that can be measured
in minutes – not just the present.)

*

Other people somewhere come into this world.

*

music on the radio

*

Walk through the words.

*

the memory of a totally perfect day near indescribable – a time
of such joys and deep happiness.

*

And then out the door into a fine drizzle.

*

As Tom once wrote "this trick doesn't work."
But what trick?   A need to...
but what/why?   and who cares?
"Better than hanging 'round street corners," said Mother Oppen.
Really?

*

These words can rest here on the page, whilst dust slowly coats
the plates. A cupboard of dishes rarely used.
Grandmothers as icons.

*

Who needs it?

*

Out to sea the continually changing horizon
the qualities of light
from left to right   east to west
a startling clarity, a rain storm, more clarity shading into a
haze, a mist. Moving all the time.
And the colours?! A whole book on the colours.

*

sullen

*

Grey dark clouds, continual rain.

*

the alignment of stars

*

bare branches.

*

chalk white boxes.

*

This could go on a long time, but won't.

*

the word is... A dressing gown hung on the door.
A quietness in the house
Clock ticks   Sound of light rain falling,
dripping from the window sill.

*

clear headed

*

Distant sounds – waves breaking on the beach, traffic a street
away.

*

Bright star maps – Orion's Belt over the ploughed fields. Following
the muddy path, crossing the swollen stream, in darkness,...

*

a blue sky. spring coming. 8.00 a.m. on the beach, sun shining.

*

The white box contains a landscape – bare branches, a night sky
set with stars, a window, a figure, curious objects.
We look in from the outside.

Magnetic pull

A bruised night sky
muffling a full moon

that pulls out the unreason
the craziness from heads

so that wandering in rooms
and streets   people who don't know

what   but fall on...
along some zigzag path

preying on and preyed upon
half blind in the half light

behind which pulses 'The Magnet'
"the mist monster" you say

"headstrong" you say
sliding into fitful sleep

lost into nightmares
of mothers and daughters

and pulled up out again
into an awake night

moonlight filling the room
the empty seafront promenade

staggering zombies or sleepwalkers
silently crash through air barriers

a small object is set on a table
the faint light catches one side of it

Moon watching: 7 nights

1st Night:

> the light of the full moon
> cuts across
> my bed
> my bare shoulder
> silver white
> summer night

2nd Night:

> the moonlit sea like old silver
> rolling across an ikon

3rd Night:

> but

> full moon:
>   "leave the phone alone
>   don't negotiate or make decisions
>   till it's passed"
> said an oracle or a
> wise woman or a smart woman
> to me some years ago

4th Night:

> yet

> the moon so clear and bright
> worshipped or feared
> both

> a presence
> a cold pure white

above the town   above the sea
cutting down   (all to size?)

month after month this
strange power or "fascination"
no answer to the "why"

an awed muddle?   when you step back?
and then get on with the "business"

but a passing glimpse
as you climb the stairs
or walk by a window

5th Night:

inland veiled moonlight
is caught on the still pond
two shafts of light fork
down on the dark fields and hills
briefly as the clouds loosen and shift

we plod on through the darkness

6th Night:

a solitary and remote obsession it seems
but joined in silence,
singular to plural, on occasion, we

thin words   thin light

7th Night:

And in the East they had parties
to do this same thing, so I hear
A platform built out on a lake
wine and instruments and poetry
to accompany the moon watch

Summer 1990

Swimming at night,
the creamy full summer moon
gilding the dark lacquered sea.
Floating in the soft swell of the waves
as though suspended...
the sea soft and warm
as a lover's skin, near heaven,
only better.

What next?

I wade out of the sea,
dry myself then sit watching
the sea, the moon,
the small lights on the distant pier.
Walk home, go to bed, dreamy
still hung in those waves.
Such precious time given or taken.

Air clamps

The building is very large that you see
across the fields, dear reader,
can you see, above the green the white
of its walls and red of the tiles?

Standing amongst all this green
whether to sigh in admiration of a vague harmony
or to rage at this fixity? Huh?

A gardener or a visitor might be moving
in the distance towards or away from that building;
or simply standing still musing or about to
step off into some irresolute, even meaningless, action.

I step off into the bushes, the hillsides of long grasses,
the sunken path now overgrown and decorated with orchids,
to emerge later, somewhat sweaty, but pleasantly glowing.

The Stuff is fixed in its grip on us
but we slip loose some times and decay
gradually eats at the structures, we hope.

In 20 years' time the white may be grey,
or still a dazzling white, but the house now
turned into a hotel for conferences, gourmet weekends.
The estate divided, the landscape farmed,
or built on even, though unlikely in this place.

A frazzled reader shoves old postcards, photos,
jigsaw puzzles into a remote drawer
wanting only to get up and out the door
into the street air, but then suddenly
dawns the weirdly controlled clamps rotating
in the sky by unseen hands.

Czech dream

1

'The last bell is ringing
The fairy tale is over'
        shout some distant Czechs
        early on a frosty evening

"A sharp new moon
in a smudged pink sky"
the story begins,
but seemed a repeated story
heard too many times before.
That tale over,
but another continues?

        "Arm in arm with you"?

2

The story began

        "Waking at five and passing into a jumble
        of dreams that with time ended by
        taking me into your arms.

        Over the weeks apart our minds race
        ahead of our bodies.
        When we meet, when they catch up,
        then like a golden light, yes?
        descends upon us wholly.

        The dream is right.
        The words wrong-foot sometimes
        but try to push through the briars,
        leap over them sometimes,
        Brer Rabbit and all."

429

But I built too much in those dreams?
Too many scars and losses behind us.
Yet this chance, come upon by accident,
precious but shakey.

3

Not the village wedding,   the mad bride's suicide,
billowing white veils against the greenery
of leaves or water

but

> "The thought of being with you.
> Dizzy floating I bite my lip
> in the middle of 'worldly commerce'."

4

"'God has many mansions' said Miss Flanagan S.R.N.
and the mansion where we dwelt...
'and which mansion did you sleep in?' she added
                                    with a sly laugh
The rosaries and mugs of sherry are duly told
Our love stained sheets tell
our mansion"

5

Yet it doesn't shelter us
stave off the unavoidable collapse.
Dreams and stories snare us
before we can get past rubbing our eyes.
A mess of fears sets in that neither
Venus nor Ganymede can dispel.
Like Cupid a blind romantic rush
tips us sprawling into a mirrored room
where self-absorbed dreamers wander
almost ghostlike.

The creators of such illusions
stand close beside us. The creatures.

6

Spoken into a mirror

    "I travel to you

    your warmth
    To stand or lie in each other's arms

    battle scars, tired of the old deceits
    we come nervously to each other
    yet surely (we think)

    Is this the clarity
    we dream of?

    Not magic but more powerful
    in its simplicity –
    us

    Guided out beyond the ramparts
    the savage boors

    Touch me   you"

and tinkling bells in the distance
and the words flatter themselves, words on words,
and the first flakes of snow falling softly,
the landscape whitening out

African violets

for Pansy Harwood my grandmother 1896-1989

Flags stream from the tops of the silver pyramids
Purple flowers present themselves to the air, the world
Chopin fights his way through all the notes, the choices

All this, and yet that emptiness

A real heart-breaker, tears in my eyes

What did I give you? At the last a pot of flowers,
your favourite colour, you said
then died soon after, the day after
I'd left you there in the bare hospital room
your eyes and voice so clear in the recognition
like so many years before   "O Travers"

And you gave me?   everything I know.

But to reduce this to yet another poem
to entertain

pages of words creating old routines

I systematically smash all those pretty pictures,
they won't do anymore.
"That was a bit unnecessary, son," you say.
I know, but their weight does you no service.

My blood is your blood,
it's as ancient as that;
pride and style that you had,
and with all a lovely generosity
I treasure.

I find myself moving as you would,
not the same but similar,
sharing your tastes and paths;
the night jasmin bower.

432

The strength of these memories
The comfort your home was

Yet it seems almost another world –
building rabbit hutches on winter evenings
in your living room, sawdust and
wood shavings on the worn carpet, easily cleared.
A house that was lived in, not exhibited.

And all those other evenings, summer or winter,
spent pickling onions, or bottling fruit,
or wrapping boxes of apples for store,
or stringing onions to hang in the shed
above the sacked potatoes,
or mending our own shoes,
all the work, cooking, making,
fixing, all done capably, easily
together.

But you now gone forever

Not sat in the corner of the couch
after your morning bath, with a cup of tea
reading the morning paper.
That ritual finished

though other "stuff" continues
as your blood continues too flow in me
no matter what I might say
(the tense continually shifts, past and present blur)
we both love(d) love and were, are natural liars,
easy with the "truth", turning facts to meet the story;
we both have a distaste for "trade" –
all the contradictions happily ignored;
we both…

Now wandering helpless around my room
the rich world about,
the flags and skies, the dreams

I talk to you again and again,
I see you again and again   sat there

Tao-yun meets Sandy Berrigan *

A wall hung with charms –
pictures, a Welsh love-spoon, beads
"for worrys"

I live with this
the touchstones, rituals, to hold off or hold to...
Clinging to the walls?

A soft hot night, and May
now, a half moon so clear
in the dark sky

All round the globe
Like Chinese poems of dear friends' separations,
brief meetings, then parting again

Shifts and changes
that can't be charmed away
only soothed by this "hollow"

I remember the taste of coffee
as late at night I entered a room
where you lay sleeping

*"Tao-yun (c400 A.D.), (poet and) wife of General Wang Nin-chih. The general was so stupid that she finally deserted him."
Arthur Waley – *170 Chinese Poems*.

Summer 1993

early in the evening
the smell of jasmin

pushes death away

in the fading light
a strong wind tugs across the sea
bright white crests on the waves

my son enters pushing his bike
my daughter runs downstairs

pushes death away

*

slid into a selfish gloom
the result of...?
An overcast summer's day by the sea,
luminous grey white clouds,
patches of bright sunshine,
but a dullness in one's heart,
if not elsewhere?
At that age...
At some point in one's life
when...   what does it matter?

The losses irreparable, irreplaceable.
The deaths of loved ones,
and one's own death hovering nearby
that would seem welcome but for...
the loved ones living and those moments
when a flower's scent or a shaft of sunlight...

*

But as though out on one's own, almost.
"The solitary" – though that too dramatic.
"The melancholic" – self-absorbed romancing
that has a sharp edge to it,
cuts deeper than your finger.

And you who reads this –
it must bore you or seem so irrelevant.
I need to write this for whatever reason
but you don't need to read it. (goodbye)

Inside the castle all's well.
Outside the angry creatures
pounce and flail
in swirling mists or black night.
Dreams horribly real.

*

changes in the past, but ahead?
Drilled into the ground
stuck waiting
the light fading,
or "dormant" some say
depending on one's cheer (glad or no).

*

surviving, not perkily ending.

just to get it over.

over the blue grey hills
angels hover in a paleing sky
still-faced   shadows cross a face
eyelash flicker   bright sunlight
such gloom?   foolish but...
 step back   still spot

In the mountains

In memory of Paul Evans

A bright full moon
in a clear black sky
over Llyn Ogwen.

Eight years pass.
A climber falls.

Now where's that leave us?

A veiled smoky moon
on a dark night,
the lake a dense black.

Absence gnawed at.
Stuck in a cleft.

A car drives by far below.
Some people returning somewhere.

Later – a chill dull day.
Jagged blocks and spikes
pump the heart heat.
Haul up through rock
onto snow covered ridge.

Did it.   Do it.   Then... ?

Then strapping on crampons
and on up – as we'd both do –
on up.   Yes,   magnificent.

A rose red gold sun in ice air.

"Where's Mr. Perky now?"

Days and nights pass
and the weight increases,
steadily pressing down.
Deaths and losses,
wrong doing, facts,
without forgiveness.
A lead cloak around your shoulders.
So tired.

What's done "is done"
and that no excuse.
Guilt and grief bound in
to the fabric, it seems forever.

Enough said.   "Stop it."
The words, the talking.

And living with all this.

The glimmer of sunlight
early in the morning.

Hard to believe
anything's final, but…

A white terrace of houses
up from the sea
where people live in rooms
once loved by others.
The little empires we build.

A faint dream, seasons passed, and
swimming through glittering waves
while a man walks by to start
another night shift.

Dreams of Armenia

like an angel of death
telling the tale again and again
never any release

the dry rustle of feathers
behind your ear
a feather brushing your neck, your cheek

then a silence
a shadow traveller
then it starts again

*

1894 August: Sasun and surrounding villages attacked by Turks
                and Kurds. 3,000 Armenians slaughtered. "The
                Armenians were absolutely hunted like wild beasts,"
                said H.S. Shipley, British representative.

1895:   Ottoman sultan puts into effect his "final solution"
                for the Armenian "problems". Special army units are
                formed. 30,000 Armenians murdered and over 8,000
                flee the country.

1896, 26-27 August: In Constantinople 6,000 murdered, the rest flee.

1896, 15-17 September: In Eghin 2,000 murdered.

1908:   "Young Turks" massacre 15,000 in Adana, and 15 to 25
                thousand in the surrounding villages. "Conservative
                estimates," say the consuls of the "Great Powers".

1915-16:   One and a half million Turkish Armenians murdered
                out of a population of three million.

The lists and details continue and continue, the facts of numberless
horrors pile up endlessly like torn bodies in the Kemakh gorge.

*

In a dream a door opens
the long dead father stands there
Many others come and go
A friend enters and stays there
fixed there   the light streaming
past his silhouette   the silver edge
a bright day outside

*

If these the last words written,
words then a death, or a silence,
let them at least praise...
 the "Armenia" I imagine?
moonlight filling a room?
Awkward symbols,
painted boards propped
against a crumbling wall.

*

Komitas the composer silent for 20 years after watching the butchery,
the massacres in a wild and empty place – neither word nor note until
his death (in Paris 1935).

*

a wooden table tilted in the courtyard
an empty glass and coffee cup on one side
the heavy scent of jasmin as the evening...

*

Like an Armenian song that tears your heart,
like an Armenian song that tears your heart
with "memories", past loves, empty plains,
empty villages, desolate highlands, clogged ravines.

All those "things" beyond any words.

*

carved stone churches like lighthouses

And in the year 301 A.D. St. Gregory the Illuminator converted
Armenia, the first Christian kingdom in the known world.

Be praised.

And later, in 874, Princess Mariam of Siunia built a nunnery on an
island in Lake Sevan. A place to meet her fisherman lover, they say.

Be praised.

All of Armenia a massive rockbound island rising out of the
surrounding plains. A light to be praised. An illuminating beauty
besieged by barbarism and death, tides of charred destruction.

*

the silence, though not a silence,
the wind in the trees, the sound of water
somewhere, someone calling, far off,
a brief snatch of bird song nearby,
the wind in the trees, the sound of

As though a trickling – very slowly – away

*

The land still there, the sun in the sky.
The eastern provinces, Russian Armenia, still there, real enough,
crops and music and industries and dancing.
The western provinces, Turkish Armenia, there, though
the people dead or driven away. An emptiness.

*

A carved archway. An elaborately carved tomb
broken in half. Stone cut like lace.
The yellow white of grasses late in summer.

Your long black hair, an occasional grey hair,
your deep brown eyes that churn my heart.
Laughing. To touch your face,
kiss your hands and shoulders.
The poplars sway in the breeze,
their leaves twirl and sparkle silver in the sunlight.
The warmth that melts all reserves.

*

... Mkhitar Heratsi sews the wounds up with silk thread, uses
mandragora as an anaesthetic, shows for the first time (1184) how
"fevers", typhoid and malaria, are infectious, uses music for relief
of nervous complaints... A medieval beacon... King Gayik Ardsruni
of Vaspurakan builds (915-921) a church on the island of Aghtamar
in Lake Van. The outside walls covered in relief carvings of biblical
scenes. A marvel to see with your own eyes... The island deserted, its
people long since dead, its churches crumbling, the towers sprouting
bushes and trees...

*

Your smile, a glance caught in the market or on the river
bank. Touching as we leave a building.
The evening stroll begins in Yerevan. Lights come on in the
small outdoor cafés. Talk. The tap of backgammon pieces.
A single man's voice   singing   singing   that gives your

heart trembling wings. Then a skirl of reeds. Oboes, piccolos,
flutes, recorders, lutes, zithers and drums.
In the hot night lying together, your eyes glisten in the
soft half-light. The animal scent of our bodies.

*

fields, meadows and orchards, vineyards and pastures in a
stony land, hard and well worked and watered.
apricots, pomegranates, melons, grapes, wheat, sunflowers,
the sheep grazing.   blossom in the trees.   roses.

*

Towns, villages, churches, graveyards destroyed.
Let off the leash to murder and plunder.

But the notes, the figures, back then – 1895 –

8 October: Trebizond, 920 killed and 200 in the surrounding
                  villages.

21 October: Erzindjan, 260 killed and 850 in the villages.

25 October: Bitlis, 800 killed.

27 October: Baiburt, "several hundred" killed.

30 October: Erzerum, 350 killed.

1-3 November: In Diyarbekir 1,000 killed and in Arabkir 2,800.

4-9 November: Malatia, 3,000 killed.

10-11 November: Kharput, 500 killed.

28 December: Urfa, 3,000 men, women and children seeking safety
                  in the cathedral were shot or burned to death there by
                  Turkish troops.

"The sickening odour of roasting flesh pervaded the town" wrote Consul Fitzmaurice.

*

a silence. a door bangs in the wind.
not a dream.

*

Since the 1880s the Turkish army trained by Germans, and fully reorganised in 1913. Liman von Sanders, the German Inspector General of the Turkish Army and Freiherr Hans von Wangenheim, the German ambassador, in 1914 assist with the "master plan" for the destruction of the Armenians, a planned genocide.

"Who remembers the Armenians?" said Hitler years later as he set on the Jews.

*

Massacres, shootings, bayoneting, hacking, thrown into the Kemakh gorge, thrown into the Black Sea, deportations, forced marches, rape, starvation, robbery. Children, men, women, the old and sick.

*

They would do this to you, my love,
and to our son.

*

A summer breeze in the trees
on the hillside, on the river bank.
But the ghosts sighing,
and the crowding savages

Postscript

1   Arshile Gorky wrote in a letter, 14 February 1944, 'What has the
     Armenian experience to add to modern life? Sensitivity. That
     is the main, the unforgettable word that has been engraved in
     my memory of it. Sensitivity to beauty, sensitivity to sadness
     and melancholy, sensitivity to the frailty as well as the nobility
     of life. Sensitivity to mental progress. It is such an important
     contribution. Sensitivity in the day of dehumanization. There
     lies our contribution to all art. Our Armenia, the sensitivity of
     Armenia, its understanding and immense experience of bad
     and good, of the beautiful and ugly, the dead and living is
     needed by all the world.'

2   Beside the many books on Armenian history as a whole,
     the most thorough account of 19th and 20th century history
     is Christopher J. Walker's *Armenia: The Survival of a Nation*
     (Croom Helm, London, 1980).

The Songs of Those Who Are On The Sea of Glass*

A hospital room in near silence
Men in beds in varying degrees of pain
A clutter and the colour white
The bright January sun
illuminating...
the beige of the building opposite
The arrangement of buildings   so beautiful
Clouds and white puffs of smoke from unseen chimneys
reflected in the black windows

Waking to see this   from on high
across the morning courtyard
It's amazing

*

The bright vision fades

A battered piece is put back
on the game board
whose endlessly complicated contradictory rules
...... absurd and with no purpose

The box chipped and coated in dust
Jamaican cigars long gone
into the blue haze

*

Osip Mandelstam calls this earth
"a Godgiven palace" "the happy heaven
...the boundless house in which we live our lives"

*

446

The living dead plod across the ice to
stare through thick glass walls
"Let me in!"   "Let me out!"

As though floating. Couldn't care less.
Which side.   Outside.   Down there.

The ice window
(that's a metaphor)
Climbing over the bones
(that's a metaphor)
Aquarium walls

Grotesque gawping fish
Nightmare stuff

A new moon high in the sky over the sea

*

Suddenly keeling over
A blur
Dream ambulances, rooms, people, tubes

Back and forth over the river

But love and duty call and pull,
Stoic virtues make it amusing,
the whimpers and begging – a story.

*

Talking in code ?

*

A rawness.   The rediscovered face in the mirror
"I know you?"   Mid-morning.
Washed and shaved
A body stitched and wired together. The Creature.

"The monster! The monster!" fleeing villagers yell
in black and white Transylvania.

"I don't need, I don't need..."

Emptiness would soothe
A bare room   no clutter

*

The sea was frozen as we approached Esbjerg
the crunch and crack of ice beneath the ferry's bow
as it ploughed on towards a grey line in the whiteness

Inland a fox trotted nervously
across snow-covered fields and streams

The warmth of the cabin bunk, of the den,
of the sun when it breaks through
and, wrapped up, you skim stones across
a small frozen pool in the mountains,
the ricochet ringing, whining,
a high singing.

*

black glass windows
across the courtyard
reflections of clouds, columns of smoke
Bright January sun
a glitter in the air
that fills rooms
(a gold-leaf annunciation)

As though reborn
not racked with loss, past if-onlys

To walk at ease with the ghosts
(not a club member yet)
warm and open and thankful

with care
it seems possible

sat up in bed in bizarre pyjamas

*title of the volume of Welsh hymns by William Williams
(Pantycelyn), published c1750: *Caniadau y Rhai sydd ar y Mor a Wydr.*

Gorgeous – yet another Brighton poem

The summer's here.
Down to the beach
to swim and lounge and swim again.
Gorgeous bodies young and old.
Me too. Just gorgeous. Just feeling good
and happy and so at ease in the world.

And come early evening a red sun setting,
the sea all silky,
small gentle surges along its near still surface.

And later
the new moon hung over the sea,
a stippled band of gold across the black water,
tiger's eye.

I walk home.
The air so soft and warm,
like fur brushing my body.

The dictionary says
"**gorgeous** – adorned with rich and brilliant colours,
sumptuously splendid, showy, magnificent, dazzling."

That's right.

Mirrors

in the mirror

                an unknown face

a blank
of flesh, colours, slight movements,
"facial muscles" the words say

something slipping away
                        unknown
                                totally unknowable

                "might discover himself not
in the mirror of Narcissus' pool but
in men and upon that arid earth"*

                        ...dark hidden motives...

... penetrating clarity...

                        ...success through what is small...

...no place to "stay"...
                        ...persons quarrelling...

...deep cunning...

                        ...repeated deliberation...

Amongst all those words
"conflict means not to love"

A hellish trembling world
or a possible heaven
at the touch or glance of the one you love

Not the lapis lazuli sky, gold leaf stars
way up above beyond the crust
overcrowded heavenly chorus
Not the black red fire world below
in the bowels of the earth
men savagely buggered with long poles
by wretched capering deformed demons

but here   and now

you make it happen   you make it happen

talking in the particular

obvious enough

gulls laugh, screech, and chunter on nearby roofs
morning light glances off the mirror
the sunlight the window the sound of the sea

*Carlo Levi's 1963 Introduction to 'Christ Stopped at Eboli'

South Coast

mauve inside of a shell

squealing terns plunging into the sea
hunting   zigzagging
along the edge of the beach

the new bright spring sunshine

these particulars   that hold one

what was it we were trying to say?
were we talking of love?
and other difficult words?

while diving through the glittering light
into out of the sea...

the ochres, whites, greys of the shingle
against the peacock blue-green of the sea
against a pale blue sky

 cloudless sparkling air

thoughts and judgements
slide and tumble after each other
untrustworthy untrustworthy
leading nowhere but...

the side of your face
a suntanned hand
a hard glance in the eyes
your mouth

the impossibility of holding onto
anything   anyone
sun sweeps its arc

moon and stars rotate
continually shifting
at night the dull hiss of the surf
sounds constant but fades or pulses
radio static

No?   is this wandering?

something slipping away
a steady reduction of time
notched off

red bands hold the white lighthouse
at the end of the harbour arm
runs and drips of red paint smudge the white edge

sand eels are put on the hook
to catch bass, I'm told

Talking Bab-Ilu

for Anne Stevenson

The words scattered or hidden
since the tower of Babel
and a jealous Jehovah
(get a new job, why don't you?
who needs it? **that** sort of stuff?).

Up and down the ziggurat stairs,
into the skies into the earth.
A gate for gods, not a confusing babble.
The language of trees, of seas,
of winds, plants, and us beasts.

Music after the flood
in the hills and mountains.
As spring comes a young bull
bellows in a high green field.
You stop and listen.

And the other sounds –
the mew of two buzzards up above,
the drumming of water down
over rock slab over rock slab,
my voice talking to myself.

Listening,   waiting,   drifting
into that space beyond words.
Forgot what I meant to say.
My hands before my eyes.
It can happen.   Clear and bright.

Late Journeys

1996-1998

Late journeys

You think you'll sleep so well tonight
warmed with the glow of feeling precious
to someone else out there.   Can it be?

You don't sleep **that** well,
but what's **that** simple?
Us animals snuffle around so eagerly.

At dusk – coral pink clouds
lined up along the horizon
like mysterious monuments symbolising "Hope".

A weighty full moon hangs over the pier,
silvers the sea, churns our hearts.
Warm silk summer nights.

The orange lights of provincial railway stations.
People walking home, people taking the last train,
shouting across streets, talking on the platform.

It seems all right
whatever may come.

Monuments

Lines of dark trees in a plantation, ivy, bramble

underfoot.

Two charred trunks stand – totems, watchers, uncaring

guardians.

Deeper in the wood a long pit filled with scribbles of

blue light.

On the edge of the wheatfield a forest of slim granite posts

maps a wave.

Naked men broad chested stand fixed on a green path their

faces whitened.

Algae on the stones. Your scent on my hand

my body.

Your body – lines beyond words, warm curve

touch.

Your eyes in the half-light. Your mouth. Lines of a shoulder

dreamed of.

In the viridian undergrowth red stone arches beset a path.

Too obscure?

Heavy metal sections bolted together form

a rough canyon.

Feel it. Cobwebs stretch from rust patina. Still water

in a sexual scoop.

This is not a dream,
I saw all this.
Sweep of your body
in a white room.
Stands of trees.

"So what?" someone snaps   "So what??"

I say

"it's amazing wonderful out there in front of

you."

A neon blue light below the dirt and chalk, a sacred

dusky glow.

Genghis Khan's hat

Genghis Khan loves his new mauve hat
sent by a feeble emperor far away.
He wears it all the time,
awake and asleep.

Drums and gongs beaten in the encampment.
Wars and skirmishes in the distance.
Coming and going. Fluttering banners.
Horses kick up dust, flying turf.

Among the tent's yellow silk draperies
we're here.
Mr. Mauve Hat is out,
History is out.

The leaves of summer trees
the look in your eyes.
On a distant steppe now
a threadbare hat lying in coarse grass.

Classicism (Satie, Finlay, et Cie..)

Afternoon light slides through a Paris apartment
The white walls and few furnishings
Simple and bare and elegant
Piano music now
The books   the couch

Timeless moment

If you were here
we would stare into each other's eyes
almost frightened so intense the love

"No fear. No harm."
say Chinese sages 3000 years ago

Caravans depart the oasis
Roman mottos grow mossy

"The Temple of Ancient Virtue"
on its knoll   the beech trees turning

Fragments creak in their chains
Grand proclamations chipped and broken   solid stone
Startled birds arpeggio and sweep off into...   other trees

The moment   we touch
naked   such a world
overwhelming   so present

A bed scented with cinnamon and vanilla
Dear timeless virtue

Vessel

for Penny and a homage to Chris Drury

Fire in the cairn on a winter mountain
Snow streaked summit   the range of grey
in the ice air

Orange flames waver in a brief home
high above mists and moor, the scattered lochans

You...   I hardly begin to say

The vast landscape we inhabit, we wander in

My mouth stopped with our kisses

To burn with love

Moss and white grass

amongst rocks and boulders

To the south pale rose clouds above the sea
the waves below a dull grey pink at dusk

To launch out
across clawed rock slabs

Thaw conditions

To get past the concrete slab
the jagged metal
stagnant pools of rust tinted water
a seeming wreck ready to lunge

Traps for the unsuspecting, insects and others

Watched by Security and cashiers

You enter the gates   you enter the wood
thousands of leaves   twigs   blades of grass
millions   countless

Vast landscapes of clouds
move purposefully above us   slowly sailing their way

You could see this so many ways as
our paths weave a braided dance   our bodies too
– but no matter how –
to get clear into the clear
across beyond the fallen pediment
the bolted laws   the grey furrows
through a winter that lasted too many years
it seemed

Tundra turns to surprise   to spring
to sunlight cutting through clouds searching the land
a dam bursting   local destruction   mud and greenery
Banks of herbs and flowers

I gnaw and kiss your shoulder   the smell of your arms
as your head thrown back   at such release
the spring we find

Dante wanders by clasping his **Vita Nuova**
He's miles away   maybe

You dismantle the walls
it takes time   we both know that
The prism's wavering rainbow scatters across the room
Swarming atoms   a delight of differences
alike

An Horatian Ode

*"I shall nudge the stars with my lifted head"**

sea sparkle   touch cloud

not denying history   but

never before,   this

the bass music   pitches and springs   just right

tears of such happiness

beauty   the bronze shape shifter

transparency   and you

what you say what you do

in your arms   I cry with joy

like two people in one body

in a well loved landscape

this coast and the hills behind

we find "the daily" amazing

*Horace - *Odes*, first ode, book 1

Beginning of a West Sussex spell

You lie naked on a mossy bank
The beech woods sigh and hiss in the wind
Soft rain sweeps through and across

No tiger pads by – of course not
No nervous deer skitters by
Your lover covers you from the rain

Now you can dream or watch the sky
your body a masked sun
your face

Tonight

breath white in the street
Tired and clumsy from work
like other citizens   men women in this town

I don't think straight or hear right
I miss what you're saying
My replies not enough

Frost glazes the parks and squares
the fields and valleys beyond
The long winter night outside

Later the sound of your breathing
                              as you sleep beside me
the beauty of your face
                              as you lie asleep beside me
Such precious sharing
our pleasures

Our warm soft night passes

I hear you   you hear me
I hear you   you hear me

I can never write enough to say... I hardly know what I'm trying to
say. To describe the gleam in your brown eyes as we lie together? The
cinnamon half-light. The clear lines – your eyes, mouth, the outline of
your ear, your jaw. The thoughts then... totally without a language,
they cut so deep.

Silk veil

A migrating tribe. The men
advance through the wood,
come out into the clearing.

The majestic pace of the moon
embedded in opal clouds
as it rises above the trees.

Its light catching their rags and faces,
a dull glitter in their eyes.
Threatening or threatened and lost?

A subdued fountain swells up with dark water,
dead leaves slowly spiral beneath its surface.
No messages.   A speechless trust.

Somewhere else – far away –
factories, offices, backyard repair shops
lie empty, locked up for the night,
their dust settling in a near silence.

The advance through to where?
Through the white stone arch,
past polished red granite carved

for our touch and caress now
stood still by the fountain's mirror
as the night passes, fades, as a

brilliant gold rose streaked sun
rises out of the trees
white frost   winter dawn.

As you rise from the bath
water diamonds glitter
in your black ripple hairs.

The history of science

Beneath the surface   swarming atoms
Landscapes decay sway and thrust
beyond presumption   hardly becalmed
though seemingly so

A man advances his chest sliced with neon
A woman advances as though made of amber
cloaked in gold silk
Pulsing flecks electric blue
Glowing yellows golden browns

Overlap / overlay

Beyond understanding   move into silence
An intensity   large scale

In face
of your sleeping face
Into dream

don't know why

patchwork fields woods
below this blue swaying tower
where we lie craddled
tugged by the wind
in each other's arms

It changes

Great sweeps of loose colours
bright and sexy as you

the sun on your face
this late morning by the sea
how I melt and you dazzle

I dance across the rooftops
never "lonely as a cow"

470

Beneath the sea   the swaying forests
wave and swirl   undulate like dancers
luminous creatures pulse and build
delicately   so slowly

and not in silence

5 Rungs up Sassongher*

1. A dark face in the silver

A year of silence   now
To write one word...   useless
To claw back something
I don't even know yet
Talking to you?   to myself?   to the "ether"?

Like an imagined sea
sheets of blank paper covering
the heaving waves
All the impossible words
words you won't hear

While outside a cold winter night
a sharp moon in a rumpled cloud sky
a real sea glinting like metal
under whose dark surface seethes a life
almost beyond imagination and far from
this emptiness I seem to live in

The prowling fish devouring fish
The warfare of molluscs and starfish
Underwater forests where...

The weak words –   "wounded"?
But some form of broken trust
It happens   People change
Courage wavers in face of the secure
or maybe just   Desires change
You chose your path   as we must do

I'm wandering   word wandering
Brooding not thinking
while you go about your "daily business"
at this same moment
dealing with its reasons and pressures
children and households   pleasures and jobs

472

But your face
the memories burn my heart
Your face
the glitter of your eyes in the half dark
as we lay naked gazing into each other
candle light   sweet touch   sweat back

now passed

As day follows night
Oh to "be new tender quick"**
not haunted by cancelled dreams
abandoned expectations
You

Legalistic eagles swoop with undeniable logic
proving their claims and explanations   faultless

"Decisive action"? or "running scared"?   both?   but

Our unconscious collusion in the unsaid
Unread codes and some form of blindness maybe
But dreams we could touch

Today I received a heart shaped shell
Today I received a copy of GRAND STREET
Today I heard Spyridoula Toutoudaki sing
Some days I feel so rich
but this dark night dull with loss

All becomes simile

"Where you are   where I would be,
half thought   thought otherwise"***

Sleepless   thought otherwise

A simple ordinary tale

And more months pass
bright sunlight fills the room
covers the sea
Along the coast
the same sun wakes you
and another day begins

2. Orchid prowed

fast moving clouds

a gold silk curtain
ceiling to floor
like a wall
dream block memory hook

you're in this too
whether you or I want it
not to be

the bright seashore

then "sleep well" I don't say to you

asleep
(you walk into my dreams)
awake
(you appear in the crowd)

once proud at your side

you steered away

gold silk
silk as your skin

laurel wreaths thrown in the sea

the white winged orchid's quiet display
a thin stem of flowers crimson mouthed

a calm magnificence beyond us

3. "The joyous lake"

A cup placed   on a saucer   and filled with coffee.
Steps across   a carpeted room   to open a window
and step out   onto a balcony   viewing the sea.

One can't ask   for much more   in hope.
A private world,   almost lost   to ghosts,
but as open   as air,   the light we breathe.

A sort of simplicity,   not babble,   to hold to
firmly but gently.   Intense and.   Beautiful as
a spray of   moth orchids   on the sunlit table.

4. Touch stones

June 1st, 1834. Port Famine, Tierra del Fuego.

"The number of living creatures of all Orders, whose existence intimately depends on the kelp, is wonderful. A great volume might be written, describing the inhabitants of one of these beds of seaweed... On shaking the great entangled roots, a pile of small fish, shells, crabs of all orders, sea-eggs, starfish, beautiful Holuthuriae, Planariae, and crawling nereidous animals of a multitude of forms, all fall out together."

July 23rd, 1834. Valparaíso, Chile.

"What a difference does climate make in the enjoyment of life! How opposite are the sensations when viewing black mountains half enveloped in clouds, and seeing another range through the light blue haze of a fine day! The one for a time may be very sublime; the other is all gaiety and happy life."

July 23rd, 1834.

"...the plants and shrubs possess strong and peculiar odours; even one's clothes by brushing through them become scented."

(Charles Darwin – *Journal of Researches into the Natural History and Geology of the Countries visited during the Voyage round the World of H.M.S. 'Beagle' under command of Captain Fitz Roy, R.N. 1839*)

5. Dolomitic ditty

dapper in my lederhosen
I will sing you a song

Mr. Marmot will whistle
an accompaniment

| CURTAIN |

like an old folk tale
the crisp winter's night
frost glittering on the

"brushing through them"

* Sassongher – peak on south-east corner of the Puez group in the Dolomites.
** George Herbert's poem *Love unknown*
*** Susan Howe's poem *Silence Wager Stories*

Evening Star

1998-2003

Salt Water*

The complexity of a coral reef
the creatures   sunlight
shafting down through crystal sea
water   the flicker of shadows
light wavering and fading
into the depths

Near the silver mirrored surface
bright yellow fish
flutter through the reef
crowded with the swaying tendrils
of coral and anemones,
smudges of algae, drifts of seaweed,
starfish and shellfish flowing
through the canyons

The sun rises three times
The sun sets three times

over sea   over land

on land
her blue grey eyes gaze at the world
in silence   blink at the world
the world goes about
its usual business

"A fine view along the coast"
to be seen from a high building's
window   one of many windows

"Polyps" the books say   coral
a tube with a mouth at the end
surrounded by tendrils to catch
small creatures
A world of soft tissue
And the colours
white   red   orange
yellow   green   blue

purple   "natural pigments"
and those too changeable
when algae "lives within the tissue"

Many species   Many depths
and the light filtered down
reducing reducing

And bright yellow fish
banded with peacock blue
flutter through the reef
Red fish   Black fish
with lemon ringed eyes
flutter through the reef

How delighted she'd be
Her blue grey eyes gazing at this world
while cradled in her mother's
her father's arms
the world going about its usual business

A ship's bows cut the salt water
a phosphorescent trail in the tropic night

The phosphorus glitter of the sea
From the Greek
phos (light) — phoros (bringing)

Like her
as she came and went

Morning star

* In memory of Joey Peirce / Harwood,
who lived 11 - 14 March 1997.

481

Pagham Harbour spring

The blur of sky and sea
this white grey morning
before the day burns
moves into blue

the sweet butter scent of gorse
the sweet scent of you
dear daughter   ghost in my head
dear daughter

the mudflats and saltings shine
as the children run by
along marsh edge and the high dyke bank
egret and oystercatcher   dunlin and sandpiper

In the distance a train passes
where a short neat man
pushes a refreshment trolley
his clean white shirt immaculately ironed
his black waistcoat just right
the quiet dignity of him
as he passes through the hours

You'd know this   the particulars
were you here
held in the wide sky arc
the children running on the dyke bank
absorbed in this world

Fragment of an indecipherable inscription

A rocky headland dreamt of.
Its road jammed with cars,
with tangled crowds, police,
authority snared in its own grip.

As dusk cloaks us I leave the road,
walk the cliff edge. Tussocks and drops.
Rock-faces in darkness. Large shadow birds.

In the distant town can we buy food?
Like refugees.   Like distant bombs.
A stumbling return. Will you still be there?

Our babe-in-arms, you, me,
us three in this bare grey landscape.
No word reaches us, not even in dreams.
As though lost and searching, almost lost.

In work

for the photographer Ben E. Watkins

amongst labour to see
in the crowd of people
before you   I mean
in front of you
and those weaving their way
through the streets behind
in sight   out of sight
A passage through

amongst labour to see
in the crowd of people
their shadows still then gone
the hopping children and lingering
adults smiling or hard-mouthed
or just going somewhere they know
with purpose or as though drifting
A featureless sky above

amongst labour to see
in the crowd of people
the viscous webs that wrap
round our faces   that bind us
not the elegant "empty" city
we dream in   but something warmer
private worlds arm in arm with each other
You cross a road   enter a building

Seasons

"A sense of tranquillity and privacy"
– the moods Morandi treasured.

And some times
it's like floating   like floating
up and beyond   beyond

Drift off or sharply here.
And the cycles, the seasons not
eternal though seemingly so.
The strata decay, tilt, and shift.
The constellations wheel through the night
sky, bursting and fading.

***

In the sunken ship's boiler an octopus
gives birth to her young, stops eating, fades away.

A spring leaf unfurls, spreads to full summer sail,
then falls in faded glory.

The salmon force their way up stream, spawn,
then exhausted die in a shadowy pool or
drift with the current back to sea.

And us too. That's it. Talking of the basics.
Unreasoning biology, its drive and cycles.

"Enjoy"
is said without irony.
And why not?

The wind rises : Istvan Martha meets Sandy Berrigan

After the goodbyes
the first steps out
across the ice and snow.

As though the first steps
of one's life. white breath.
one foot after another.

A black wind-torn night
and the sound of footsteps
crunching on unseen ice.

A glaring light trembles
on the side of a distant cowshed.
We get older.

The past autumn a memory
that now warms us.
A journey back to the city.

An old woman and her grandchild
climbing into the provincial train
carrying baskets of dark plums.

Dogs barked at the edge of a village
as crumbling cement walls faded
into a soft smoky dusk.

The last clamour of rooks,
a distant car barely seen not heard,
the clatter of a helicopter flying low home.

From that dusk into this night
so quick despite the weeks.
Shocked back into the present.

In your cabin you lean forward
to sew a quilt or read a letter.
Leagues away I enter this darkness.

In the black cold I...   you...
A curtain is pulled closed.
To reach sleep one way or another.

But wherever, the ghosts are with us.
We live with them, that loss.
Loved ones gone one way or another.

Dead or alive they are with us
sharing a view, a joke, some music.
Guiding or grieving us.

Is that what getting old is?
Learning to live like this – that strength
increasingly needed. Or sink into gaga?

And by day the thud of machines,
the high whine of the saw mill,
the clicking of keyboards and tills.

The swish of a broom as a man
sweeps the gutter, the swish of your broom
as you sweep the homes of the wealthy.

Winter birds clear against a grey sky.
As night falls snow falls
on near silent factories, heavy forests.

You lean towards the light, pause.
"Neighbour-calls in the dark".
Tender-hipped you dream, dear heart.

Not forever in this chilling night,
I know, there are places to go.
Stumbling over frozen ruts and furrows.

One foot after another
steering through half-known outlines,
the black silhouettes of hills and trees.

The ghosts are quiet,
minding their own business,
warming their hands in Kapolcs or Capel.

Pole star "to a foreign land"
where no one will follow
in black or white or "golden gown".

Young woman in Japanese garden

The day so cold. Your breath white,
coming out in small trailing clouds.
The trees snow laden in the Snow Garden.
A pause in the ritual, step by step.
The pale late afternoon light that
makes you think you're there, so present
– crunch of snow and the red gate post –
but you're not.

                    The trick is played
– look again – appearances shift.
The trees are in blossom
early on this cold spring evening.
Cigarette smoke trails from your mouth.
A mouth too perfect. Make-up, hair,
all too perfect.   The chill
in the air, and somewhere in you?
Your coat still damp from the rain.

Mistaken again. And the fictions pile up.
Dreams of elsewhere. A set of
elaborately wrapped boxes to be
placed on a highly polished table.
Small beautiful gifts held inside.
Behind you, in the corner of the park,
the gardeners' shed is locked.
They're at home with their wives,
or on their way home carrying groceries.

Poem to accompany Chris Schwarz's photo titled "Smoke Japan".

Safe-past-words?

1

A voice says something
                    but inexplicable
The words float in and out
                    flash pictures
Nights of dreams that, on
                    waking, shred your heart
And then...

The vines are cut, pruned with skill
To the south dunes ripple and shift
around marram grass and splayed fences
A man leans on a table beside
a large pot plant (a pelargonium)
ninety years ago   The soft colours

Am I Leonid Andreyev?   Are you Ivan Belousov?
Am I Ivan Belousov?   Are you a pelargonium?
It's as daft and remote as that, sometimes

Your heart neat in a matchbox
placed on that cloth covered table

"Look closer   Look closer"

The log wall   the potted palm
the crude comic figures on the cloth
and – at the centre – the matchbox
decorated with a line of
three red stars, or are they hearts?

And
on the horizon gold flecks
                    of distant glories

2

Man talk   Woman talk

the blindness and vanity

and all the contradictions

And a hundred years before Andreyev
'Princess Caraboo' appeared in Bristol
talking "convincing gibberish"
then fleeing to the Americas

But your heart

in the words   beyond the words
beyond the masks and good intentions

A long journey
that fades with potato starch
courtesy of the Lumière brothers
A long journey
that passes through shadows and
out

Alfred Wallis

Near the harbour
the mad old man rages
The demons that persecute him
Granite hard
and grazing cruel

Ships in his head
Houses in his head
Shining sweeps of paint in his head
might save him   but don't

Erik Satie

As simple as that

a piano in a cluttered room
high above the suburbs
factory chimneys railway bridges

to make a heart melt and lurch

On the train back to the centre
a crazy woman repeating repeating
"un voleur des anges   un voleur des anges"
angel thief   angel thief
again and again

To calm her...   Nothing
can touch her

Cwm Nantcol

for Anne Stevenson and Peter Lucas

1

Light slanting down on this high green valley.
Wind blowing, bending the reeds, hawthorn trees,
the scattered clumps of rowans.

Massive slabs of rock,
like ribs down the sides of the cwm,
clawed and scoured, ground and polished
by the glaciers of "Ancient Times".
And now silver birch, oaks, tender mosses
grow in the shadows of these purple grey bluffs.

Such an emptiness. Here where sheep die
trapped in a fence or drowned in the river,
where a single track winds up into the mountains,
ends at the last farm, a stream, cattle
up to their shanks in a bog, a leaning
telephone pole among giant scattered boulders.

A near silence broken by the sound of
a raven's wing-beat as it flies
high above, fast across a clear blue sky;
the sound of waterfalls in the distance.

That's it, all that's present, or so it feels.

But why this fascination? the many returns
to this place? A comfort? Seeming timeless moments
when stood here in the sweep of the mountains.

2

The Polish general in that shrinking army camp, near late 1940's Nantwich, planted out his garden. Wherever he was, planted out the same garden – his only gravity among all the moves and changes. The neat rows of raddish, onions, cabbage, carrots, and dill to go on the potatoes. And lots of flowers – marigolds, sweet williams, sweet peas. A home. And a deep pit to store potatoes for the winter. A clamp. A deep safe cellar.

3

And back here in the west a high sprung hare
gallops away, disturbed on the hillside.

Later, the winter sun warm on my face,
I sit on a rock surrounded by bog myrtle,
the colours of the mountains, the patches of
blond gold grasses and red copper bracken.
A stillness beyond words.

Not denying the distant city.

The darkness of late afternoon is near
and sudden. A pale line of sea on the horizon.

Five pieces for five photos

for Lou Esterman wherever he may be.

1. The Surveyor's Office at the Custom House, Salem, where Nathaniel Hawthorne worked 1846-1849.

It's a dream, an escape of sorts that does work in its fashion – the solitary life, "peace", and no demands. A neat life, marred by an ageing fussiness, the fading of friendships, times of undeniable loneliness. And yet those days when bright sunlight holds the room and there is an indescribable quiet.

I know what is in every drawer, on each shelf. Inscribe in the ledger these details?   Hesitant.   No, let it be.

Outside the door the sound of people running down the stairs

2. Packing OK Sauce at George Mason & Co. Ltd., Fulham, London, c1920.

It's as though the war is over. The women stand around. A formal pause in their work. Not rows of shell cases, but bottles of sauce to be lined up, boxed, dispatched. Their relaxed beauty – not fooled but amused by this odd occasion, the photo of the workers, the busy production line.

What a daydream. Not shells to be fired at the Hun. But brown sauce to be rocketed over the priests of this small world of ours. All those self-appointed spiritual officials, gurus, shamans. Who needs them and their elaborate power games? their prohibitions and idiot explanations? We should gloop OK sauce over them when they're in full flight. The women and men at the OK Sauce factory would probably agree (or I dream they would) that's the best solution. We'd let those fools stew in their own foolishness. Though the OK workers would probably be more charitable, and more indifferent, than me about all this.

In the factory – if this were Thessaloniki – we'd all sing rebetiko songs at the tops of our voices, amongst the clatter of machines. What a real joy. Nena Venetsanou I dream of you. I kiss your sauce flavoured fingertips.

3   **View of Site Workers from Above.**

The details of our "trade" and
the people we've worked with.

Who'll know our histories?
the skills and terms as shadows grow.

Be ignorant of such knowledges,
details and procedures, at your peril.

What do you need to know?
To listen to what's said,

understand the language
that makes things work.

Whether to install an emergency coupling
or work in a child protection unit.

The railwayman. The social worker.
"honouring their world" is the phrase.

Alternatively

"You're working on the railways? You must be joking."
said the grand lady, before returning to her Kent 'estate'.

4. Sand Storm Sweeping Over Khartoum, 1906.

"It came out of nowhere," they say. No, it didn't. Nothing does.

Clouds suddenly cloak the mountains blown from somewhere, on a wavering spring day. If we'd paid attention we'd have guessed it. "The Cloud of Unknowing", we joke, working by compass along a now featureless ridge.

But there are those who with clear eyes stare ahead, with some sort of certainty in the world. T.E. Lawrence blue eyed (courtesy of Peter O'Toole), D.H. Lawrence brown eyed (I guess). Knowing what they're after through all the clouds and storms, sand or otherwise.

Such confidence is daunting.
Let them fight on. I'll hunker down behind this rock, or if you like, for the sake of fiction, this dune. Wait till it's blown over, then continue. There's room in this world for us crafty folk too. Foxes aren't daft, nor am I.

5. Mother and Child in a Restaurant Garden.

> We smile at the children
> absorbed and open in their world,
> with warm hearts
> watch them and their young parents.
>
> We're older, our bodies too –
> your silken sagging breasts,
> my scrawny arms.
> Yet when we laugh together,
> are happy in each other's company,
> touch, embrace, feel that love,
> then...   All the tussles fade.
> Moments of anger and estrangement
> between couples, within families,
> resentments, lies, and unfading scars,
> disappear like rocks in the mist.

Blown pink roses hang on their stems
in the garden or hedgerow.
Their scent not powerful nor obvious
until you put your face in their petals.

There are dusty plateaux around Rudina in Hercegovina. Only the hardiest grasses can grow in their near barren soil, fit only for flocks of goats and sheep. Of the few that live there most families leave in the winter, unable to bear its hardships. It's the embodiment of the vukojebinje of south Slavic lore. This Serbo-Croat word translates as "the land where wolves fuck".

To come from there and make something
– is that a question or an exhortation?

A present for Anne Stevenson
on her 70th birthday

Five flowers shaped like daisies
and two bunches of thin delicate leaves
– as though from an olive tree –
all made of fine fragile gold.

"Early Minoan jewellery" the card says
"from the cemetery at Mochios."

I don't know how they would be worn,
nor who would have worn them.
Pinned to a dress or a robe?
by rich and powerful people?
though maybe not so dark a tale.

But just to hold one between my fingers
and wonder at it, and its history.

You'd know how to handle this,
their beauty, and stories bronzed or sour,
and show the strands we weave – "in language
that puts its clothes on carefully."
A clear music. Sharp eyed for any foolishness.

The marvel of such making,
whether the golden flowers of Crete or your poems.

2500 BC
(say that out loud)

The quotation in lines 16-17 is from
Anne Stevenson's poem *In Passing*.

Dream of blue paint

Down steep wooden steps
from a verandah of sorts
in a country I've never known.
The wood worn and bleached,
painted a pale blue.
A tropical landscape maybe
or at least warmer than here.
Central America or Australia or Turkey.

No one comes down these steps
or goes up to the sprawling house
beyond. The hours pass.
I'm not sure what will happen.
It feels safe here
wrapped in the daydream's quilt,
the seashell's passive armour.

To walk back up into the shade
and sit in the near still air.
A dry heat and hint of a breeze to come.
The book instructs "limitation".
An orange butterfly flutters by.
"Lost" someone says, far below.

To float out of this dream on theatre wires?
Gauze winged and modestly spangled.
Fairy wand to dispel the troubles
no matter how deep the seams.
Will it work? Just relax. Wait.

"You will die, running-dog."

The service sector

The white doll's house
is set down by the sea.

A peacock green sea
flecked with brilliant white breakers.

A pale blue sky,
no smudge of a cloud.

White buildings line the shore
and this small house joins them.

Small eyes peep out.
Giant eyes peer in.

Trucks and cars drive by,
dogs zigzag pissing obsessively.
The town's bustle.

Time to put on minute coats, step out,
drive around in the matchbox car.
Best not.

How to explain, through the nervous chatter,
the demands and dangers
out there?

The words for duty or just doing your job,
and the warnings and not failing.
A strong south-west wind pulls,
tugs the matchbox car and passers-by.

A crescent of hills backs the town,
fields sun-bleached to olive and gold.
People walk that chalk ridge, the close cropped turf.
Chatter chatter.

Then a voice says – out of nowhere –
        "Why you no listen?"
A comedian, dressed as a Japanese businessman,
echoing the thoughts of everyone who serves.

Hampton Court shelter

That hue of light you find on a summer afternoon
when a rain storm batters the gardens, stitches the heavy river.
Like dusk but not.

You and I in a room set with windows overlooking that river.
A room panelled with large mirrors, long smoky mirrors
whose foxed glass reflects our dusky selves, maybe our ghosts.
And inbetween – the window seats and views of a flowing watery world.

That this 17th century pavilion, built for privacy and banquets,
could have been where voyages were planned, trade calculated
and profit, much profit, inbetween the laughter.

That the elaborate maze-like gardens that surround this pavilion
are where people wandered talking,
are where we will soon wander in a fine rain
unaware of anything beyond, caught in the moment's delight

as we weave our way through the flower beds, the sunken gardens,
the arched corridors of wisteria, pergolas of laburnum,
honey scented lime walks, our myths and histories laid aside.
Floating in any century, timeless, we romantically imagine.

If the myths were put aside, and we... ?
Would the mirrors be clear and glitter?   a rainbow
flickering on their bevelled edges?   I doubt it.

"So what are you going to do
with the rest of your life?"

from

Take a Card, Any Card

: An Ikonostasis

52 pieces to be shuffled as you will

2003-2004

Lying on the edge of sleep,
sliding sideways, it feels,
back to – again and again –
those memories visited too often.

The past and what-might-have-been.
Like layers peeled back
the shifting strata, not bedrock,
that bring heavy pain.

Those instinctive yelps for help
call more on the dead
than the living, it seems,
though that's not real.

But my mind near bursting remembering
wrong choices, selfishness and inaction,
elders neglected, children failed.
Easy to say, but true enough. No excuse.

Waking into a grey midwinter morning
the roofs wet with mist.
The seatown set for action.

People get out of bed, wash and dress
and head for work down the front steps,
down the damp street.

A young woman sets off with her friends
to choose a bridal gown,
nervous and laughing and dreaming.

♣

The old pier slumps into the sea after a winter storm. Wealthy residents collect the wreckage from the beach, planks they don't need. Battered bits of wood to sit with all those other oddments so proudly haggled for in the drizzle at a Sunday market.

Dear Reader,
Do you ever consider what age you will be when you die? and what will happen to your possessions?

♦

On a cold winter night
the full moon rises above the rooftops,
steers through the sky as
the hours pass, nights and days pass.

There's this space now
– do I mean time? –
when clear decisions could be made
and then acted on.
Such is the illusion.

♥

You smile out of the photo,
holding your baby daughter.
And her now a capable nurse
with her own family.
And you dead twelve years.
And the days pass.

♠

On the shelf

Tiger you're snarling, but you don't know why.
Your eyes large with desperation, and what?
Life on a dusty shelf suddenly hits you.
The company of a grey dog with green eyes,
an alpine cow with bell and flowers,
a croaking frog, and a balding monk hand-puppet,
is useless, irrelevant.

A little dog trots by in the street outside
ready for combat.

♣

"This scroll commemorates
Sergeant D.N.L. Harwood
Royal Air Force
held in honour as one who
served King and Country in
the world war of 1939-1945
and gave his life to save
mankind from tyranny. May
his sacrifice help to bring
the peace and freedom for
which he died."

What public citation now would have such clear
honesty?   Though words will never do them
justice.

And his brother made sure his men brought all
their rifles back in the evacuation and – like so
many other survivors – led a life forever besieged
by memories and nightmares and dreams of what
might have been.

♦

At the meeting of two mule tracks
in a remote country chapel
the ikonostasis glows in the half light
on this hot dazzling afternoon.
The wooden screen, that keep us
from the bare damp sanctuary,
painted with rows of saints and martyrs,
archangels, The Virgin, Christ Pantocrator,
fables and deeds of courage.
Here and there the deep colours a little
chipped and scratched, the paint cracked
and flaking. Some woodworm,
some splits in the boards.

At home on this northern island
a wall studded with memories.
Pictures of what's held dear,
of the people we love (dead or alive),
of places and art and those moments of glory.
Pictures that feed a need we can barely explain,
that remind us of our own history, of what's ahead,
that map our hearts' every detail.
These objects we each choose to hang or
pin on our walls, to accompany us as the weeks pass.
Private and domestic.
In the lamp light come evening
the colours glow.

♥

Being one of Life's corporals I know
my place in the scheme of things.

♠

Orchids

On this late February morning
sunlight floods a table,
a table full of orchids.

A delicate Moth Orchid (Phalaenopsis)
whose pure white petals surround
a mouth marked inside with crimson flecks
and smudges of pale yellow.

A Dendrobium, tall and sturdy, whose
green white flowers unfurl with clear purpose,
whose apparent simplicity is far from true.

A Cymbridum, "dripping with exotic splendour",
yellowy green petals attending a rich
purple blotched mouth that leads deep
down a yellow grooved tongue into a red speckled throat,
the stems glistening with drops of sticky sap.

These worlds stood on a long pine table, stained and knotted,
the grain's patterns picked out in the sunlight.
The wood warm and silky.   Touch.

In the Royal Botanic Gardens a notice said :
"The 25,000 described species range
from subtle and dainty to flamboyantly glamorous."
From the cool mountain forest to
those Asian tropical nights we dream of.

And here on this northern island,
come June, I'll walk the chalk hills searching
among the short cropped grasses for
the Common Spotted Orchid, the Fragrant Orchid,
the Pyramidal Orchid, the Bee Orchid,
and maybe even find Burnt Orchids
on that airy slope overlooking Folkington.
Small modest flowers, our "native" orchids.

Their delicate and complex markings.
Their near infinite forms, cunning and amazing.
Their grace almost bird-like.
Near beyond words.

Liam O'Gallagher lived in an apartment in Chinatown in San
Francisco. His bed was in the middle of the room surrounded by
louvered screens. Lying on his bed on a June afternoon – it felt
like being on a ship in the Tropics. A boat slowly going down-
river – a river so wide you could barely see the shore.

♣

a grey sea a grey sky
a seamless day with no hours
flecks of snow on my coat
family far away
in foreign lands or waterlogged graves.

♦

No.31, the last tram, is about to leave the terminus. Poorly dressed people queue to climb on, standing in the rain like sleepwalkers on this black enamel night under the glaring street lights. Is it Saturday? What was Brobat (1/- in 1950 prices)?

......but......

......which was strange (

). Then...

Here come the Munchkins – drunk as usual – heading for Gloom City.

♥

Don't be afraid, said the perky optimist.
Dying?   Flowers come and go.   We're no different,
except their passing may be neater, simpler.

Meanwhile stolid grey-muzzled old dogs
plod along behind their impatient owners.
Scrawny old cats, their fur all tufty,
stare at the world or the wall.

I never thought I'd be writing this letter
to you, to anyone.

♠

Ikon

The wood panel cracked, the ikon
chipped, scratched, the paint flaking.
So many years she's looked out
with that nervous certainty.
This image repeated on so many smoke stained boards.

The pure virgin, immaculate mother
of myth or mistranslation.
Drawn in by her look, an offered calm,
certainty amongst the storms and doubts,
a motherly embrace that's longed for.

"There, there", we imagine, she says.
"Don't fret."   But we do,
knowing, beyond the sentimental glow,
the havoc caused by the pure, the sure,
by those who know what's best, what's right for us.

It's not like that, not *that* easy.
Edgy, yet wanting the contradictions.
Faced by the legions of the faithful
– "God protect us", as one says –
the muddled muddle, laugh with the changes. But

the rabbi with his family in their living room
at 10 Krochmalna Street.
The monk with his 'brothers'
at 23 Cambridge Road.
Good men though remote, confined.

Attended by two faded angels
and an evolving mollusc.

♣

A kaleidoscope scatter of muted colours –
ochres, fauns, greys, pale washed-out blues.

Fragments of buildings, pavements, ledges,
indecipherable floors, words, phrases.

Microscope slides of rock structure,
mica, or animal tissue.

Some form of exhaustion.
Money, politics, the whole shebang of

daily living with its twists and turns.
Dumb powerless confusion, or resignation?

A few clear words would help.
Shrug of the shoulders.

♦

For years I'd thought – without really looking –
your delicate watercolour was of bindweed
with its flaring white trumpets, "grandmothers' nightcaps",
on a green twisting vine.
But no – I now see it's a spray of jasmin.
My favourite scent whether in a Greek lane at midday,
or in my grandmother's garden as dusk approaches
and the war planes' drone is completely forgotten,
or some backyard in New York where you saw it,
where you breathed in that scent.

♥

R

In the pop-up alphabet book
the rabbit postman strides on
in a faded blue uniform, cap on his head,
bag over his shoulder, a letter in his paw.

A letter in his paw... ?   For who?
And where is he anyway? The setting
is vague, if not non-existent.
Remote as those landscapes
seen on old postage stamps.
Violet islands, ochre oak trees.

Is the letter for me?   but
I'm too young to read it, so
will never know if it's for me,
whether it contains greetings or
a declaration of love or
the announcement of incomprehensible disaster.

Times when
years go by, it seems,
then one day "it" all falls into place.
The lock opens.
Don't know why, but...
and I'm standing there
looking at you.

The public gardens are full of cherry blossom.
I am not a Japanese poet.

I don't know the connections.

♦

New moon over the palace.
New moon over the sea.

Dark evening clouds
pushing across the paleing sky.

Seatown lights – the promenade, pier,
decaying bandstand, Grand Hotel.

Drunk kids in the police car
parked across the empty pavement.

Factories, post offices, law offices,
corner shops shut, and in darkness.

Gilded balustrades – nice phrase.
Something significant? – not really.

Lists are made for whatever reason.
Later while dreaming

figures hurry or loiter
in the streets, moon gone.

Lights go off, come on.
The world ticks its way.

♥

So what?

On the plane the man was dreaming of licking the intimate parts of his woman friend. By the bulkhead a rabbinical student was swaying saying his prayers. Another man was sitting thinking of nothing in particular. A woman flicked through a magazine again, bored and irritated. A cat in the hold crouched on the floor of its cage, ears flattened, terrified.

In three or four hours where will they be? Sniffing the fresh spring air of their home country on a railway platform? Or returned to too many cares and duties that numb such moments?

There are too many questions here.

♠

Dear Joe

A tall slim vase holds
white, yellow, and purple iris
set amongst various greenery
– Queen Anne's lace? –
as well as four roses, or
are they peonies?
The gouache has faded
over nearly forty years.
It's hard to be sure.

Fourteen butterflies flutter
around the vase, your picture,
on that summer's day.
A Vermont meadow outside your
studio window?   or New York?
It could be either, and not matter.
The sheer pleasure of this world
you made, patiently, carefully.
A neat pencil line under
the near transparent colours.

Side by side
(and so long ago)
your picture and

Your large white bed
surrounded by a ring of lit candles.
To enter that world, or retreat
to walking the night streets?

Regrets?   Of course.

The bundle of stuff we hold inside us.

♣

lying on the beach eyes closed
        listening to the
crash of the waves and drag
        of the shingle

♦

The last of summer – an evening when
the room is heavy with the scent of lilies
and a full moon floats in a bed of small clouds.
The windows open, the warm soft night air.

Antique memories flood in – a velvet dusk
in an orchard overlooking Canterbury,
making love with you among the apple trees.
Decades ago, but still here set in my head

like a... ?   I don't know what.
It's there just like my bones are there.

It's like Cornell's boxes. Not a nostalgia that sees the past as
somehow better but that captures the sadness, the undeniable
fact, of time passing, life passing.

♥

A matchbox becomes a car,
the carpet's pattern a road.
We drive off on hands and knees.
Time is forgotten.
Winter or summer
it's a long road.

♠

A stillness in the room –
sunlight slanting in on a table,
two chairs, a chest of drawers.
In this light the wood a yellow gold
or, at times, the colour of straw.
All except that one small chair,
its chestnut brown seat so lovingly polished
that it mirrors the surrounding room.

There is a silence, a sense of silence,
but this scene is not entirely silent.
Men and women can be heard working outside, and
someone's chopping wood in the barn.

The clarity of such moments
that don't stand still but seem to,
like a rest or reminder of
that simple happiness dreamt of, beyond words.

Inside the drawers and a box on the table
the hidden beauty of dovetail joints.
How the wood fits together.

♣

"Courage, traveller."
cut into a slate memorial
beside a little used mountain path.

The mew of a buzzard circling above.
The honk of a raven as it flies high overhead.
The sound of horns clashing as
two wild goats tussle for power.

"Courage, traveller."

This late September –
clear skies and hot sun
and all around a spread of mountains
and to the west the sea
stroking the land.

"To the enduring memory of Janet Haigh who ever as late as
her 84th year despite dim sight and stiffened joints still loved
to walk this way from Talybont to Penmaenpool. This stone
was placed in 1953 by her son Mervyn sometime bishop of
Winchester. Courage traveller."

♦

Printed in the United Kingdom
by Lightning Source UK Ltd.
125937UK00001BA/10/A